D1480526

551.46 Mar
Marine science : an
  illustrated guide to
  science

OCT 1 3 2006

$49.50
ocm71432242

WITHDRAWN

WITHDRAWN

SCIENCE VISUAL RESOURCES

MARINE SCIENCE

An Illustrated Guide to Science

The Diagram Group

CHELSEA HOUSE
PUBLISHERS
An imprint of Infobase Publishing

Marine Science: An Illustrated Guide to Science

Copyright © 2006 The Diagram Group

Editorial: Gordon Lee, Jamie Stokes

Design: Anthony Atherton, Richard Hummerstone,
                        Lee Lawrence

Illustration: Peter Wilkinson

Picture research: Neil McKenna

Indexer: Martin Hargreaves

All rights reserved. No part of this book may be reproduced or utilized in any form or by any means, electronic or mechanical, including photocopying, recording, or by any information storage or retrieval systems, without permission in writing from the publisher. For information contact:

Chelsea House
An imprint of Infobase Publishing
132 West 31st Street
New York NY 10001

For Library of Congress Cataloging-in-Publication data,
please contact the publisher.

ISBN 0-8160-6166-1

Chelsea House books are available at special discounts when purchased in bulk quantities for businesses, associations, institutions, or sales promotions. Please call our Special Sales Department in New York at 212/967-8800 or 800/322-8755.

You can find Chelsea House on the World Wide Web at
http://www.chelseahouse.com

Printed in China

CP Diagram 10 9 8 7 6 5 4 3 2 1

This book is printed on acid-free paper.

Introduction

Marine Science is one of eight volumes of the **Science Visual Resources** set. It contains seven sections, a comprehensive glossary, a Web site guide, and an index.

Marine Science is a learning tool for students and teachers. Full-color diagrams, graphs, charts, and maps on every page illustrate the essential elements of the subject, while parallel text provides key definitions and step-by-step explanations.

Geography of the oceans provides an overview of the physical dimensions of the bodies of water that cover 70 percent of Earth.

Geology of the oceans examines the geological processes that have shaped Earth's surface and features that are unique to the marine environment. It covers the regions of intense volcanic activity that lie deep beneath the sea, and the shifting boundaries between water and land.

Chemistry of the oceans is concerned with the nature of seawater and with the global cycles that carry vital elements, such as carbon and nitrogen, from the oceans to the atmosphere to the land, and back to the ocean again.

Ocean-atmosphere system details the engines that drive global climate. The cycling of heat from warmer to cooler latitudes, the impact of Earth's rotation on ocean currents, and the daily ebb and flow of the tides are covered here.

Biology of the oceans is an overview of the wealth of plant and animal life that lives in, on, or near the oceans. Food chains stretching from bacteria to blue whales are described, as well as the unique communities that thrive in the pitch black of the deep ocean floor. Every class of animal and plant found in the marine environment is articulated.

Marine exploration and **Marine economics** focus on the human relationship with the sea. It covers the technology that has allowed explorers to span the globe and probe the depths of the ocean. The vital role of marine food sources in the health and wealth of the world is also examined.

Contents

1 GEOGRAPHY OF THE OCEANS

2 GEOLOGY OF THE OCEANS

3 CHEMISTRY OF THE OCEANS

4 OCEAN-ATMOSPHERE SYSTEM

5 BIOLOGY OF THE OCEANS

6 MARINE EXPLORATION

7 MARINE ECONOMICS

APPENDIXES

© Diagram Visual Information Ltd.

Key words

heat sink
polar
precipitation
temperate
tropical

The importance of water

- Water is vital for life on Earth. Most organisms mainly consist of water. For example, the human body is usually composed of at least 65 percent water.
- The distribution of water on land largely determines the occurrence and abundance of terrestrial flora and fauna. In environments where there is little water available, such as deserts, there is little or no animal or plant life. In environments where there is a lot of water available, such as rain forests, there are more plant and animal species than anywhere else. Rain forest covers only about six percent of Earth's surface, but contains more than 50 percent of all known animal and plant species.
- Water dissolves many kinds of substances and is a major transporter of chemicals between land and sea.
- Water is the planet's most potent heat transporter. It acts as a massive heat sink that carries tropical heat to temperate and polar regions.
- The presence of water in the atmosphere generates weather and climate. Clouds, for example, form from condensing water droplets. They trap sunlight, release precipitation, and act as a heat-insulating layer around Earth.
- Water heats up and cools down slowly and so moderates temperature changes in coastal areas.
- As liquid or ice, water is a powerful erosive force that shapes the planet's surface.

Earth's water

The oceans

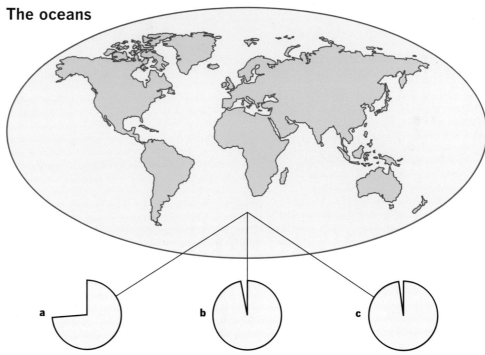

a The oceans cover 71 percent—139 million square miles (361 million km²)—of Earth's surface.

b They contain more than 97 percent—323 million cubic miles (1,348 million km³)—of Earth's surface water.

c About 98 percent of Earth's living space is found in the oceans.

The partition of surface water

saltwater = 97.55%   freshwater = 2.45%

The partition of water on Earth's surface

Seas and oceans	Ice	Groundwater	Lakes and rivers	Inland saltwater	Atmosphere	
97.54	1.81	0.63	0.009	0.007	0.001	% of total water
–	73.9	25.7	0.36	–	0.04	% of fresh water

These figures do not include the tiny fraction of available water contained within living organisms.

Earth's oceans

Pacific Ocean

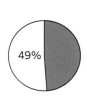

49%

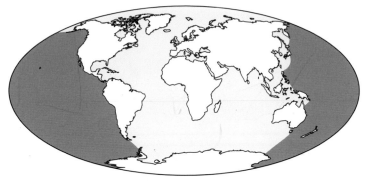

Atlantic Ocean

25%

Indian Ocean

22%

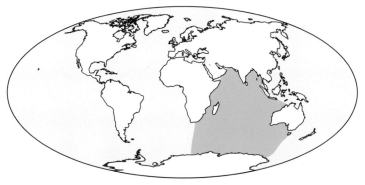

Arctic Ocean

4%

The Southern Ocean

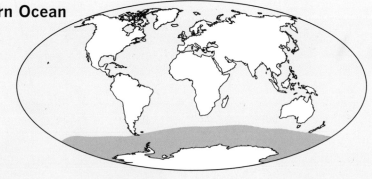

Key words

coast seawater
latitude
Ocean

Ocean

- The *Ocean* is the continuous expanse of seawater that covers 71 percent of Earth's surface.
- The *oceans* are the four major subdivisions of the Ocean—the Pacific, Atlantic, Indian, and Arctic oceans, plus the Southern Ocean.
- The Pacific Ocean extends from the west coast of North, Central, and South America to the east coast of Asia and Australia.
- The Atlantic Ocean extends from the west coast of Europe and Africa to the east coast of North, Central, and South America.
- The Indian Ocean extends from the east coast of Africa to the west coast of Australia.
- The Arctic Ocean extends from the north coasts of Europe and Asia to the north coast of North America.
- The Southern Ocean extends from the coast of Antarctica to latitude 65°S. Comprising the southern parts of the Pacific, Atlantic, and Indian oceans, its limits were officially set in 2000 by the International Hydrographic Organization.

Facts about

Ocean (excluding seas)
Area in square miles (km2)
Mean depth in feet (m)
Volume in cubic miles (km3)

- *Pacific Ocean*
  63,800,000 (165,250,000)
  14,040 (4,280)
  169,610,000 (707,000,000)

- *Atlantic Ocean*
  31,830,000 (82,440,000)
  10,920 (3,330)
  65,830,000 (274,400,000)

- *Indian Ocean*
  28,355,000 (73,440,000)
  12,760 (3,890)
  68,510,000 (285,600,000)

- *Arctic Ocean*
  5,440,150 (14,090,000)
  3,240 (988)
  3,338,000 (14,000,000)

© Diagram Visual Information Ltd.

© Diagram Visual Information Ltd.

Key words

mid-ocean ridge
trench

Seafloor topography

- The seafloor is not flat and featureless.
- Valleys and mountains on the seafloor are often deeper or higher than similar features on land.
- The Mariana Trench in the Pacific Ocean reaches a depth of about 36,000 feet (11,000 m) below sea level and 16,700 feet (5,100 m) below the surrounding seafloor. The deepest valley on land is Hell's Canyon, Oregon, which is 7,875 feet (2,400 m) at its maximum depth.
- The tallest mountain emerging from the sea is Mauna Kea, Hawaii, which rises 33,465 feet (10,200 m) above the seafloor. The tallest mountain on land is Mount Everest, which rises 29,030 feet (8,848 m) above sea level.
- The longest mountain range on Earth is the mid-ocean ridge system that extends for 40,000 miles (64,000 km) along the seafloor. It is four times longer than the Himalayas, Andes, and Rocky Mountains combined.

The Eastern Hemisphere

Major topography

1 Mid-Indian Ridge

2 Australian–Antarctic Rise

3 Ryūkyū Trench, Japan

4 Mariana Trench, North Pacific

5 Japan Trench

6 Kermadec Trench, South Pacific

7 Tonga Trench, South Pacific

The Western Hemisphere

Major topography (continued)

8 Aleutian Trench, North Pacific

9 Southwest Pacific Plateau

10 East Pacific Rise

11 Peru–Chile Trench

12 Puerto Rico Trench

13 Mid-Atlantic Ridge

Key words

island chain	seafloor
lithospheric plate	spreading
magma	subduction
mid-ocean ridge	trench

Mid-ocean ridges

- Mid-ocean ridges are found on the seafloors of all of the world's oceans.
- They are undersea mountain ranges that mark the boundaries between divergent lithospheric plates.
- They are formed from the upwelling magma that drives divergent plates apart and causes seafloor spreading.

Trenches

- Trenches are very deep, steep-sided depressions in the seabed.
- They are formed where one lithospheric plate slides beneath another in a process known as subduction.
- Trenches are often associated with volcanic island chains. These form on the side of the trench formed by the non-subducted plate.

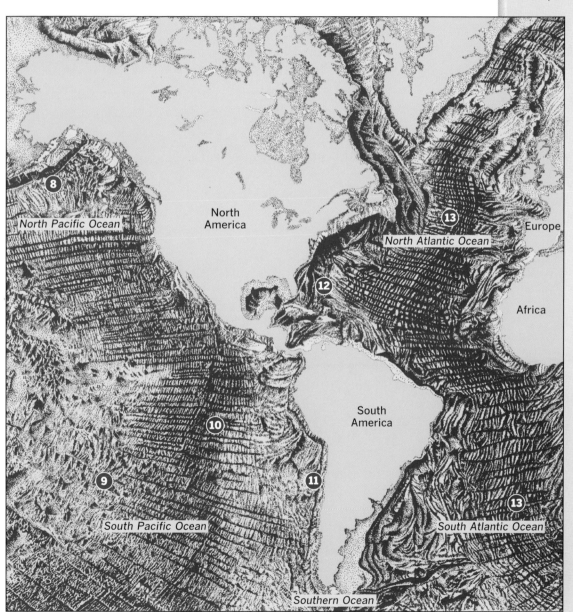

© Diagram Visual Information Ltd.

Major seas

© Diagram Visual Information Ltd.

Key words

bay
gulf
ocean
sea

Seas

- A *sea* is a region of an ocean that either covers a defined geographical area, or has a defining characteristic.
- The Caribbean Sea is an example of a sea that covers a geographical area. It is a region of the Atlantic Ocean that lies off the coasts of South and Central America.
- The Sargasso Sea is an example of a sea that has a defining characteristic. It is a part of the Atlantic Ocean where there are almost no surface currents. Large quantities of a seaweed known as sargassum grow there.
- A sea may also be a large body of saltwater that is connected to the ocean by a narrow channel, such as the Mediterranean Sea is.
- A sea may also be a large body of saltwater that is not connected to the ocean, such as the Caspian Sea.

Bays and gulfs

- *Bays* and *gulfs* are seas that are mostly enclosed by land.
- There are no internationally-agreed conventions on the relative sizes of bays and gulfs, but gulfs are usually larger than bays.
- Hudson Bay on the northeast coast of Canada is an example of a bay.
- The Gulf of Mexico on the south coast of the United States is an example of a gulf.

Atlantic Ocean

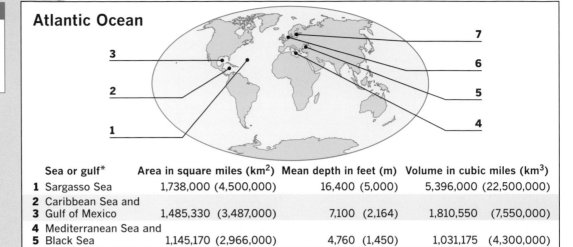

Sea or gulf*	Area in square miles (km²)	Mean depth in feet (m)	Volume in cubic miles (km³)
1 Sargasso Sea	1,738,000 (4,500,000)	16,400 (5,000)	5,396,000 (22,500,000)
2 Caribbean Sea and **3** Gulf of Mexico	1,485,330 (3,487,000)	7,100 (2,164)	1,810,550 (7,550,000)
4 Mediterranean Sea and **5** Black Sea	1,145,170 (2,966,000)	4,760 (1,450)	1,031,175 (4,300,000)
6 North Sea	222,010 (575,000)	305 (93)	12,710 (53,000)
7 Baltic Sea	162,930 (422,000)	180 (55)	5,510 (23,000)

Pacific Ocean

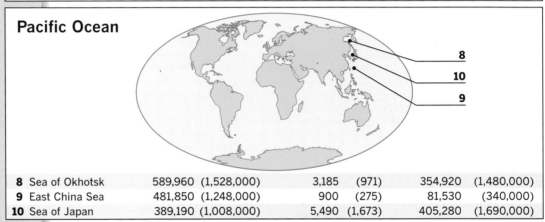

Sea	Area in square miles (km²)	Mean depth in feet (m)	Volume in cubic miles (km³)
8 Sea of Okhotsk	589,960 (1,528,000)	3,185 (971)	354,920 (1,480,000)
9 East China Sea	481,850 (1,248,000)	900 (275)	81,530 (340,000)
10 Sea of Japan	389,190 (1,008,000)	5,490 (1,673)	405,280 (1,690,000)

Indian Ocean

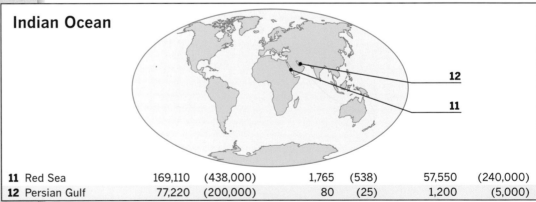

Sea or gulf	Area in square miles (km²)	Mean depth in feet (m)	Volume in cubic miles (km³)
11 Red Sea	169,110 (438,000)	1,765 (538)	57,550 (240,000)
12 Persian Gulf	77,220 (200,000)	80 (25)	1,200 (5,000)

Arctic Ocean

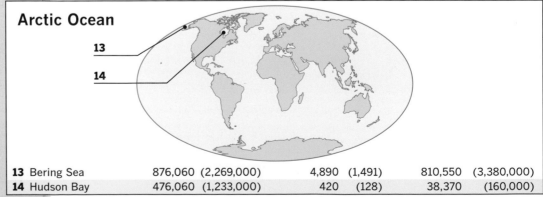

Sea or bay	Area in square miles (km²)	Mean depth in feet (m)	Volume in cubic miles (km³)
13 Bering Sea	876,060 (2,269,000)	4,890 (1,491)	810,550 (3,380,000)
14 Hudson Bay	476,060 (1,233,000)	420 (128)	38,370 (160,000)

*All data is approximate. There are no precise, internationally agreed boundaries for these bodies of seawater.

Pacific Ocean

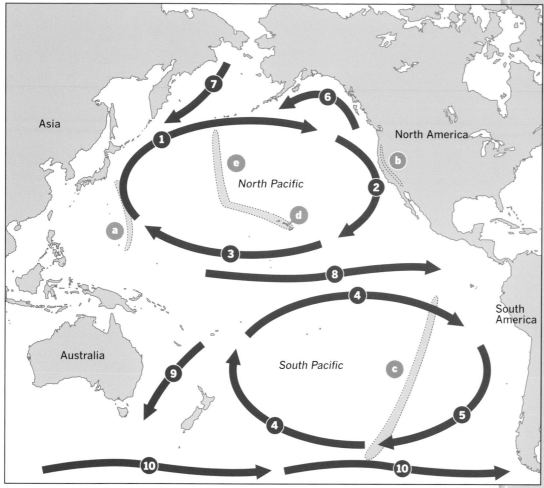

© Diagram Visual Information Ltd.

Key words

current	plate
fault	boundary
gyre	seamount
hot spot	spreading
mid-ocean	ridge
ridge	trench
ocean	

Pacific Ocean

- The Pacific Ocean is the world's largest ocean.
- It stretches from the west coast of North, Central, and South America to the east coast of Asia and Australia.
- The Pacific Ocean contains more water than all of the other oceans put together.
- The Pacific was named by the 16th-century Portuguese explorer Ferdinand Magellan, who believed the ocean to have a gentle nature (*pacific* means "calm"). In reality however, the Pacific experiences severe tropical storms (typhoons).
- The Pacific Ocean is surrounded by destructive plate boundaries that border landmasses. They create an arc of volcanic and earthquake activity sometimes known as the "Ring of Fire."
- It is the oldest of the world's oceans and is gradually shrinking as the Atlantic Ocean slowly expands.
- The Pacific Ocean is usually divided into the North Pacific and the South Pacific.

Major geologic features

a The Mariana Trench is the world's deepest trench.

b The San Andreas Fault is 745 miles (1,200 km) long.

c The East Pacific Ridge, a spreading ridge, is 6,550–9,850 feet (2,000–3,000 m) high and 1,550 miles (3,500 km) long.

d Volcanic activity at the Hawaiian Hot Spot has generated the Hawaiian–Emperor Seamount Chain.

e

Surface currents

The North Pacific Gyre

1 Kuroshio Current

2 California Current

3 North Equatorial Current

The South Pacific Gyre

4 South Equatorial Current

5 Peru Current

Other

6 Alaska Current

7 Oyashio Current

8 Equatorial Countercurrent

9 East Australia Current

10 Antarctic Circumpolar Current

Facts about

Area
63,800,000 square miles (165,250,000 km²)

Volume
169,600,000 cubic miles (707,270,000 km³)

Mean depth
14,043 feet (4,280 m)

Deepest point
36,163 feet (11,022 m) in the Mariana Trench

Key words

basin	mid-ocean ridge
coast	ocean
current	sea
gyre	trench
latitude	

Atlantic Ocean

- The Atlantic Ocean is the world's second largest ocean.
- It occupies an S-shaped basin that extends from the east coasts of North, Central, and South America to the west coasts of Europe and Africa.
- The land area that drains into the Atlantic is four times greater than the land area that drains into the Pacific or Indian oceans.
- The Atlantic is usually divided into the North Atlantic Ocean and the South Atlantic Ocean.
- The boundary between the North and South Atlantic is defined by the region where the two dominant surface currents, the North Atlantic Gyre and the South Atlantic Gyre, pass each other (about 8°N).
- The Atlantic Ocean was named after the Greek god Atlas, who held up the heavens.
- The Atlantic Ocean is the youngest of the world's oceans. It began to form fewer than 100 million years ago, when the North and South American landmasses began to separate and move away from Europe and Africa.
- The Atlantic is still expanding today as volcanic activity along the Mid-Atlantic Ridge continues to push the Americas further away from Europe and Africa.

Facts about

Area

31,830,100 square miles
(82,440,000 km²)

Volume

65,830,300 cubic miles
(274,525,000 km³)

Mean depth

10,925 feet (3,330 m)

Deepest point

27,495 feet (8,380 m) in the
Puerto Rico Trench (**d**)

© Diagram Visual Information Ltd.

Atlantic Ocean

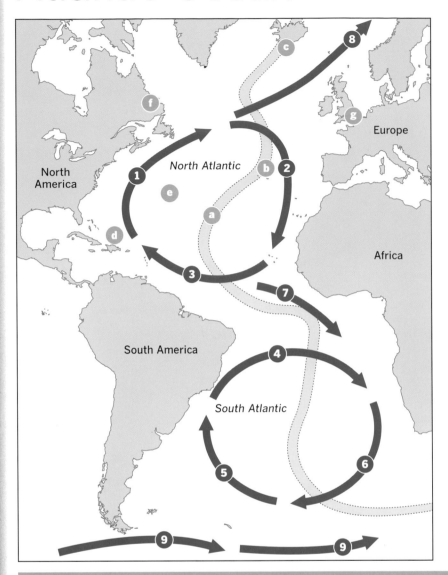

Major geologic features

a The Mid-Atlantic Ridge runs the length of the ocean basin. At 7,020 miles (11,300 km) long and up to 13,100 feet (4,000 m) high it is part of the world's longest mountain chain, the mid-ocean ridge system. Associated volcanic activity has produced islands such as the Azores, west of Portugal **b** and Surtsey, Iceland **c**

d The Puerto Rico Trench is the world's second deepest trench.

Surface currents

The North Atlantic Gyre encircles the Sargasso Sea e :

1 Gulf Stream

2 Canary Current

3 North Equatorial Current

The South Pacific Gyre:

4 South Equatorial Current

5 Brazil Current

6 Benguela Current

7 Equatorial Countercurrent

8 North Atlantic Drift. Fed by the Gulf Stream, it warms northwest Europe. Labrador **f** and London **g** lie at similar latitudes, but London is some 18°F (10°C) warmer in mid-winter, largely because of the heating effect of the North Atlantic Drift.

9 Antarctic Circumpolar Current

Indian Ocean

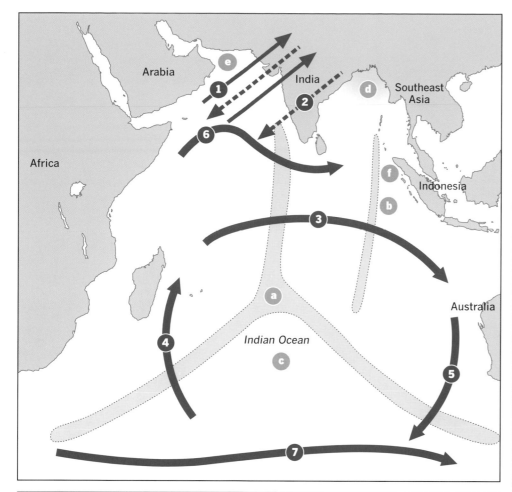

Key words

coast	mid-ocean ridge
current	monsoon
Gondwana	ocean
gyre	sediment
hot spot	upwelling

Indian Ocean

- The Indian Ocean is the world's third largest ocean.
- It extends from the east coast of Africa to the west coast of Australia and is bounded in the north by southern Asia.
- The Indian Ocean's currents are unique because its northern surface current reverses direction for part of the year (the monsoon). This is due to seasonal weather changes across the landmasses that encircle the northern part of the ocean.
- The world's first civilizations developed around the Indian Ocean and it was the first ocean to be crossed extensively by regular trade routes.
- The Indian Ocean has formed during the 125 million years since the breakup of Gondwana.

Major geologic features

a The mid-ocean ridge system. The major site of seafloor spreading, it is an inverted Y-shape.

b Ninety East Ridge. About 2,000 miles (3,000 km) long, it is the world's longest straight-line feature. It is probably the product of the Kerguelen Hot Spot **c**

d Ganges-Brahmaputra Fan, south of Bangladesh. About 930 miles (1,500 km) across, it is the world's largest sediment fan.

Surface currents

The Indian Ocean, unlike the Pacific and the Atlantic, is entirely enclosed by land on its northern side. One consequence of this is the monsoon wind system of the northern Indian Ocean that reverses direction seasonally. The Indian Ocean does not have a Northern Hemisphere gyre.

1 In summer, the southwesterly monsoon winds from the southern Indian Ocean cause deluges in India. The summer winds generate upwellings that enhance phytoplankton productivity in the Arabian Sea **e**.

2 In winter, northeasterly winds suppress the upwellings and lower productivity.

The South Indian Gyre

3 South Equatorial Current

4 Somali Current

5 West Australia Current

Other currents

6 North Equatorial Current

7 Antarctic Circumpolar Current

Facts about

Area
28,355,200 square miles (73,440,000 km²)

Volume
68,510,000 cubic miles (285,681,000 km³)

Mean depth
12,760 feet (3,890 m)

Deepest point
24,445 feet (7,450 m) in the Java Trench (**f**)

© Diagram Visual Information Ltd.

Arctic Ocean

© Diagram Visual Information Ltd.

Key words

coast
continental shelf
current
mid-ocean ridge
ocean

Arctic Ocean

● The Arctic Ocean is by far the smallest and shallowest of the four true oceans.

● Unlike the other true oceans, it is virtually landlocked with only narrow channels connecting it to the Atlantic and Pacific oceans.

● It extends from the north coast of North America to the north coasts of Europe and Asia.

● The central region of the Arctic Ocean is covered by permanent ice at least 10 feet (3 m) thick. During the winter the ice covers almost the whole of the Arctic to the shores of the surrounding landmasses.

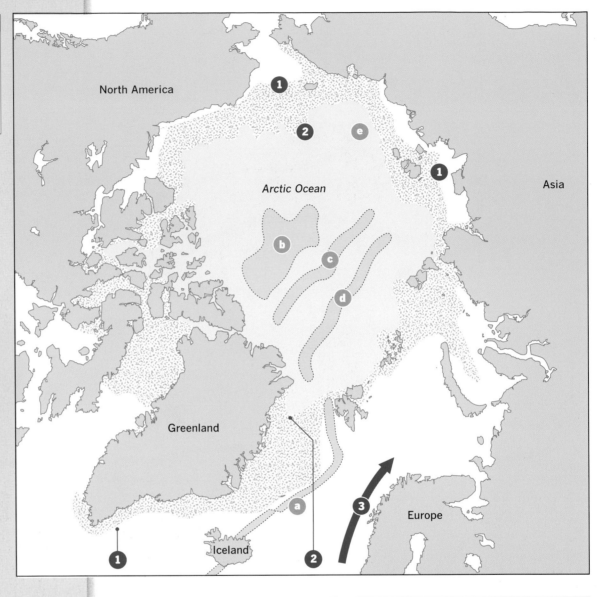

Facts about

Area

5,440,000 square miles (14,090,000 km²)

Volume

3,338,350 cubic miles (13,920,920 km³)

Mean depth

3,240 feet (988 m)

Deepest point

18,052 feet (5,502 m) on the Polar Abyssal Plain

Major geologic features

There are a series of roughly parallel ridges across the seafloor of the Arctic ocean:

a Mid-Atlantic Ridge

b The Alpha Ridge

c The Lomonosov Ridge: the current site of seafloor spreading.

d The Nansen Cordillera. This is near continuous with the Mid-Atlantic Ridge **a**.

e North of Eurasia, the continental shelf is extremely wide, at about 1,000 miles (1,600 km) across.

Climatic features

Large areas of the Arctic Ocean are permanently covered by ice. The amount of ice cover varies from season to season and is influenced by the presence of warm currents:

1 In winter, sea ice is 10 feet (3 m) thick or more and covers most of the Arctic Ocean.

2 Even in summer, the shrinking ice covers about half the Arctic Ocean.

3 The Norwegian Current. An extension of the North Atlantic Current, its warm water keeps the Norwegian coastline free of ice throughout the year.

Southern Ocean

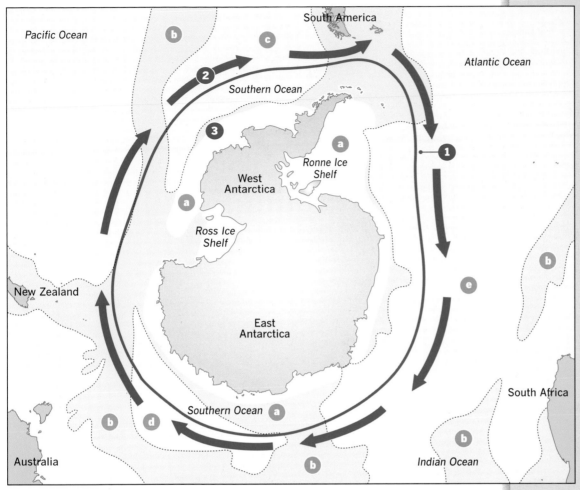

© Diagram Visual Information Ltd.

Key words

basin
convergence
current
mid-ocean ridge
ocean
sea level

The Southern Ocean

- The Southern Ocean, also known as the Antarctic Ocean, is not usually regarded as a true ocean because it lacks bordering landmasses.
- In nautical terminology however, the southern regions of the Atlantic, Indian, and Pacific oceans have long been referred to as the Southern Ocean.
- Its status as an ocean and its official limits were set by a decision of the International Hydrographic Organization in 2000.
- The Southern Ocean surrounds the continent of Antarctica and extends north to latitude 65°S.
- Antarctica is the coldest region on Earth. Many coastal areas have mean annual temperatures of only –22°F (–30°C).
- Ice coverage of the Southern Ocean increases by seven times from the height of summer (March) to the height of winter (September).
- The Antarctic Circumpolar Current is the world's largest ocean current in terms of the amount of water it moves. It always flows from west to east.

Major geologic features

a Antarctica's continental shelf is extremely deep at 1,200–1,600 feet (370–490 m) below sea level. It is depressed by the weight of ice on Antarctica's landmass.

b Mid-ocean ridge system. Beyond the continental shelf, parts of this system enclose the deep ocean basin. This is subdivided into:

   c The Southeast Pacific Basin

   d The South Indian Basin

   e The Atlantic-Indian Basin

Climatic and current features

1 Antarctic Convergence around 50–55°S. Here cold polar water at surface and deep levels interacts with warm subpolar waters at midwater level.

2 Antarctic Circumpolar Current. Situated north of the Antarctic Convergence, this current forms the southerly boundary of the southern gyres of the Pacific, Atlantic, and Indian oceans. It is the only major surface current that circles the globe.

3 In winter, sea ice increases to more than six times its summer extent.

Facts about

Area

13,500,000 square miles (35,000,000 km²)

Deepest point

16,400 feet (5,000 m) approximately

Caribbean Sea and the Gulf of Mexico

© Diagram Visual Information Ltd.

Key words

basin	ocean
current	sea
eddy	strait
gulf	
isthmus	

Caribbean Sea

- The Caribbean Sea is situated between South and North America and bounded by Central America in the west and a string of islands including the Greater and Lesser Antilles in the east.
- There are more than 7,000 islands in the Caribbean, for example Cuba and Puerto Rico.

Gulf of Mexico

- The Gulf of Mexico is bounded on three sides by the United States and Mexico.
- The southeast of the Gulf is bounded by Cuba.

Facts about

Gulf of Mexico

Area

596,140 square miles (1,544,000 km²)

Maximum depth

13,220 feet (4,029 m)

Caribbean Sea

Area

750,190 square miles (1,943,000 km²)

Maximum depth

25,218 feet (7,686 m) in the Cayman Trench (**f**)

Major geologic features

Geologically, the Caribbean Sea is believed to be a fragment of Pacific Ocean crust separated from the rest when the Isthmus of Panama was formed some 3 million years ago. The wider Caribbean comprises four comparatively deep ocean basins:

- **a** Isthmus of Panama
- **b** Gulf of Mexico
- **c** Yucatán Basin
- **d** Colombian Basin
- **e** Venezuelan Basin
- **f** Cayman Trench

Major currents

- **1** Warm surface water flows from the Atlantic Ocean into the Caribbean Sea. Shallow sills prevent cold deep water from entering.
- **2** Warm water from the Caribbean Sea enters the Gulf of Mexico via the Yucatán Channel.
- **3** Large eddies retain the water within the Gulf, warming it further.
- **4** The water discharges through the Florida Strait.
- **5** The water then feeds the Gulf Stream.

Locator map

Sargasso Sea

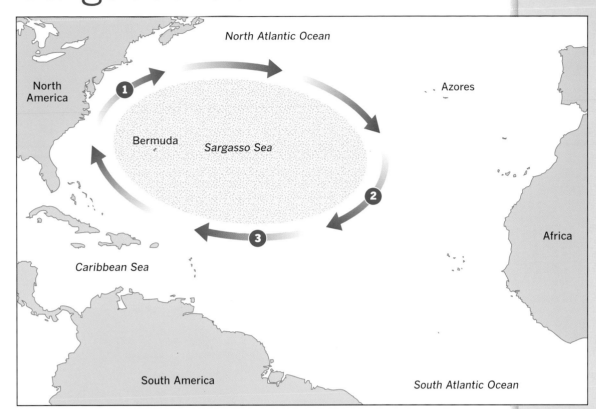

North Atlantic Ocean

North America

Azores

1

Bermuda   *Sargasso Sea*

2

Africa

3

Caribbean Sea

South America

South Atlantic Ocean

Key words

current   longitude
fauna   ocean
flora   salinity
latitude   sea

Sargasso Sea

● The Sargasso Sea is a region of the North Atlantic Ocean that lies between latitudes 25° and 35°N and between longitudes 40° and 70°W. It covers an area approximately 700 miles (1,200 km) from north to south and 2,000 miles (3,200 km) from east to west.

● It is an unusual sea in that its limits are defined not by land boundaries but by ocean currents.

● The ocean currents that surround the Sargasso Sea move water quite rapidly, but the water within the sea barely moves at all: it is an irregular oval of slow-moving clear water.

● Large quantities of a seaweed known as sargassum weed accumulates near the surface of this slow-moving water. There is a unique community of creatures adapted to life among this surface weed.

● Salinity levels in the Sargasso Sea are very high because there is little movement of water into or out of it. There is also therefore little inflow of nutrients.

● The animals adapted to living in this environment are not specialized to feed on any one type of sargassum weed because they need to be able to eat any kind of plant material that is available.

Major currents

Boundary currents
The Sargasso is encircled by fast-moving currents:

1 The Gulf Stream to the west and north

2 The Canary Current to the east

3 Equatorial Drift to the south

Locator map

Sargasso flora and fauna

1 The Sargasso is patchily covered with a floating carpet of sargassum weed, mostly *Sargassum natans*. The weed is inhabited by superbly camouflaged fish, such as:

2 Pipefish (*Syngnathus pelagicus*)

3 Sargassum anglerfish (*Histrio histrio*)

Facts about

Area

1,737,750 square miles
(4,500,000 km²) approximately

Maximum depth

24,600 feet (7,500 m) approximately

© Diagram Visual Information Ltd.

Mediterranean Sea

© Diagram Visual Information Ltd.

Key words

ocean
precipitation
runoff
salinity
sea
strait

Mediterranean Sea

- The Mediterranean Sea is situated between Europe, Africa, and Asia.
- It gets its name from the Latin *mediterraneus* which means "in the middle of land."

Connections

1 Strait of Gibraltar to Atlantic Ocean
2 Dardanelles to Sea of Marmara
3 Sea of Marmara to Bosphorus
4 Bosphorus to Black Sea
5 Suez Canal to Red Sea

Sea currents

- In the Mediterranean, sea-surface evaporation is about three times greater than precipitation and runoff. Sea level is maintained by water flowing in from the Atlantic Ocean.
- The water in the eastern Mediterranean is slightly warmer and more saline than that in the western Mediterranean.
6 Atlantic cold water enters through the Strait of Gibraltar and travels along the North African coast.
7 Warm, more saline, water returns to the Atlantic along the European coast.

Facts about

Area
1,145,000 square mile (2,966,000 km²)

Mean depth
4,760 feet (1,450 m)

Maximum depth
16,707 feet (5,092 m) in the Hellenic Trough

Connections

Sea currents

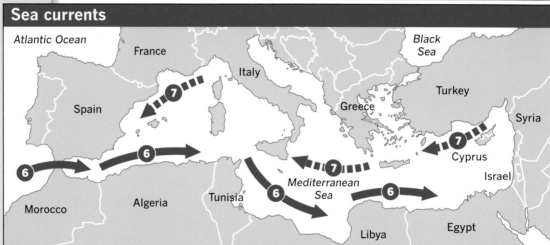

Component seas

Component seas

Geographically, the Mediterranean includes several other seas, including:

a The Tyrrhenian Sea

b The Adriatic Sea

c The Ionian Sea

d The Aegean Sea

Locator map

North Sea

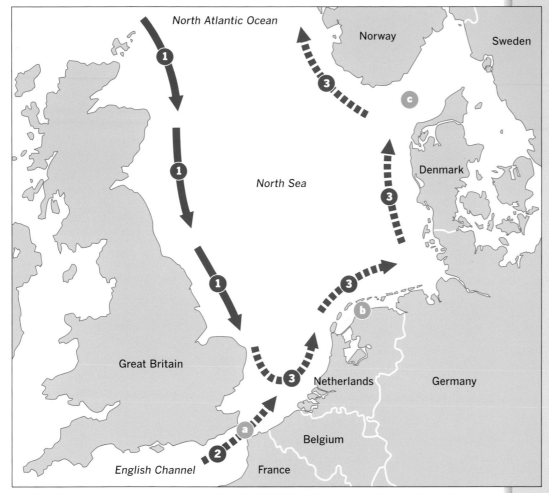

Key words

continental	ocean
crust	runoff
current	sea
land bridge	sea level
Northern	strait
Hemisphere	

North Sea

- The North Sea is a shallow northeastern arm of the Atlantic Ocean.
- It separates Great Britain from mainland northern Europe.

Evolution

- Movements of Northern Hemisphere landmasses between 225 and 65 million years ago established the beginnings of the North Sea's current shorelines.
- As recently as 18,000 years ago the North Sea did not exist. Its northern half was buried beneath an ice sheet and its southern half was covered in woodland and scrub. Since then, this low-lying region of continental crust has become flooded as sea levels have risen following postglacial warming.
- About 10,000 years ago, the land bridge between Dover, England, and Calais, France became submerged, forming the Straits of Dover. Much of the northern Netherlands was also submerged at this time.

Major geologic features

- **a** Straits of Dover
- **b** Northern Netherlands
- **c** Skagerrak entrance to Baltic

Current features

Cold northern stream

1 Cool water from the North Atlantic sweeps down the east coast of Scotland and England.

Warm southern stream

2 Warm water from the Atlantic Ocean enters the North Sea through the Straits of Dover **a** and helps keep the North Sea free of ice all year.

Mixed waters travel north

3 The circulation pattern in the North Sea is counterclockwise. Pollutant-laden runoff from the UK, France, Belgium, the Netherlands, and Germany is carried northward toward Denmark and Norway.

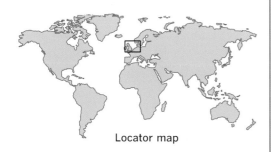

Locator map

Facts about

Area
222,010 square miles (575,000 km²)

Average depth
305 feet (93 m)

Maximum depth
2,380 feet (725 m) at Skagerrak (**c**)

© Diagram Visual Information Ltd.

© Diagram Visual Information Ltd.

Key words

current	rift valley
gulf	sea
monsoon	spreading ridge
ocean	

Red Sea

- The Red Sea is a northward extension of the Indian Ocean. It separates Africa from the Arabian Peninsula.
- The Red Sea is an example of a recently-formed sea that is expected to continue becoming wider.

Component parts

- **1** Gulf of Suez
- **2** Gulf of Aqaba
- **3** Main body of the Red Sea

Connections

- **4** The Strait of Bab el Mandeb connects the Red Sea to the Gulf of Aden and Arabian Sea.
- **5** The Suez Canal connects the Red Sea to the Mediterranean Sea.

Evolution

- The Red Sea is a flooded rift valley.
- It is widening from its spreading ridge in the axial trough **6** at the rate of about 0.5 inches (1.25 cm) per year.

Circulation

- **a** In summer, water currents flow southward, out of the Red Sea. Water is drawn out by currents in the Arabian Sea that are driven by the southwest monsoon winds.
- **b** In winter, water is driven into the Red Sea by reversing Arabian Sea currents and the northeast monsoons.

Facts about

Area

169,100 square miles (438,000 km²)

Mean depth

1,765 feet (538 m)

Maximum depth

9,580 feet (2,920 m) in the axial trough (**6**)

Red Sea

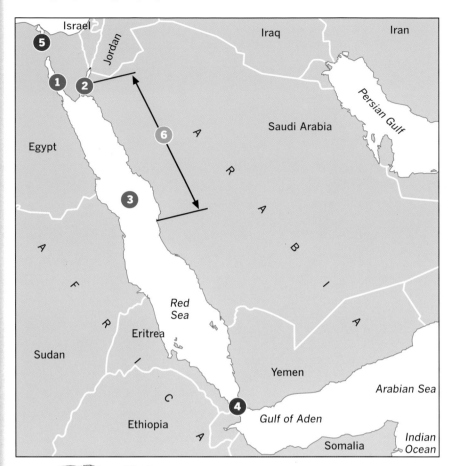

Locator map

Circulation

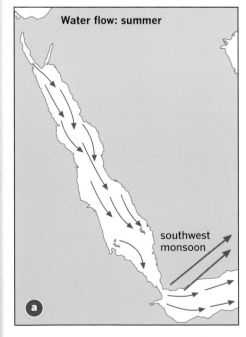

Water flow: summer

southwest monsoon

a

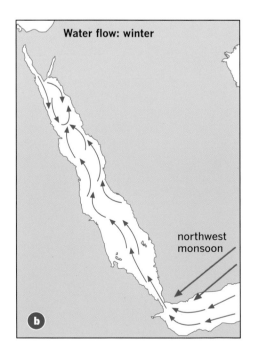

Water flow: winter

northwest monsoon

b

Persian Gulf

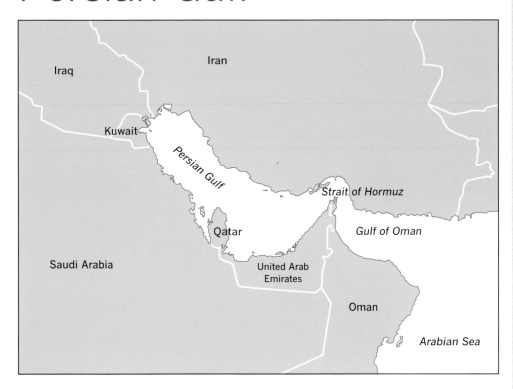

© Diagram Visual Information Ltd.

Key words

gulf	sea
lithospheric plate	strait
monsoon	subduction
ocean	tide

Persian Gulf

- The Persian Gulf is a shallow enclosed sea connected to the northern Indian Ocean via the Strait of Hormuz.
- The Gulf is less than 330 feet (100 m) deep over much of its area.
- It is polluted by oil discharges and agricultural and domestic waste. However, the strong circulation and high water temperatures tend to degrade and disperse pollutants rapidly.
- Strong tides flush water out through the Strait of Hormuz and into the Gulf of Oman and beyond. Pollutants are dispersed into the larger and deeper Arabian Sea in the Indian Ocean.

Evolution

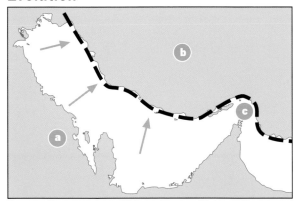

Locator map

- The Persian Gulf region is an area of active subduction, with the Arabian plate **a** to the southwest sliding beneath the Asian continental plate **b** to the northwest.
- It is feasible that within the next 100,000 years the Strait of Hormuz **c** could close as a result of this tectonic movement.

Circulation

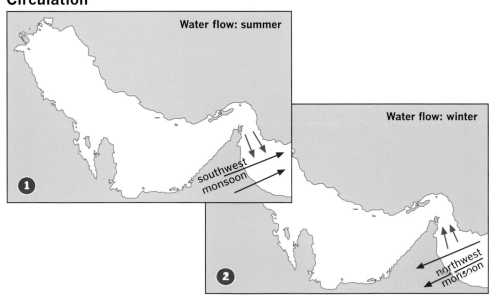

1 In summer, net surface water flow is out of the Persian Gulf, driven by the southwest monsoon winds.

2 In winter, net surface water flow is into the Persian Gulf, driven by the northwest monsoon winds.

Facts about

Area
77,200 square miles (200,000 km²)

Average depth
80 feet (25 m)

Maximum depth
560 feet (170 m)

© Diagram Visual Information Ltd.

Key words

abyssopelagic zone	epipelagic zone
atmosphere	fauna
bathypelagic zone	mesopelagic zone
depth zone	photosynthesis
	thermocline

Depth zones

- *Depth zones* are theoretical partitions of the water column referred to by biological oceanographers.
- These partitions are based on physical conditions and the biological communities that are adapted to living there.

Physical conditions: Light

- Organisms inhabiting the various depth zones are adapted to the abundance and quality of ambient light.
- In clear seawater, most of the available sunlight is absorbed within the top 660 feet (200 m).
- The remaining light is predominantly of blue and green wavelengths; the other wavelengths—violet, yellow, orange, and red—have already been absorbed.

Pressure

- Pressure increases by one atmosphere for each 33 feet (10 m) of depth.
- In the deepest parts of the ocean, at depths of greater than 33,000 feet (10,000 m), the ambient pressure is in excess of 1,000 atmospheres.

Temperature

- Sunlight warms the surface waters and turbulence transfers heat downward to depths of 660–990 feet (200–300 m).
- Below this, there is a steep temperature gradient, the thermocline, extending down to 2,650–3,300 feet (800–1,000 m).
- The deep ocean is almost uniformly cold, at between 30 and 39°F (−1 and 4°C).

Depth zones

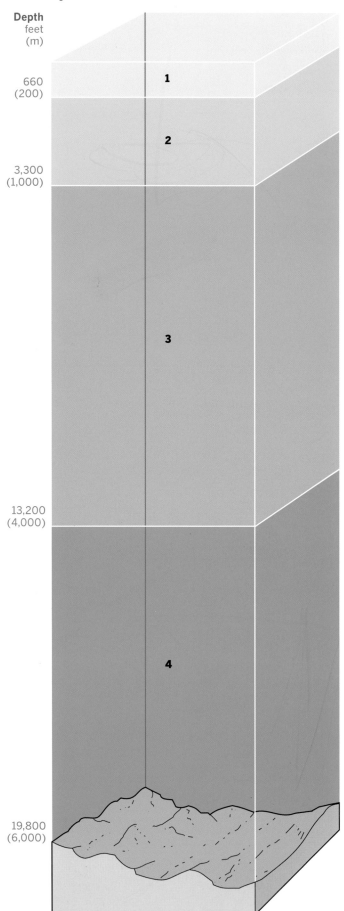

1 The *epipelagic zone*, also called the euphotic or sunlit zone, is the upper region of the water column. It receives sufficient sunlight to sustain photosynthesis. Most marine life depends, directly or indirectly, on plant production in this zone.

2 The *mesopelagic zone*, sometimes called the twilight zone, receives diffuse sunlight but in insufficient amounts to sustain photosynthesis. Most creatures inhabiting this zone:
- migrate to the epipelagic zone to feed, or
- rely on a rainfall of dead bodies or fecal matter sinking from the surface waters.

3 The *bathypelagic zone* receives no sunlight. Animal life is relatively sparse and consists mostly of crustaceans, squid, and relatively small fish. The latter have capacious mouths for engulfing the occasional prey item that may be as large as the predator itself.

4 The *abyssopelagic zone* is essentially an extension of the bathypelagic zone down to the seafloor, but supports an even sparser fauna.

The first oceans

Key words

atmosphere · · · · · · · · outgassing theory
cometary theory
element
heavy water
ocean

Outgassing theory

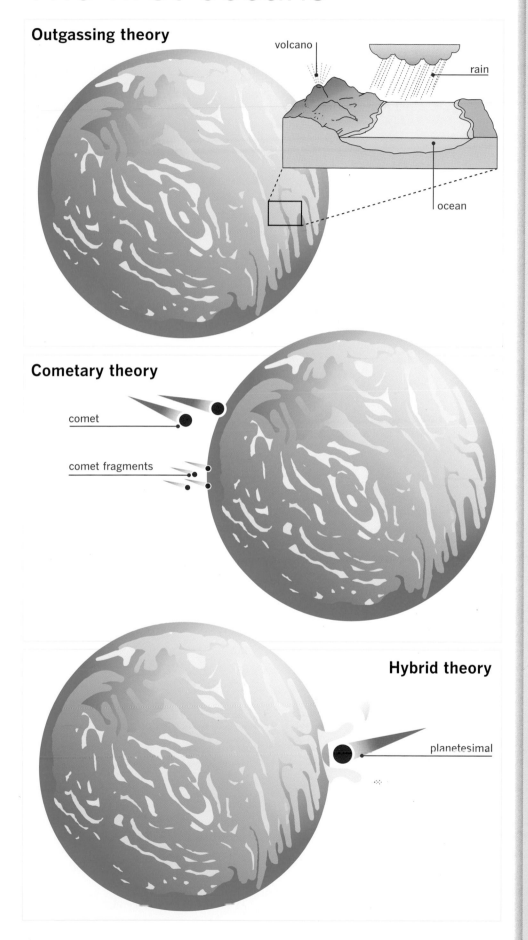

Cometary theory

Hybrid theory

Outgassing theory

- *Outgassing theory* states that the water in Earth's oceans originated with the gases that were released from the planet's interior soon after it coalesced into a single body.
- The early Earth is thought to have been a mainly molten ball. In this state, the heavier elements were separated out from the lighter, and these lighter elements (gases such as hydrogen and helium) escaped from the surface.
- At first Earth would have been so hot that most of these gases would have immediately boiled off into space.
- As Earth cooled, some of these gases would have been trapped by Earth's gravity to form an atmosphere.
- This atmosphere would have increased Earth's reflectivity so that less sunlight would have reached the surface, allowing the planet to cool further.
- Eventually, the atmosphere and the surface would have cooled to a point at which water droplets could condense and fall as rain.

Cometary theory

- *Cometary theory* states that some of Earth's water probably originated from comets that impacted Earth.
- However studies of the water content of comets suggest that most of Earth's water could not have come from comets. Cometary water contains a higher proportion of heavy water than Earth's oceans.

Hybrid theory

- Although it is unlikely that a significant proportion of Earth's water originated from comets, much of it may have come from the large bodies known as planetesimals that came together to form Earth.
- The remainder probably resulted from outgassing.

© Diagram Visual Information Ltd.

Key words

continental crust
oceanic crust
plate boundary
spreading ridge

Oceanic and continental crust

Earth's crust

- Earth's *crust* is the thin, solid layer of rock that forms the outer skin of the planet.
- There are two types of crust: oceanic and continental.

Oceanic crust

- *Oceanic crust* is the part of Earth's crust that forms the ocean floor.
- Oceanic crust is 4–7 miles (6–11 km) thick and has an average density of about 1.7 ounces per cubic inch (3 g/cm^3).
- It consists mostly of basalts, the majority of which have been formed within the last 200 million years.
- Oceanic crust is generally much younger than continental crust because it is constantly being destroyed at convergent plate boundaries and created at spreading ridges.

Continental crust

- *Continental crust* is the part of Earth's surface that forms the continents.
- Continental crust is 20–25 miles (30–40 km) thick with a maximum thickness of about 45 miles (70 km) and has an average density of about 1.6 ounces per cubic inch (2.7 g/cm^3).
- It consists of two basic layers: an upper layer dominated by granites and a lower layer dominated by basalt and diorite. These rocks are usually much older than oceanic crust rocks.

Oceanic crust

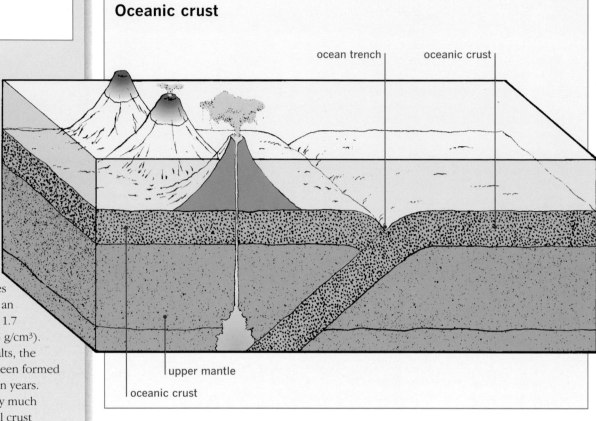

ocean trench   oceanic crust

upper mantle

oceanic crust

Continental crust

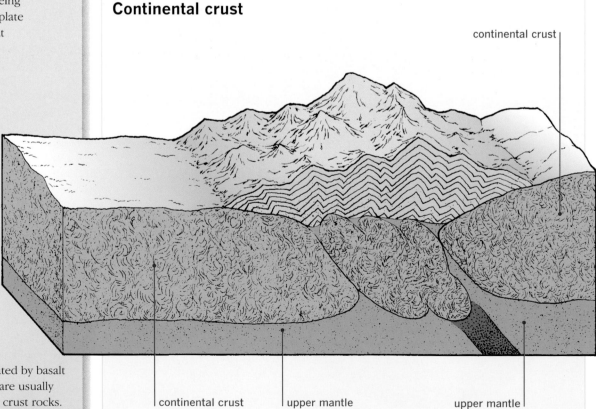

continental crust

continental crust   upper mantle   upper mantle

© Diagram Visual Information Ltd.

Primeval continental drift

250 million years ago

180 million years ago

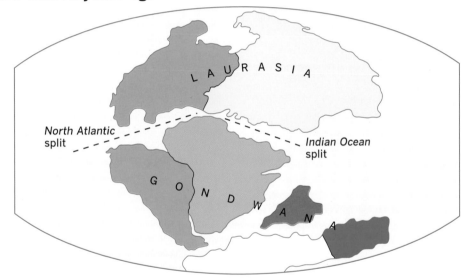

100 million years ago

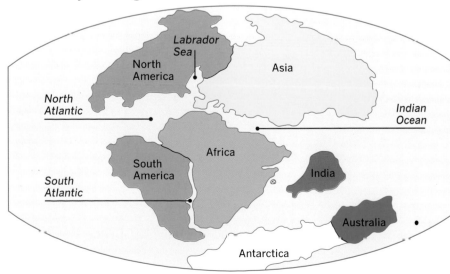

Key words

continental drift	Pangaea
Gondwana	Panthalassa
Laurasia	
ocean	

Continental drift

- *Continental drift* is the theory that the continents are very slowly moving in relation to one another.
- Geologists believe that the present-day continents once formed a single landmass that has since broken apart.

250 million years ago

- Two hundred million years ago there was just one landmass on Earth. It is referred to as *Pangaea*, which is Greek for "all land."
- The continental crust that makes up today's landmasses was a part of Pangaea.
- The great ocean that covered the rest of the globe is called *Panthalassa*, which means "all sea."

180 million years ago

- By 180 million years ago Pangaea had begun to break up.
- The first split to occur opened up what became the North Atlantic and Indian oceans. The landmass to the north of this split is known as *Laurasia* and the landmass to the south as *Gondwana*.
- Antarctica also split away from Pangaea and started to drift slowly southward.
- India split from Antarctica and began to drift northward.

100 million years ago

- By 100 million years ago the North Atlantic and Indian Ocean splits had grown wider.
- Africa and South America had begun to separate as the South Atlantic Ocean began to open up.
- The Labrador Sea, which eventually separated Greenland from North America, had also begun to open.
- India was moving strongly northward on a collision course with the southern coast of Asia.

© Diagram Visual Information Ltd.

© Diagram Visual Information Ltd.

Key words

continental drift
ocean

60 million years ago

- By 60 million years ago South America had separated from Africa completely and was drifting toward collision with the southern tip of North America.
- The North Atlantic continued to widen and eventually detached North America from Europe altogether.
- India continued to move northward.
- Australia remained attached to Antarctica.

Present day

- Today North America and Europe are separated by an ever-widening North Atlantic Ocean.
- South America and Africa are separated by an ever-widening South Atlantic Ocean.
- Greenland has become isolated from North America and Europe.
- India has impacted with Asia.
- North and South America have joined.
- Australia has separated from Antarctica and migrated northward.

50 million years in the future

- Both the North and South Atlantic will have continued to grow wider.
- Australia will have continued its northward drift.
- India will have been propelled eastward with the rest of Asia.
- Africa will have drifted slowly northward, closing the Mediterranean.
- Africa's Rift valley will have widened to form the beginnings of a new ocean.
- The Red Sea will have widened and become continuous with the Mediterranean.
- North and South America will have become detached again as North America continues to drift north west.

Recent continental drift

60 million years ago

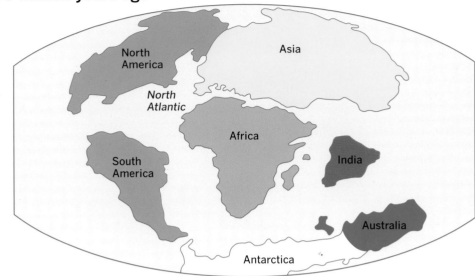

Present day

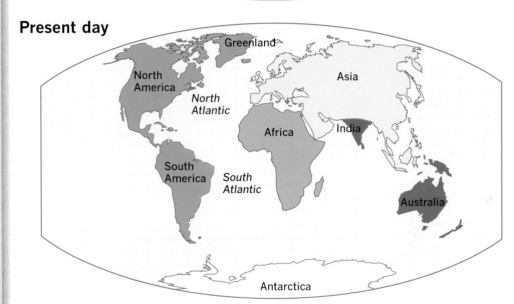

50 million years in the future

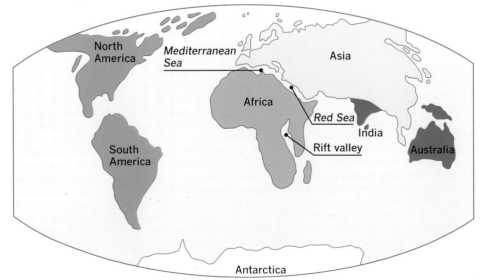

Seafloor spreading

Key words

magma
mid-ocean ridge
oceanic crust
sea-floor
  spreading

The process of seafloor spreading

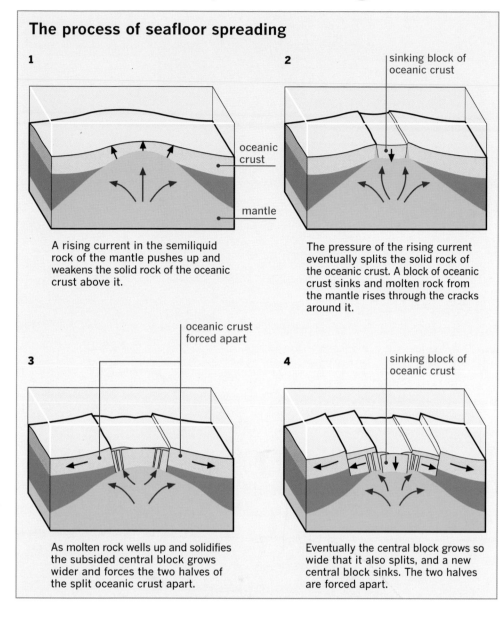

1

oceanic
crust

mantle

A rising current in the semiliquid rock of the mantle pushes up and weakens the solid rock of the oceanic crust above it.

2

sinking block of oceanic crust

The pressure of the rising current eventually splits the solid rock of the oceanic crust. A block of oceanic crust sinks and molten rock from the mantle rises through the cracks around it.

3

oceanic crust forced apart

As molten rock wells up and solidifies the subsided central block grows wider and forces the two halves of the split oceanic crust apart.

4

sinking block of oceanic crust

Eventually the central block grows so wide that it also splits, and a new central block sinks. The two halves are forced apart.

Seafloor spreading

- *Seafloor spreading* is the process by which seas become wider as volcanic processes create new seafloor material (oceanic crust).
- A *mid-ocean ridge* is a volcanically active site where new oceanic crust is created.
- Magma wells up from the center of the ridge and quickly solidifies as it is exposed to the cold water.
- Solidified magma is soon pushed outward by new magma upwellings. With each upwelling, the oceanic crust spreads further outwards from the ridge.

Magnetic polarity reversal

- When magma emerging from ocean ridges solidifies, it effectively records the orientation of Earth's magnetic field at that point in time.
- Iron-bearing minerals in the magma are orientated by Earth's magnetic field and are locked in that position when the rock solidifies.
- Studies of oceanic crust have shown that Earth's magnetic field has reversed polarity many times in the past.
- Rock on the seafloor consists of bands of solidified magma with alternating magnetic orientations.
- These bands indicate that Earth's magnetic field reverses polarity at irregular intervals of between 100,000 and 25 million years.

Fossilized magnetic polarity reversals

Bands of rock that have recorded reversed polarities are found running parallel to spreading ridges. The existence of these bands is thought to prove the process of seafloor spreading over geologic time.

oceanic crust formed during a period of reversed polarity

oceanic crust formed during a period when polarity was the same as today

6   4   2   0   2   4   6

Age in millions
of years

spreading ridge

© Diagram Visual Information Ltd.

© Diagram Visual Information Ltd.

Key words

continental crust	subduction
magma	upwelling
mid-ocean ridge	Wilson Cycle
oceanic crust	
rift valley	

Wilson Cycle

- The *Wilson Cycle* (after J. Tuzo Wilson 1908–93) describes the creation, evolution, and eventual destruction of an ocean.

1 Embryonic stage

- An upwelling of hot mantle material stresses the continental crust above and may cause it to begin to split.
- A rift valley results from this splitting.

2 Juvenile stage

- As the rift deepens, seawater will eventually flood in.
- Upwelling magma seeps to the surface and begins to form oceanic crust.
- Oceanic crust forms on either side of the magma upwelling, pushing the two halves of the flooded valley further apart (seafloor spreading).
- A new ocean is being formed.

3 Mature stage

- As seafloor spreading continues, the ocean matures and the coasts continue to move apart.
- A mature ocean features a mid-ocean ridge and a continental margin.

4 Declining stage

- An ocean begins to shrink when the amount of new oceanic crust being formed at ridges is exceeded by the amount being subducted beneath other crustal plates at trenches.
- Older oceanic crust tends to sink beneath newer crust because it is cooler and floats lower on the mantle.
- Where oceanic crust is subducted there is a high incidence of volcanic and earthquake activity.

5 Terminal stage

- The shrinking ocean eventually becomes isolated from the rest of the oceans and may drain.
- Continents are eventually drawn into collision, forming mountain ranges.

The Wilson Cycle

1 Embryonic stage

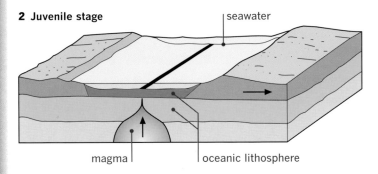

rift valley

continental lithosphere (continental crust and upper solid mantle)

asthenosphere (semifluid upper mantle)

2 Juvenile stage

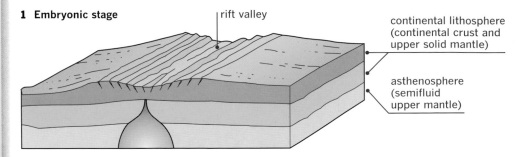

seawater

magma

oceanic lithosphere

3 Mature stage

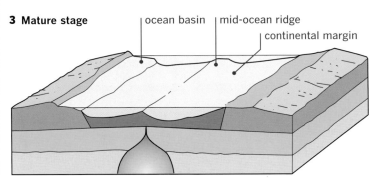

ocean basin

mid-ocean ridge

continental margin

4 Declining stage

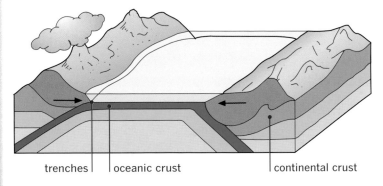

trenches

oceanic crust

continental crust

5 Terminal stage

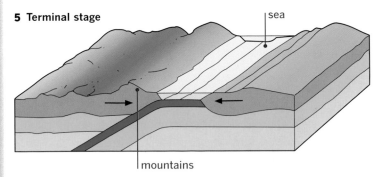

sea

mountains

Major lithospheric plates

Key words

convergent boundary	lithospheric plate
	mantle
divergent boundary	transform boundary

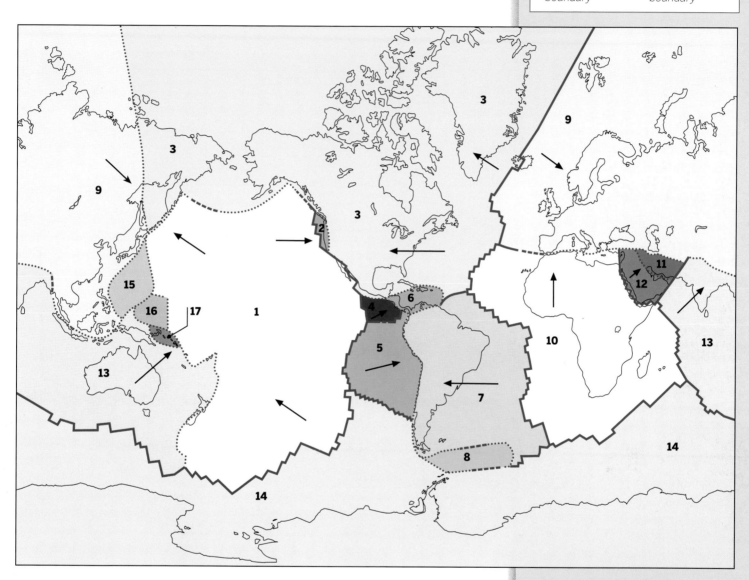

convergent plate boundary (where adjacent plates come together)

divergent plate boundary (where adjacent plates move apart)

transform plate boundary (where adjacent plates move past one another)

direction of plate movement

1 Pacific plate
2 Juan de Fuca plate
3 North American plate
4 Cocos plate
5 Nazca plate
6 Caribbean plate
7 South American plate
8 Scotia plate
9 Eurasian plate

10 African plate
11 Iranian plate
12 Arabian plate
13 Indo-Australian plate
14 Antarctic plate
15 Philippine plate
16 Caroline plate
17 Bismarck plate

Lithospheric plates

- A *lithospheric plate* is one of the solid, but distinct, segments that make up the outer surface of Earth.
- Lithospheric plates are mostly solid and float on the semiliquid mantle beneath.
- Lithospheric plates float because they are less dense (on average) than mantle material.
- Lithospheric plates move around Earth's surface, collide, and interact with each other.
- Their motion is thought to be driven by convection currents in the mantle.

© Diagram Visual Information Ltd.

Plate boundaries

© Diagram Visual Information Ltd.

Key words

convergent
  boundary
divergent
  boundary
lithospheric plate
mid-ocean ridge

plate boundary
spreading ridge
subduction
transform
  boundary
trench

Plate boundaries

- *Plate boundaries* are the regions where lithospheric plates meet.
- Lithospheric plates are either moving apart, colliding, or sliding past each other.

Divergent boundary

- A *divergent boundary* is a region where lithospheric plates are moving apart.
- They occur where oceanic crust is being laid down at a spreading ridge. These are common at mid-ocean ridges.

Convergent boundary

- A *convergent boundary* is a region where two lithospheric plates are colliding.
- The denser plate usually sinks beneath the other. This is known as *subduction*.
- Older portions of lithospheric plate are usually denser than younger portions. This is because older portions are cooler.
- Deep depressions in the ocean floor known as *trenches* are common where subduction occurs.

Transform boundary

- A *transform boundary* is a region where two lithospheric plates move past each other at a fracture called a transform fault.
- Friction between the plates causes frequent earthquake activity along transform boundaries.

Divergent boundary

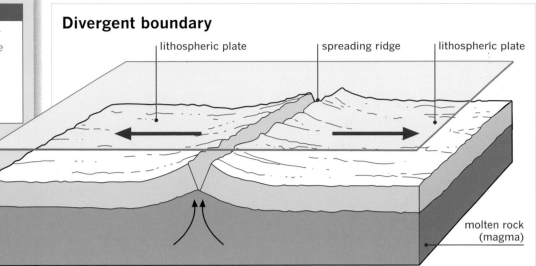

lithospheric plate · spreading ridge · lithospheric plate

molten rock (magma)

Convergent boundary

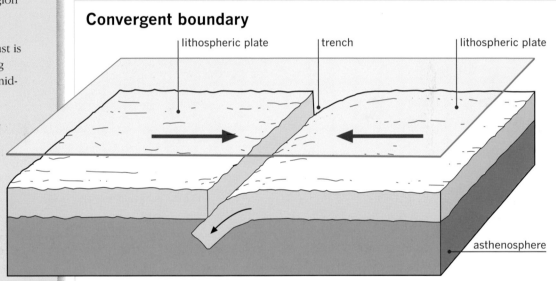

lithospheric plate · trench · lithospheric plate

asthenosphere

Transform boundary

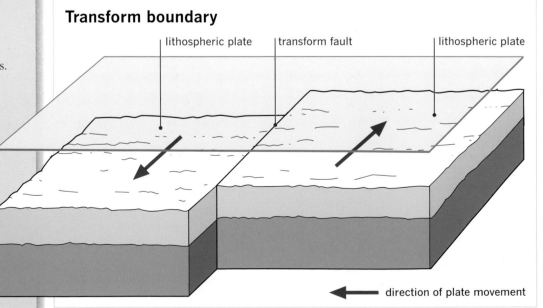

lithospheric plate · transform fault · lithospheric plate

← direction of plate movement

Seamounts and guyots

Volcanic island formation

Key words

guyot	*spreading ridge*
magma	*upwelling*
mid-ocean ridge	*volcanic island*
oceanic crust	
seamount	

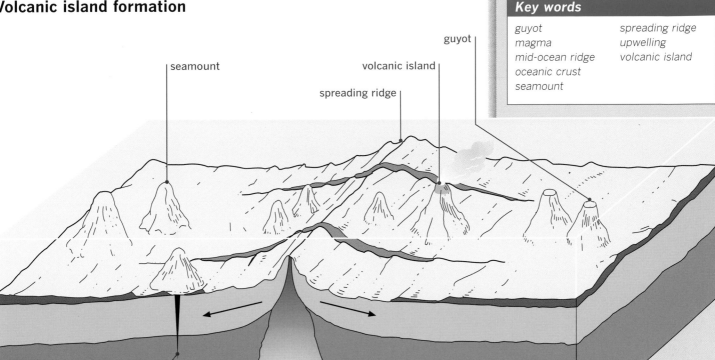

seamount   spreading ridge   volcanic island   guyot

tension fracture

Guyot formation

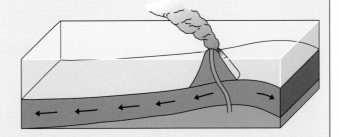

1 A volcanic island is formed at an oceanic spreading ridge.

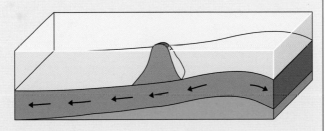

2 The volcanic island moves away from the spreading ridge, and as it sinks, wave action erodes its top.

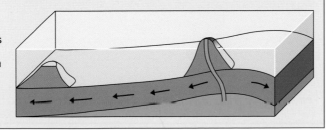

3 The submerged island moves further away from its source and the top is flattened to form a guyot: a flat-topped seamount. Meanwhile a new volcanic island is formed at the spreading ridge.

Volcanic features

- Several geologic features are associated with mid-ocean ridges.
- Most volcanic activity takes place along the axis of the spreading ridge and consists of magma upwellings that build oceanic crust.
- Further away from the ridge, tension fractures allow magma to escape and form other volcanic features.
- A *seamount* is a submerged volcano that forms close to a mid-ocean ridge.
- Seamounts may grow in height until they break the surface of the ocean and become volcanic islands.
- As a seamount moves with the oceanic crust further from the spreading ridge, it will eventually become inactive.
- As an inactive seamount moves even further from the spreading ridge, the underlying crust subsides and it may become submerged again.
- A *guyot* is an inactive seamount that has emerged from the ocean as a volcanic island, been eroded flat by the action of weather and waves, and become submerged again.

© Diagram Visual Information Ltd.

© Diagram Visual Information Ltd.

Key words

hot spot	seamount
island chain	volcanic island
lithospheric plate	
magma	
oceanic crust	

Volcanic island chains

- A *volcanic island chain* may form when oceanic crust moves over a persistent *hot spot* in the mantle (**1**).
- Magma is forced to the surface above the hot spot and builds a seamount (**2**) that eventually emerges as a volcanic island (**3**).
- As the island moves away from the hot spot with the oceanic crust, volcanic activity ceases and the island may begin to subside.
- A new seamount forms above the hot spot, eventually breaking the surface as a new volcanic island (**4**).
- Over millions of years a chain of seamounts and volcanic islands emerges.

Hawaiian and Emperor chains

- A mantle hot spot has created the Emperor seamount chain and the Hawaiian Islands over 70 million years.
- The Emperor seamount chain now consists of submerged seamounts (**a**).
- About 25 million years ago, the Pacific plate changed direction (**b**) and the Hawaiian chain began to form (**c**).
- Today, Hawaii is a volcanically active island, and to its southeast Loihi is an active seamount that has yet to rise above sea level.

Growth of the Hawaiian Islands

Development of volcanic island chains

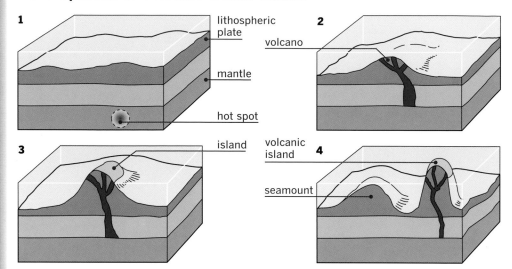

The development of Hawaii

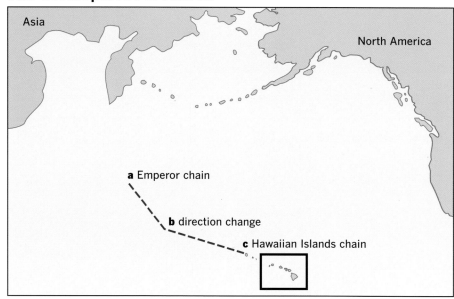

Hawaii today

Loihi: a volcanically active seamount

Hawaii: a volcanically active island for 0.8 million years

Maui: a volcanically inactive island for 0.8 million years

Molokai: a volcanically inactive island for 1.3 million years

Oahu: a volcanically inactive island for 2.2 million years

Kauai: a volcanically inactive island for 3.8 million years

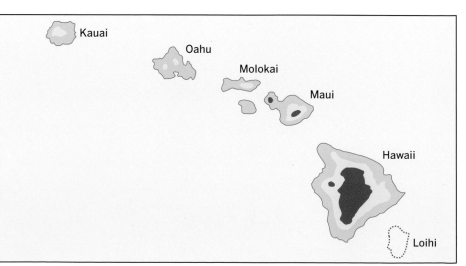

Profile of an ocean

Continental margin

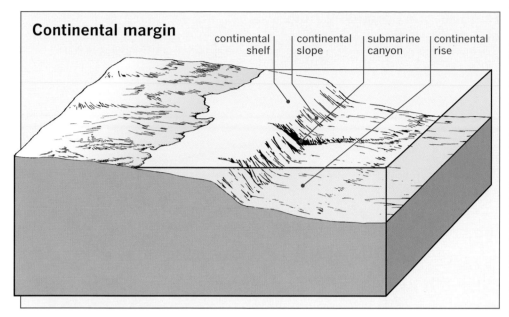

continental shelf | continental slope | submarine canyon | continental rise

Spreading ridge

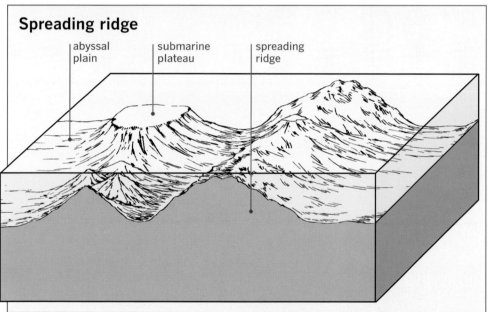

abyssal plain | submarine plateau | spreading ridge

Oceanic trench

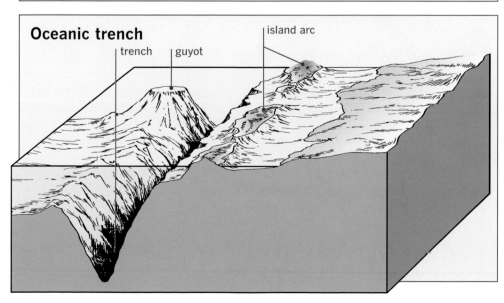

island arc | trench | guyot

Key words

abyssal plain
continental rise
continental shelf
continental slope
guyot
island arc

spreading ridge
submarine
  canyon
trench

Continental shelf

● A *continental shelf* is a continent's true rim: it descends to an average depth of 650 feet (200 m). Continental shelves occupy about 7.5 percent of the ocean floor.

Continental slope

● A continental slope is a steep slope descending from the continental shelf. Such slopes occupy about 8.5 percent of the ocean floor.

Submarine canyon

● Clefts in the continental slope called submarine canyons are cut by turbid river water flowing out to sea.

Continental rise

● The continental rise is a gentle slope below the continental slope.

Abyssal plain

● This is the sediment-covered deep-sea plain about 11,500–18,000 feet (3,500–5,500 m) below sea level.

Submarine plateau

● High seafloor tablelands are called submarine plateaus.

Spreading ridge

● These submarine mountain chains are generally 10,000 feet (3,000 m) above the abyssal plain.

Trench

● Trenches are deep steep troughs.

Guyot

● Guyots are flat-topped seamounts that have been volcanic islands before becoming submerged.

Island arc

● A curved row of volcanic islands, usually on the continental side of a trench, is called an island arc.

© Diagram Visual Information Ltd.

Spreading ridges

Features of a spreading ridge

Key words

asthenosphere
magma
mantle
mid-ocean ridge
oceanic crust
spreading ridge
transform fault
upwelling

transform fault · spreading unit · spreading axis · ocean floor

upwelling magma

upper mantle

asthenosphere

oceanic crust

Spreading ridges

- A *spreading ridge* is a region of the ocean floor where new oceanic crust is being created by upwelling magma from the layer of semiliquid rock known as the asthenosphere.
- This magma forces its way through the upper mantle and emerges on the ocean floor.
- The magma cools to form oceanic crust and is forced away from the axis of the ridge by more upwelling magma. The ocean floor spreads outwards on both sides of the ridge.
- As the newly formed oceanic crust is pushed away from the ridge, it cools.
- Cooling causes the new oceanic crust to buckle and subside.
- Stresses cause faults to open up perpendicular to the axis of the spreading ridge. These are known as *transform faults*.
- Transform faults divide the ridge into a series of offset spreading units.

© Diagram Visual Information Ltd.

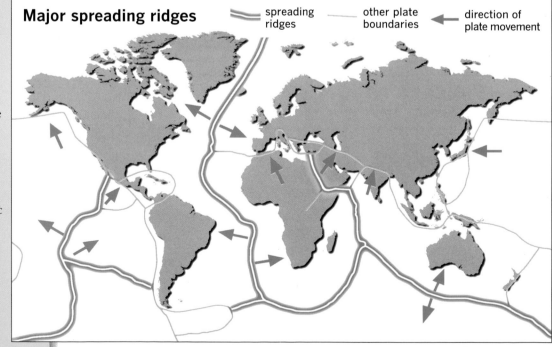

Major spreading ridges — spreading ridges · other plate boundaries · direction of plate movement

Trenches

Key words

asthenosphere   subduction
continental crust   trench
island chain   volcanic island
magma
oceanic crust

Island arc and trench systems

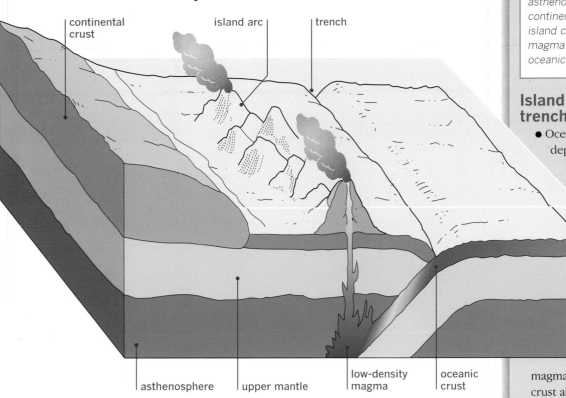

continental crust   island arc   trench

asthenosphere   upper mantle   low-density magma   oceanic crust

Continental arc and trench systems

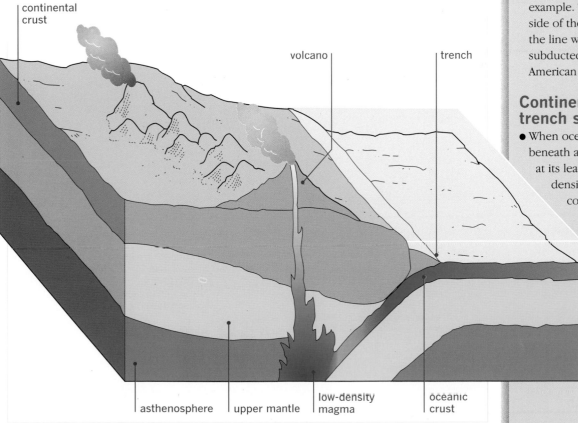

continental crust   volcano   trench

asthenosphere   upper mantle   low-density magma   oceanic crust

Island arc and trench systems

- Ocean trenches are deep depressions on the ocean floor. They are typically 2–2.5 miles (3–4 km) deeper than the surrounding ocean floor and hundreds of miles long, but narrow. An ocean trench forms when a tectonic plate is subducted beneath another.
- Melted material from the subducted plate mixes with water to produce a low density magma that tends to rise through the crust above. This volcanic activity creates a chain of islands behind the trench.
- The Aleutian Islands off Alaska are an example. They lie along the landward side of the Aleutian trench that marks the line where the Pacific plate is subducted beneath the North American plate.

Continental arc and trench systems

- When oceanic crust is subducted beneath a plate with continental crust at its leading edge, the resulting low-density magma rises through the continental crust to form a chain of volcanoes close to the shore.
- The Andes Mountains of South America are an example. They lie parallel to the region where the Nazca plate is subducted beneath the South American plate.

© Diagram Visual Information Ltd.

© Diagram Visual Information Ltd.

Key words

abyssal hills	continental slope
abyssal plain	mid-ocean ridge
alluvial fan	shelf break
continental	submarine
margin	canyon
continental rise	trench
continental shelf	turbidity current

Continental margin features

- The *continental margin* is the portion of a continent that extends beneath the ocean. It consists of several regions:

- The *continental shelf* is a gentle slope that extends from the shoreline out under the water to the edge of a steep cliff known as the continental slope. The top of this cliff is known as the *shelf break*.

- The *continental slope* is a steep slope that extends from the shelf break down to a more gentle slope known as the *continental rise*.

- The *continental rise* is a gentle slope extending from the bottom of the continental slope to the generally flat region known as the *abyssal plain*. The continental rise is made up of sediments that have slid off the continental slope.

- Valleys cut into the continental slope are known as *submarine canyons*. They are river or glacial valleys that were formed when sea levels were much lower than at present. They may also be formed by seismic activity causing undersea "avalanches" of sediment known as *turbidity currents*.

- The *abyssal plain* is the almost flat, featureless plain that makes up most of the ocean bed. It may be interrupted by abyssal hills, mid-ocean ridges, trenches, or other volcanic features.

- An *alluvial fan* is a fan-shaped layer of sediment on the abyssal plain deposited by a turbidity current.

Continental margins

Continental margin

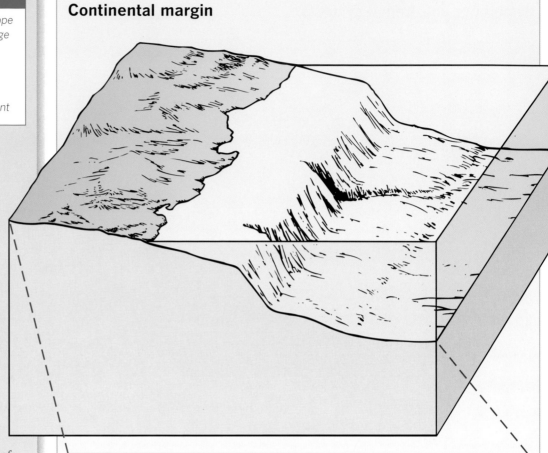

Continental margin features

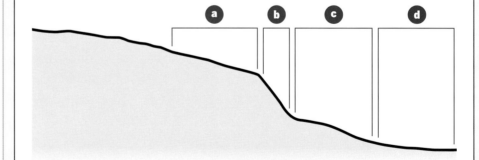

a **Continental shelf**
Slope typically 0.1°, depth less than 1,300 feet (400 m)

b **Continental slope**
Slope typically 3–6°, depth down to 6,500–13,000 feet (2,000–4,000 m)

c **Continental rise**
Slope range 0.1–1°, depth 8,200–16,500 feet (2,500–5,000 m), formed from deposition of material flowing down canyons

d **Abyssal plain**
Generally flat, depth 10,000–16,500 feet (3,000–5,000 m) but may contain trenches down to 26,000 feet (8,000 m) or more

Continental margins of North America

Key words

continental
margin

Ocean depths around North America

- 0–500 feet
  (0–150 m)

- 500–10,000 feet
  (150–3,050 m)

- 10,000–20,000 feet
  (3,050–6,100 m)

- more than 20,000 feet
  (6,100 m)

Canada

United States

Pacific Ocean

Atlantic Ocean

Mexico

West coast
The west coast of the United States has a narrow, active continental margin.

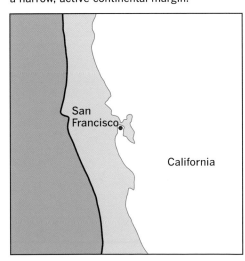

San Francisco

California

East coast
The east coast of the United States has a broad, passive continental margin.

South Carolina

Charleston

Florida

Continental margins

- An *active continental margin* is a margin where there is interaction between lithospheric plates (convergent or transform boundaries). They tend to have narrow, steeply sloping continental slopes.

- A *passive continental margin* is a margin where there is no interaction between lithospheric plates. They tend to have broad, gently sloping continental slopes.

© Diagram Visual Information Ltd.

Seafloor sediments

© Diagram Visual Information Ltd.

Key words

biogenous
  sediment
cosmogenous
  sediment
hydrogenous
  sediment

sediment
terrigenous
  sediment

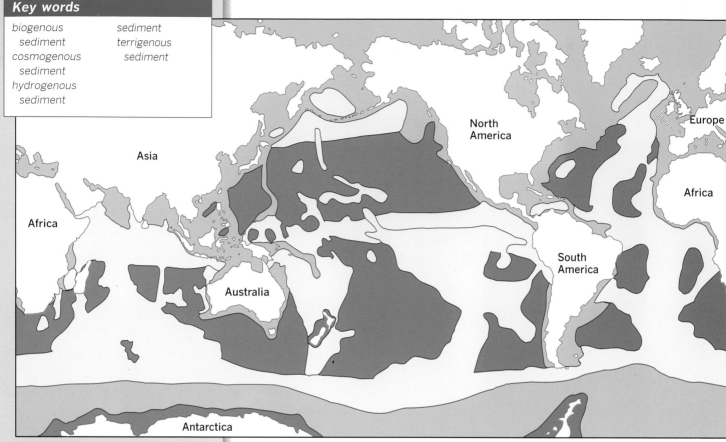

mostly
terrigenous

mostly
biogenous

mostly red clay
with some hydrogenous

Sediments of the seafloor

- A *sediment* is a layer of particles that has settled on the ocean floor.
- *Terrigenous sediments* are formed from particles that originated on land. An example is the mud carried into the sea by a river.
- *Biogenous sediments* are formed from particles that came from living things. An example is the shells of tiny creatures living in the sea.
- *Hydrogenous sediments* are formed from particles that crystallize out of seawater.
- Red clay is a kind of terrigenous sediment that is common where no other kind of sediment is usually deposited.
- Different kinds of sediment are more common across certain regions of the seafloor. For example, terrigenous sediments are more common close to the edges of continents.
- The size of sediment particles, known as grains, are classified according to the Wentworth scale.

Sediment grain sizes
Grain sizes according to the Wentworth scale

Particle size range (inches)	Particle size range (metric)	Particle or aggregate name
>10.1	256 mm	boulder
2.5–10.1	64–256 mm	cobble
1.26–2.5	32–64 mm	very coarse gravel
0.63–1.26	16–32 mm	coarse gravel
0.31–0.63	8–16 mm	medium gravel
0.157–0.31	4–8 mm	fine gravel
0.079–0.157	2–4 mm	very fine gravel
0.039–0.079	1–2 mm	very coarse sand
0.020–0.039	0.5–1 mm	coarse sand
0.010–0.020	0.25–0.5 mm	medium sand
0.0049–0.010	125–250 μm	fine sand
0.0025–0.0049	62.5–125 μm	very fine sand
0.00015–0.0025	3.90625–62.5 μm	silt
0.00015–0.000039	3.90625–1 μm	clay
>0.000039	>1 μm	colloid

Biogenous sediments

Calcareous sediments

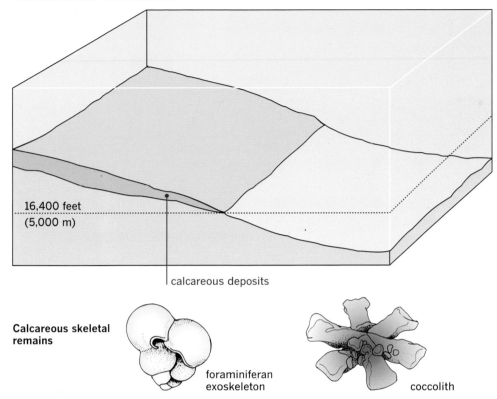

16,400 feet
(5,000 m)

calcareous deposits

Calcareous skeletal remains

foraminiferan exoskeleton

coccolith

Siliceous sediments

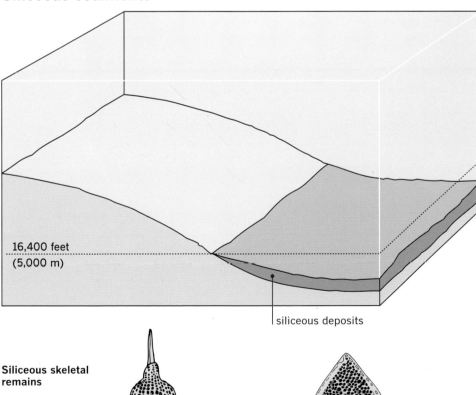

16,400 feet
(5,000 m)

siliceous deposits

Siliceous skeletal remains

radiolarian exoskeleton

diatom exoskeleton

Key words	
biogenous sediment	sediment siliceous
calcareous sediment	sediment subtropical
plankton	temperate

Biogenous sediments

- *Biogenous sediments* are sediments formed from the remains of once-living organisms.

Calcareous sediments

- *Calcareous sediments* are biogenous sediments formed from calcium carbonate. The calcium carbonate comes from the exoskeletons of tiny creatures such as foraminiferans and coccoliths.
- Foraminiferans and coccoliths are single-celled animals that live in the oceans in huge numbers.
- Calcareous sediments are found at moderate depths in subtropical and temperate waters.
- They are not found at depths greater than 14,800–16,400 feet (4,500–5,000 m) because high pressure, high carbon dioxide concentrations, and low temperatures dissolve calcium carbonate.
- The relatively shallow Atlantic Ocean has about two-thirds calcareous sediment coverage, while the deeper Pacific Ocean has about one-third coverage.

Siliceous sediments

- *Siliceous sediments* are biogenous sediments formed from the glasslike (siliceous) exoskeletons of tiny creatures known as diatoms, radiolarians, and silicoflagellates.
- Siliceous sediments are found in cooler and deeper waters than calcareous sediments.
- They accumulate where deposition of calcareous exoskeletons is low, where there are high concentrations of dissolved silica, and at depths greater than 14,800–16,400 feet (4,500–5,000 m) where calcium carbonate tends to dissolve.

© Diagram Visual Information Ltd.

© Diagram Visual Information Ltd.

Key words

continental crust	sediment
estuary	terrigenous
glacial sediment	sediment
glacier	turbidity current
iceberg	

Terrigenous sediments

- *Terrigenous sediments* are sediments formed from material that originated from continental crust.

Deep-sea clay

- Deep-sea clay covers large areas of the deep ocean floor.
- It consists of material conveyed from land by wind and water currents.
- Deposition from other sources is very low in these areas.
- Deposition rates are very low—typically 0.04 inches (1 mm) per thousand years.

Coarse terrigenous sediments

- Coarse sediments are typically deposited by rivers via estuaries.
- They are found primarily in shallow waters on the continental shelf.
- Turbidity currents can also convey coarse sediments to the deep ocean floor.
- Large river estuaries, such as the Ganges-Brahmaputra fan in the Bay of Bengal, can extend well beyond the continental shelf.

Glacial sediments

- Glacial sediments are found primarily on continental shelves where glaciers flowed during periods of low sea level.
- They are of mixed coarseness, from clay to boulder-sized particles.
- They are also found in deeper water where free-floating icebergs have melted and deposited their sediment.

Terrigenous sediments

Deep-sea clay

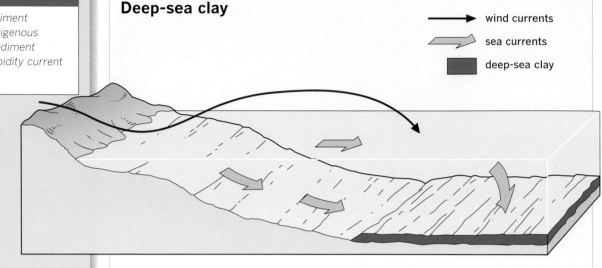

→ wind currents

⇒ sea currents

■ deep-sea clay

Coarse terrigenous sediments

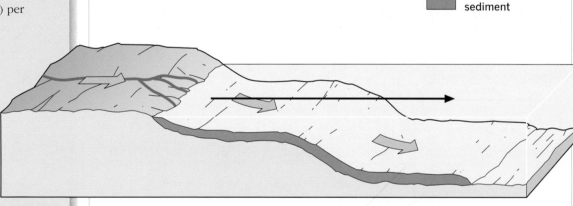

→ strong river current

■ coarse sediment

Glacial sediments

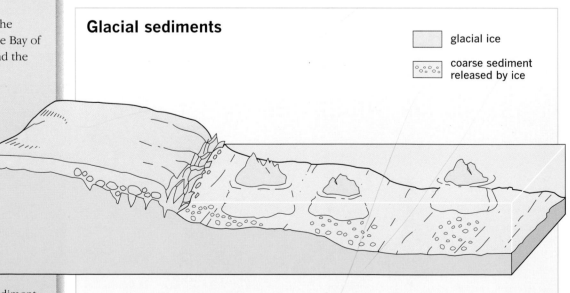

☐ glacial ice

▨ coarse sediment released by ice

Hydrogenous sediments

Hydrothermal vents

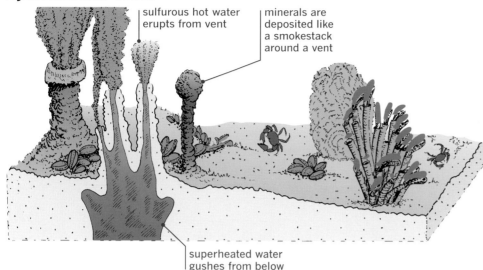

sulfurous hot water erupts from vent

minerals are deposited like a smokestack around a vent

superheated water gushes from below

Black smoker

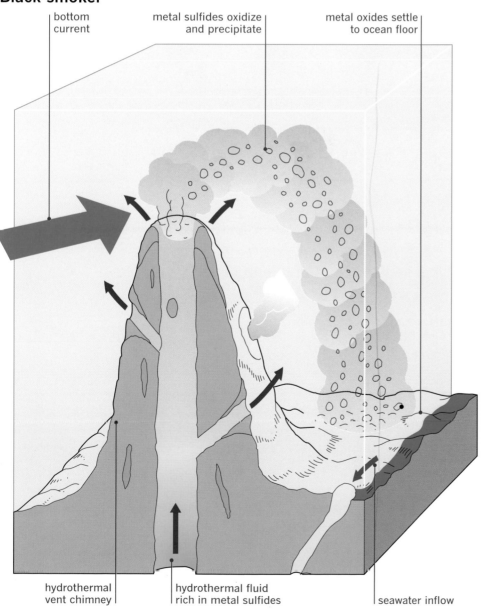

bottom current

metal sulfides oxidize and precipitate

metal oxides settle to ocean floor

hydrothermal vent chimney

hydrothermal fluid rich in metal sulfides

seawater inflow

Key words

black smoker	manganese
diffuse vent	nodule
hydrogenous	sediment
sediment	white smoker
hydrothermal	
vent	

Hydrogenous sediments

- *Hydrogenous sediments* are sediments composed of minerals precipitated from seawater.

Calcium carbonate deposits

- Seawater is saturated with calcium ions (Ca^{2+}).
- Where carbonate ion (CO_3^{2-}) concentration is high and carbon dioxide (CO_2) concentration is low, calcium carbonate is precipitated ($CaCO_3$), mainly as aragonite and calcite.

Manganese (polymetallic) modules

- *Manganese nodules* are small, roughly spherical nuggets of metals that form on the deep ocean floor.
- They typically contain manganese dioxide (30 percent), iron oxide (20 percent), and a combination of cobalt, copper, and nickel.
- It is not known how or why they form but they are thought to grow at a rate of 0.04–8 inches (1–200 mm) every million years.

Hydrothermal vent deposits

- Seawater flows into crevices near mid-ocean ridges where it is heated and dissolves minerals from the rocks.
- When this heated water is expelled again, it meets cold ocean water and some of its dissolved chemicals are precipitated as sediments.

Types of hydrothermal vents

- In diffuse vents: water is expelled at up to 86°F (30°C).
- In white smokers, water is expelled at 390–570°F (200–300°C).
- In black smokers, sulfide-rich water is expelled at 570–750°F (300–400°C).

© Diagram Visual Information Ltd.

Transport routes of oceanic sediment

© Diagram Visual Information Ltd.

Key words

aeolian transport
authigenesis
biogenous
  sediment
coastal erosion
hydrothermal
  vent
iceberg
micrometeorite
sediment
turbidity current
volcano

Origins of oceanic sediment

Origins of oceanic sediment

Material is transported into the oceans by many routes:

a *Fluvial transport*: riverborne terrigenous (land-originated) sediment.

b *Aeolian transport*: terrigenous sediment blown on the wind.

c *Coastal erosion*.

d *Fallout* from ash clouds produced by volcanoes and (**e**) *high-altitude jetstreams*.

f *Micrometeorites* from space.

g *Mass gravity flow*: Debris flows and turbidity currents.

h *Ice-rafting*: release of glacial sediment from icebergs.

i *Hydrothermal activity*: chemicals extracted from rock by hot water.

j *Submarine volcanic activity*.

k *Biogenic debris*: sediment accumulating from the waste and dead bodies of organisms.

l *Authigenesis*: addition of material by chemical reaction between accumulated sediment and dissolved substances in the overlying water.

Principal sediments of the deep ocean

carbonates   silicates
sand and mud

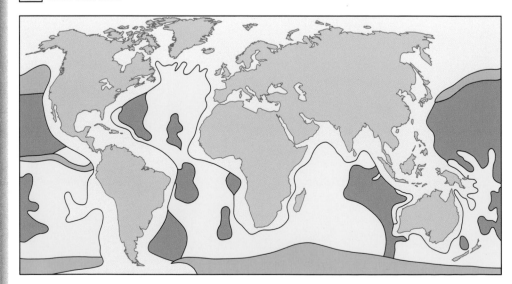

Coastal formation

Key words

bay
coastline
erosion
headland
sediment
wave action

1 New coastline
Prominent headlands prior to the action of shoreline processes.

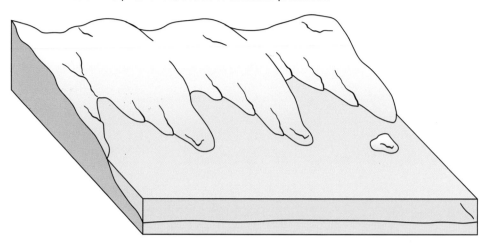

2 Shoreline processes around a headland

shallow water of bay

curved arrow showing wave refraction (bending)

shallow water near headland

headland

settled particles in bay

waves

3 Eroded coastline
The prolonged action of shoreline processes has removed the headlands.

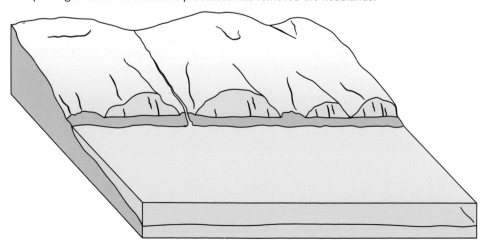

1 New coastline
- A coastline is initially established by forces such as volcanic action, tectonic movement, or the deposition of glacial or riverborne sediment.
- A new coastline may also be formed when sea levels rise or fall dramatically. In either case, rocks and formations that have not previously been in contact with the sea become subject to shoreline processes.

2 Shoreline processes
- *Shoreline processes* are the effects on a shoreline caused by waves and currents. They include erosion and the transportation of sediment.
- *Wave action* is the action of waves in the erosion and transport of sediment along a coastline.
  - Waves are refracted by headlands in such a way that their energy rapidly erodes both sides of a headland.

3 Eroded coastline
- Shoreline processes tend to straighten coastlines because headlands are eroded and the resulting sediment is deposited in the intervening bays.

© Diagram Visual Information Ltd.

© Diagram Visual Information Ltd.

Key words

erosion	wave
high tide	wave action
low tide	wave-cut
sea level	platform
strata	

Wave erosion

- Wave action erodes coastlines.
- The erosive force of waves is greatest at mean sea level.
- Soft strata erode more rapidly than hard strata.
- The angle of strata also influences the results of wave erosion.

Erosion of coastal land

- Wave action erodes a notch in the coastline between the high and low tide levels.
- As this notch deepens, the material above tends to collapse and a cliff is formed.
- Wave action continues to cut the notch deeper into the base of the newly formed cliff.
- More material above the notch collapses and the cliff becomes higher.
- A *wave-cut platform* is a near-horizontal shelf at the level of the low-tide mark. It is formed as wave action continually undermines and collapses the cliff face at the same level.
- On the seaward side of the platform, eroded material may settle as beach deposits before being removed by waves and currents and deposited elsewhere.

Steep cliffs

- Steep cliffs tend to form where the coastal rocks are hard and where coastal rock strata are tilted seaward.

Gentle cliffs

- Gentle cliffs tend to form where the coastal rocks are soft and where coastal rock strata are tilted landward.

Cliff formation

Erosion of coastal land

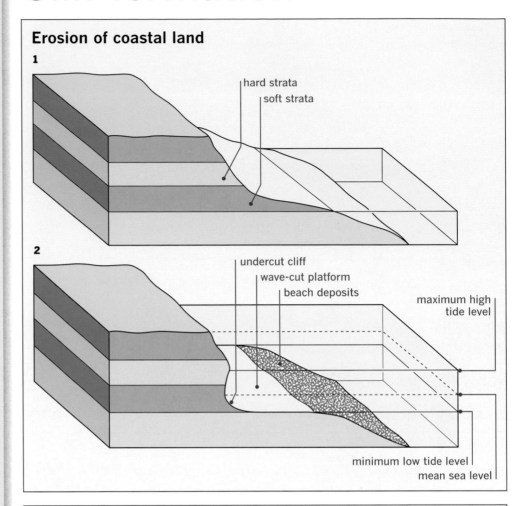

1 — hard strata / soft strata

2 — undercut cliff / wave-cut platform / beach deposits / maximum high tide level / minimum low tide level / mean sea level

Steep cliffs

Gentle cliffs

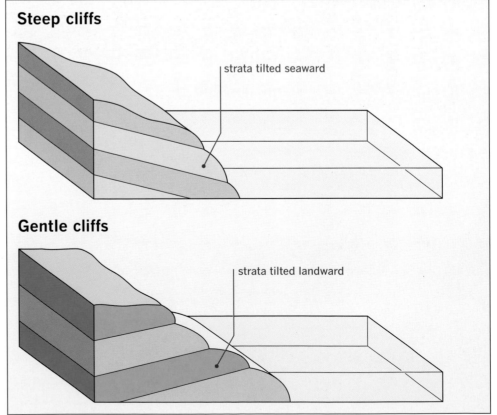

strata tilted seaward

strata tilted landward

Slopes and depositions

Key words

longshore current
longshore drift
prevailing wind
sediment
shore

shore deposition
shore slope
wave
wave action

Shore slope

On a gently sloping shore, material from the lower part of the shore (**a**) tends to be eroded and deposited on the upper shore (**b**). On a more steeply sloping shore, the situation is reversed. Most beaches are at near-equilibrium conditions between the two extremes.

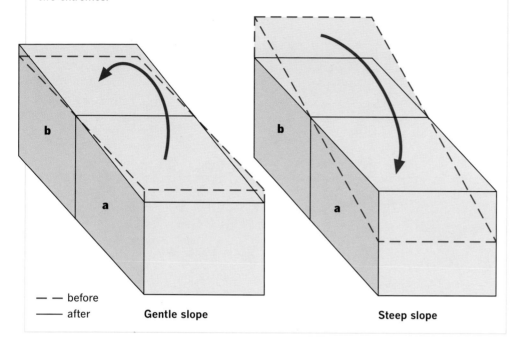

— — before
——— after

Gentle slope   **Steep slope**

Longshore drift

a Waves usually strike a depositional shore at an angle.
b Sand picked up by incoming waves is washed up the beach (swash) at an angle.
c The backwash returns directly down the beach.
d The overall effect of swash and backwash is to move sand or shingle along the beach, an activity otherwise known as longshore drift.

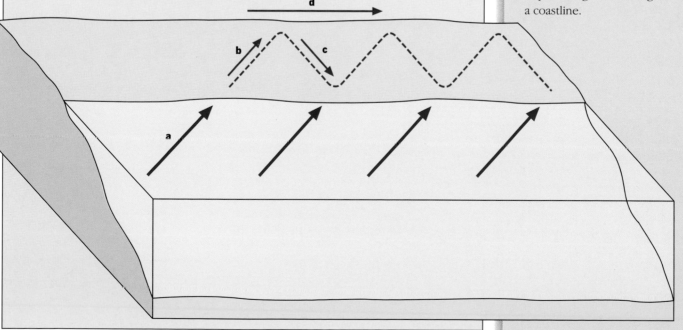

Shore deposition

- *Shore deposition* refers to the deposition of sediments and other material along the shore.
- Most of this sediment is transported to the ocean by rivers. A smaller proportion of the sediment is the result of wave action eroding the shore.

Shore slope

- The steepness of a shore's slope determines the kind of wave action erosion that takes place.
- Wave action tends to deposit sediment on gently sloping coastlines and remove sediment from steeper coastlines.

Longshore drift and longshore current

- *Longshore drift* is the tendency for wave action to move material in the direction of prevailing winds along the length of a shore.
- *Longshore current* is the tendency for material to be moved in the direction of prevailing winds along the length of a coastline.

© Diagram Visual Information Ltd.

© Diagram Visual Information Ltd.

Key words

bay	sea arch
blowhole	sea cave
coastline	sea stack
erosion	strata
headland	

Erosion patterns

- A newly established coastline is commonly composed of different strata. Some strata are more erosion-resistant than others.
- These variations in erosion resistance tend to determine the evolution of the coastline's form over time.

Bays and headlands

- A *bay* forms when less-resistant strata are eroded quicker than surrounding strata.
- *Headlands* are composed of more-resistant strata and are left protruding into the ocean as the less-resistant strata around them are eroded.

Headland erosion

- Headlands are exposed on three sides to wave action.
- *Sea caves* form as wave action cuts passages into weaknesses in the strata.
- A *blowhole* is a passageway connecting the roof of a sea cave with the surface of the land above. At high tide, waves force water up into a blowhole causing a geyser of water and pressurized air to erupt from the top of the blowhole.
- A *sea arch* forms when a sea cave is eroded right through a headland.
- *Sea stacks* are the remains of collapsed sea arches.

Landforms of marine erosion

Features of an erosion-dominated shore

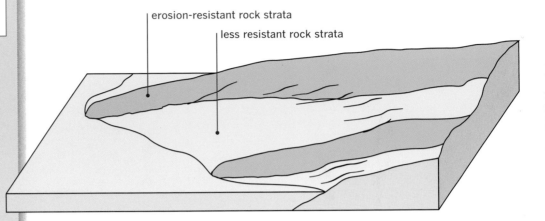

erosion-resistant rock strata

less resistant rock strata

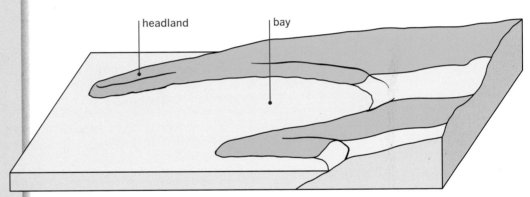

headland   bay

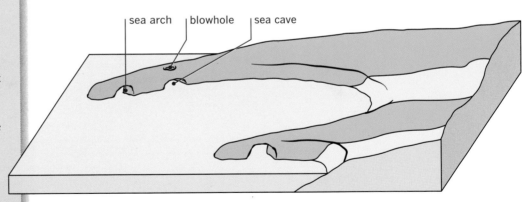

sea arch   blowhole   sea cave

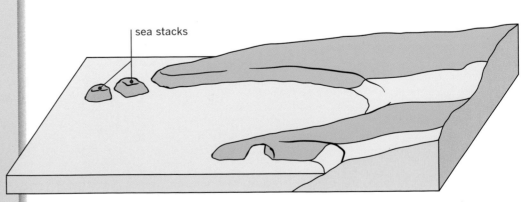

sea stacks

Landforms of marine deposition

Depositional shores

Key words

bar	lowland beach
barrier island	sediment
bay-head beach	shore
boulder beach	spit
erosion	tombolo
longshore current	
longshore drift	

Boulder beach

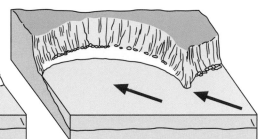

Bay-head beach

Lowland beach

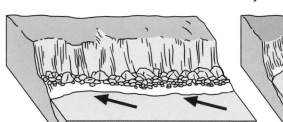

Spit

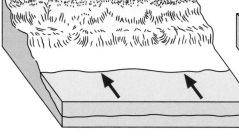

Bar

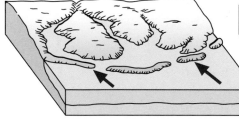

Tombolo

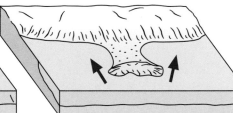

Barrier islands

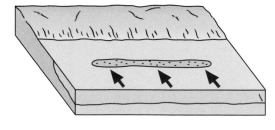

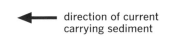 direction of current carrying sediment

Depositional shores

- A *depositional shore* is a shore on which more sediment is deposited than is removed.
- Depositional shores receive sediment from rivers, from biological processes in shallow waters, and from currents carrying material from erosion sites.
- Longshore currents and longshore drift carry much of the material that arrives at depositional shores.
- Where this material is deposited it forms one of the several landforms characteristic of a depositional shore.

Boulder beach

- A *boulder beach* is a narrow band of boulders and shingle at the base of a cliff.

Bay-head beach

- A *bay-head beach* is a crescent of sand lying in the bay between two headlands.

Lowland beach

- A *lowland beach* is a broad, gently sloping sandy beach, usually backed by wind-blown dunes.

Spit

- A *spit* is a peninsula of sediment deposited on the down-current side of a headland.

Bar

- A *bar* is a spit that entirely or almost entirely closes off a bay.

Tombolo

- A *tombolo* is a finger of land connecting an island to the shore.

Barrier island

- A *barrier island* is an island formed from the remains of a spit or bar.

© Diagram Visual Information Ltd.

© Diagram Visual Information Ltd.

Key words

bay	shore
estuary	shore slope
high tide	wave-cut
low tide	platform
sand dune	

Shore

- A *shore* is the region that lies between the extreme low water spring tide mark and the highest part of the coastline that comes into contact with storm waves.
- Shores vary depending on their composition and their exposure to the sea.

Rocky shores

- *Rocky shores* form where high, rocky landforms are in direct contact with the sea on exposed coastlines.
- They are characterized by cliffs and a flat, wavecut platform that is likely to be strewn with fallen rock.
- Typical particles are greater than 0.08 inches (2 mm) in size, formed from the breakdown of fallen rock from the cliff face.
- Beach slopes are greater than ten degrees.

Sandy shores

- *Sandy shores* form on sheltered coastlines where suspended particles of small to moderate size are deposited.
- Typical particle sizes are in the range 0.0025–0.08 inches (0.063–2.0 mm) and beach slopes are in the range 1–9 degrees.

Muddy shores

- *Muddy shores* form on very sheltered coastlines along estuaries or bays.
- Typical particle sizes are less than 0.0025 inches (0.063 mm) and beach slopes are less than one degree.

Shore types

Rocky shore

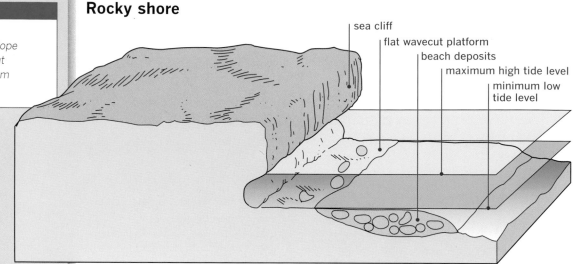

sea cliff
flat wavecut platform
beach deposits
maximum high tide level
minimum low tide level

Sandy shore

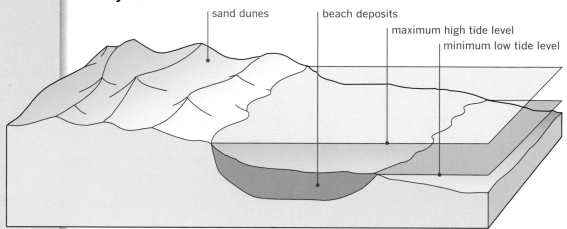

sand dunes
beach deposits
maximum high tide level
minimum low tide level

Muddy shore

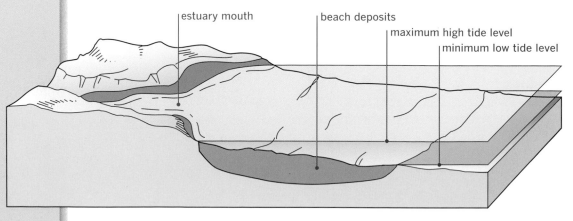

estuary mouth
beach deposits
maximum high tide level
minimum low tide level

Estuary types

Drowned river valley

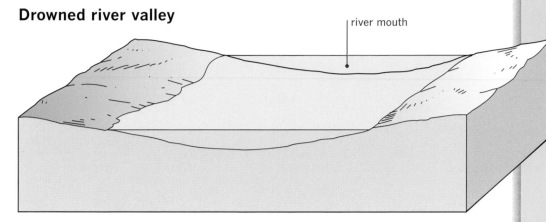

river mouth

Bar-built estuary

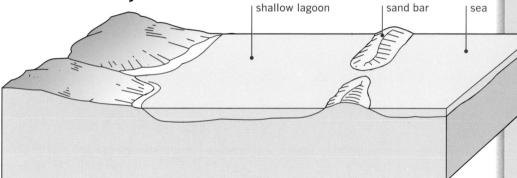

shallow lagoon   sand bar   sea

Tectonic estuary

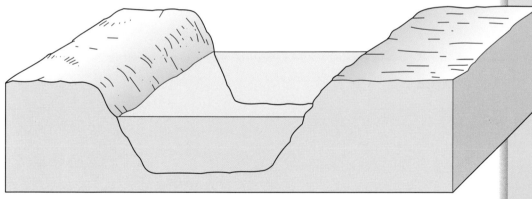

Fjord

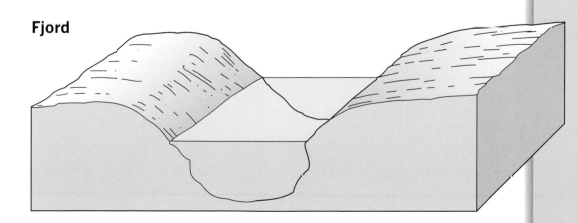

Key words

bar	river valley
bar-built	sea level
estuary	tectonic
estuary	estuary
fjord	
lagoon	

Estuaries

- An *estuary* is a partially enclosed body of water that is open to the sea and into which river water flows.
- Estuaries are commonly river valleys that have been flooded by rising sea levels.

Drowned river valleys and coastal plain estuaries

- *Drowned river valleys* and *coastal plain estuaries* are the most common form of estuary.
- They are formed when rising sea levels inundate river mouths and lowland areas.
- Examples include the Delaware estuary and the Thames estuary, England.

Bar-built estuaries

- *Bar-built estuaries* consist of shallow lagoons separated from the sea by sand bars or barrier islands that have been deposited by wave action.
- Examples include Laguna Madre, Texas, and Waddenzee, the Netherlands.

Tectonic estuaries

- *Tectonic estuaries* are formed when land subsides or is folded below sea level by geologic movement.
- Examples include San Francisco Bay, California.

Fjords

- A *fjord* is a deep, steep-sided, U-shaped valley cut by glaciers and subsequently inundated by sea level rise.
- Examples include Glacier Bay, Canada.

© Diagram Visual Information Ltd.

© Diagram Visual Information Ltd.

Key words

estuary
salinity
tide

Water mixing

- Where river water meets ocean water in an estuary the degree to which saltwater and freshwater mix between the head and the mouth depends on the depth and volume of the estuary.
- The head of an estuary is the end closer to the river. The mouth is the end closer to the sea.
- Freshwater is less dense than seawater and so tends to flow over the top of it.

Vertically-mixed estuary

- In shallow, low-volume estuaries, saltwater and freshwater mix readily enough for salinity to increase steadily with distance from the head of the estuary.

Slightly-stratified estuary

- In a slightly deeper estuary, two water layers can be identified: a freshwater layer, which becomes increasingly saline as distance from the head of the estuary increases, and a seawater layer, which becomes less saline as it approaches the head of the estuary.
- A zone of mixing separates the two.

Highly-stratified estuary

- In deep estuaries, the freshwater level increases in salinity as distance from the head of the estuary increases.
- The seawater level remains at near-normal salinity right up to the head of the estuary.

Salt wedge estuary

- In very deep, high-volume estuaries, the freshwater layer does not increase in salinity until it reaches the mouth of the estuary.
- A zone of transition from fresh to seawater is found beneath the surface.
- A wedge of seawater advances and retreats beneath the surface layer with the tides.

Estuarine salinity

Vertically-mixed estuary

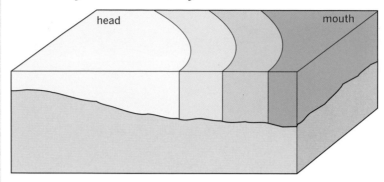

Slightly-stratified estuary

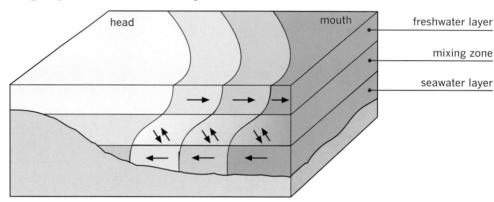

Highly-stratified estuary

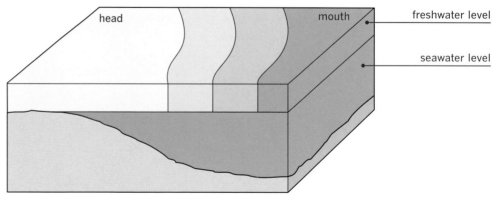

Salt wedge estuary

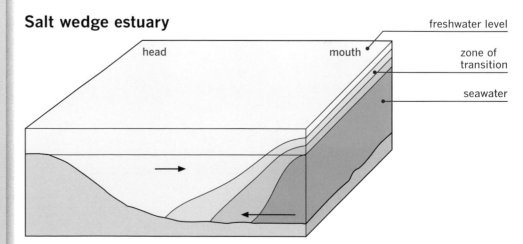

Sea level change in recent geologic time

Key words

atmosphere
glacier
ice age
ice cap
sea level

Sea level change

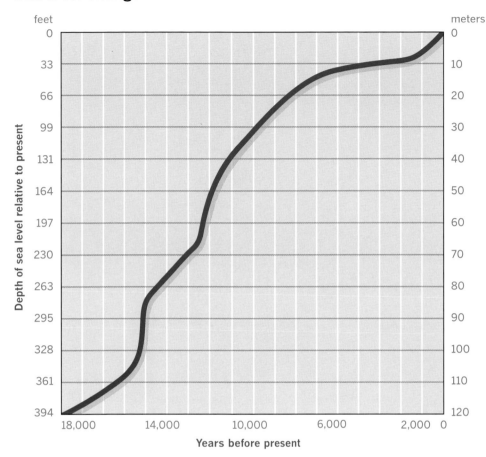

Temperature change

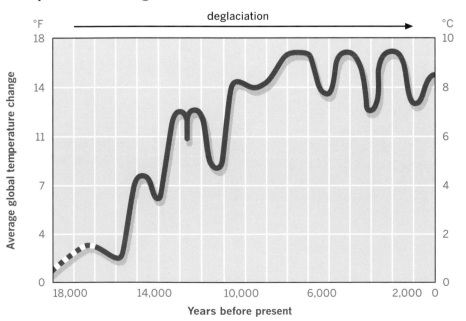

Global sea level

- Global sea level has been rising since the peak of the last ice age about 20,000 years ago.
- The most rapid rise occurred between 20,000 and 6,000 years ago.
- Between 6,000 years ago and the year 1900, global sea level rose at a constant but slower rate.
- Between 1900 and the present day global sea level has also risen at a constant but slightly increased rate.
- Global sea level is thought to have risen by a total of about 395 feet (120 m) in the last 20,000 years.
- Average global temperature has risen by about 18°F (10°C) over the same period.

Factors for change

- Many factors contribute to global sea level changes:
- Increasing temperatures cause glaciers to melt, which adds water to the oceans.
- Increasing temperatures also cause the water in the oceans to expand, increasing the overall volume of the oceans. This factor is thought to be more significant than the addition of water from melting ice.
- Ice that is floating on the ocean, such as the Arctic ice cap, does not contribute to sea level rise when it melts. The ice is floating on the ocean and therefore already displacing a volume of water equal to the volume of water that would be added to the ocean if the ice melted.
- The amount of water retained in the atmosphere and trapped on land also influences global sea levels.

© Diagram Visual Information Ltd.

© Diagram Visual Information Ltd.

Key words

asthenosphere	ice age
erosion	isostasy
eustasy	lithospheric plate
glacier	sea level
global warming	

Isostasy

- *Isostasy* refers to the state of equilibrium of the lithospheric plates floating on the asthenosphere. It is a geologic concept used to explain the differences in topographical height at different points on Earth.

- Lithospheric plates float on the denser, semiliquid material of the asthenosphere. The thickness and density of a lithospheric plate determines how high or low it floats.

- A lithospheric plate will always tend toward settling at isostatic equilibrium. This equilibrium point can change as mass is added to or removed from a lithospheric plate, or as the plate cools and becomes denser.

- Mass may be added during ice ages when thick layers of ice are loaded onto continents. Mass may be removed by erosion or by the large-scale melting of ice sheets.

- *Isostatic rebound* is the rapid uplifting of land from which ice sheets and glaciers have been removed by warming as the land seeks its new isostatic equilibrium.

Eustasy

- *Eustasy* refers to the rise and fall of global sea levels irrespective of changes in the isostatic equilibrium of the land. It is measured relative to the center of Earth rather than relative to any coastline.

- For example, geology indicates that Baffin Island in northern Canada has seen a fall in sea level of almost 100 feet (30 m) over the past 9,000 years. This is due to the fact that isostatic rebound has uplifted Baffin Island since the melting of the ice sheets that covered it during the last ice age. Although sea levels have fallen relative to Baffin Island, they have actually been eustatically rising continuously for the last 9,000 years.

Isostasy and eustasy

Isostasy

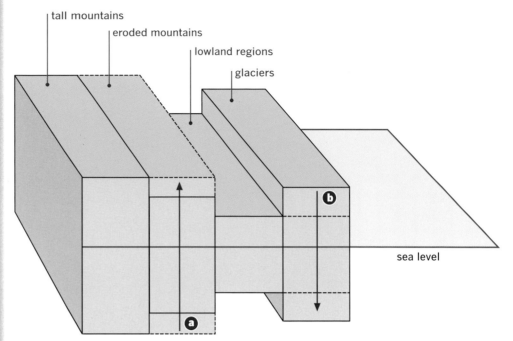

When mountains are eroded, they lose mass and float higher on the mantle **a**. When glaciers fill a valley, the locality increases in mass and sinks lower in the mantle **b**. Isostatic adjustments—with land rising or falling by hundreds of feet (meters) when mass is removed or added—take place quite slowly, over thousands of years.

Isostasy and eustasy

a isostatic sea level fall

b eustatic sea level rise

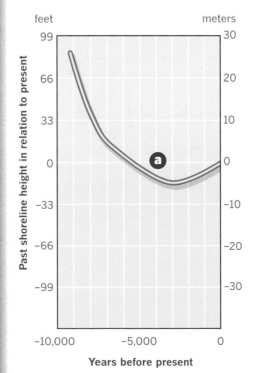

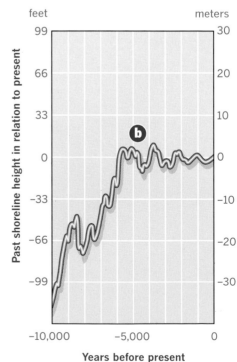

Global sea level change

Range of sea level change predictions

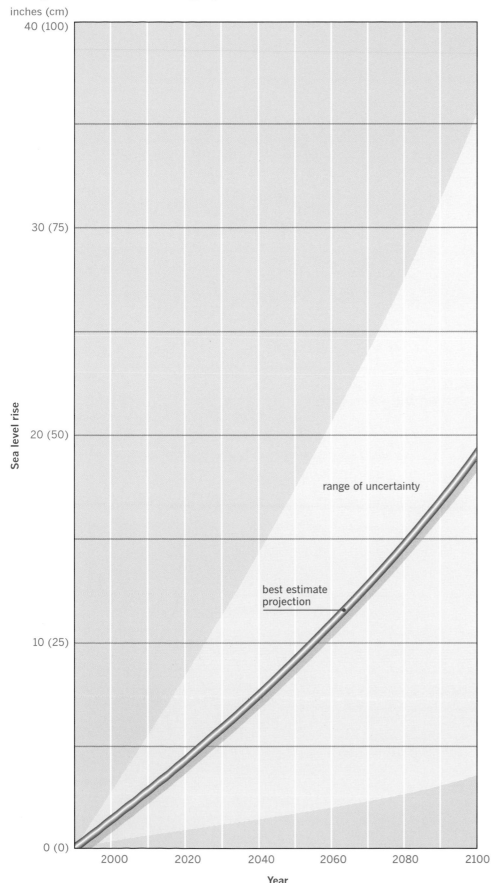

inches (cm)

Sea level rise

40 (100)

30 (75)

20 (50)

10 (25)

0 (0)

range of uncertainty

best estimate projection

2000   2020   2040   2060   2080   2100

Year

Key words

glacier
global warming
greenhouse gas
sea level

The recent past

● According to the most recent Intergovernmental Panel on Climate Change (IPCC) report in 2001, global sea level has risen by 4–10 inches (10–25 cm) in the last 100 years.

● The IPCC concluded that the bulk of this rise probably resulted from global warming, followed by the thermal expansion of water and the partial melting of glaciers and ice sheets.

● During the period 1880–1980, there was an apparent global warming of about 1.8°F (0.6°C). This temperature rise may be due in part (if not largely) to increases in atmospheric concentrations of greenhouse gases, especially carbon dioxide.

The near future

● In the IPCC's 2001 report global average surface temperatures were predicted to increase by 2.5–10.4°F (1.4–5.8°C) by the year 2100. This estimate assumed a business-as-usual scenario (emissions of greenhouse gases continuing at current rates).

● A best estimate sea level rise of about 19 inches (48 cm) was predicted by the year 2100: estimates range from 3.5–35 inches (9–88 cm). This sea level rise would not be uniform globally.

● A mean sea level rise of 19 inches (48 cm) by the year 2100 would be sufficient to cover some low-lying tropical islands entirely, such as parts of the Maldives and Marshall Islands in the Pacific.

● A similar sea level rise would flood about 15,500 square miles (40,000 km²) of China and would impact seriously on Bangladesh and other flood-prone countries in the northern Indian Ocean.

© Diagram Visual Information Ltd.

© Diagram Visual Information Ltd.

Key words

hydrogen
bonding
molecule

Water

- A drop of water contains at least one billion water molecules.
- The physical properties of water are largely determined by hydrogen bonding between the constituent water molecules.

Water molecule

- A water molecule comprises two hydrogen (H) atoms and one oxygen (O) atom joined by covalent bonds. The three atoms are set at an angle of 105°.
- The molecule is polar: overall it is electrically neutral, but it has an unequal distribution of charge on its surface. The hydrogen atoms have a slight positive charge (δ^+) while the oxygen atom has a slight negative charge (δ^-).

Bonding between water molecules

- The slightly positive regions of one water molecule are electrostatically attracted to the slightly negative region of a neighboring water molecule. This weak electrostatic attraction is a hydrogen bond.
- Hydrogen bonds are much weaker than the covalent bonds within a water molecule. Nevertheless, hydrogen bonds exert a profound influence on the physical and chemical properties of water.

Water molecules

Water molecule

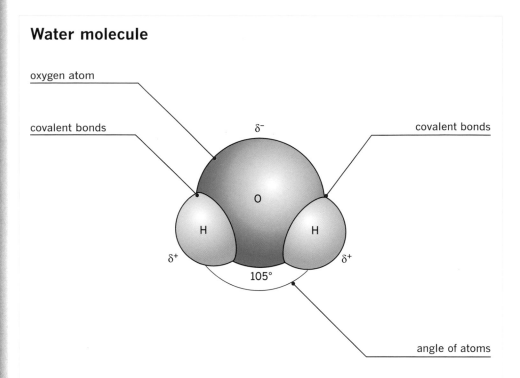

Bonding between water molecules

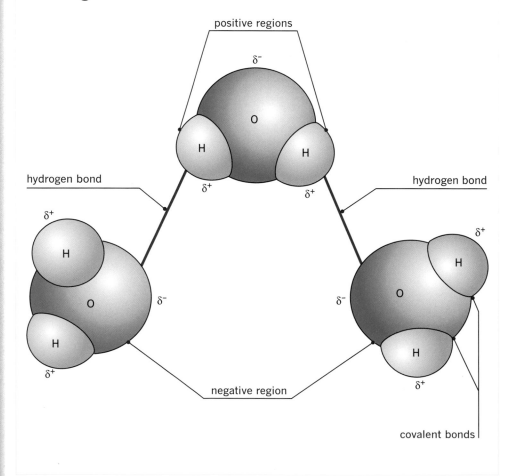

Physical states of water

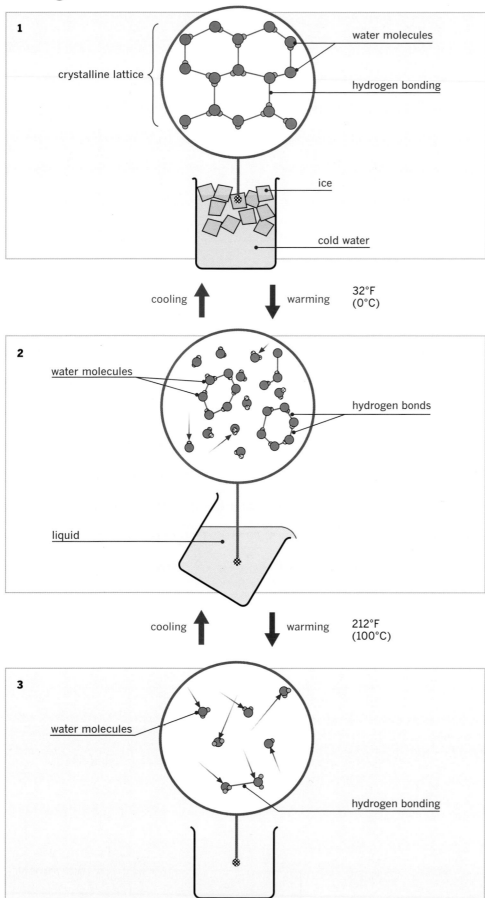

1

crystalline lattice

water molecules

hydrogen bonding

ice

cold water

cooling   warming   32°F (0°C)

2

water molecules

hydrogen bonds

liquid

cooling   warming   212°F (100°C)

3

water molecules

hydrogen bonding

Key words

atmospheric
  pressure
hydrogen
bonding

A unique compound

● On Earth, water is unique in that it exists in all three physical states—solid, liquid, and gas—under normal atmospheric conditions.

● Hydrogen bonding between water molecules accounts for many of water's unusual thermal (heat) properties.

Physical states

1 At pressure of one atmosphere (standard sea level pressure) water freezes at 32°F (0°C). In its solid state—ice—water molecules are held together in a crystalline lattice by hydrogen bonding. Water expands slightly as it freezes so that ice is less dense than cold water, and floats.

2 At normal atmospheric pressure, ice melts to form a liquid at temperatures above 32°F (0°C). Liquid water boils to a gas at 212°F (100°C). In their liquid state, water molecules move about relatively freely and form temporary hydrogen bonds with passing neighbors. Under the force of gravity, the liquid fills the bottom of a container into which it is placed, but flows when the container is tilted.

3 In their gaseous state, water molecules move freely and tend to distribute themselves randomly throughout any container into which they are placed. Hydrogen bonding is negligible.

© Diagram Visual Information Ltd.

Water's special properties

Key words

heat capacity	solvent
latent heat of fusion	surface tension
latent heat of vaporization	

Property	Significance
Present in all three physical states—solid, liquid, and gas—at ambient temperatures on Earth's surface.	• Water vapor evaporating from the sea surface helps transport heat from warm, low latitudes to cool, high latitudes. • The presence of ice and water in polar regions moderates climates in those regions. • Ice formation in polar waters during winter produces hypersaline seawater that sinks, delivering oxygen to the deep ocean.
A higher heat capacity than any common solid or liquid other than ammonia.	• Large amounts of heat energy are transported in ocean currents traveling from low to high latitudes. This cools tropical regions, warms polar regions, and thus moderates Earth's climate. • Water warms up and cools down more slowly than land or air, and so ocean water has a moderating influence on coastal regions. • Over much of the world's oceans, surface temperatures fluctuate less than 3.6°F (2°C) in a 24-hour period. By contrast, surface temperatures on landmasses may fluctuate by 27°F (15°C). • Water provides a thermally stable environment for marine organisms.
A higher latent heat of fusion than that of any substance other than ammonia.	• When ice forms or melts a large amount of heat is released or is absorbed. At high latitudes, ice formation and melting act as a thermostat, keeping water and atmosphere at temperatures around the freezing point of water (28.7°F or −1.8°C).
A higher latent heat of vaporization than that of any other common substance.	• Heat energy is absorbed from the ocean when evaporation takes place at low latitudes. The heat energy is released when water vapor condenses and falls as precipitation at high latitudes. This effect helps moderate global climate, which would otherwise be much more extreme at the poles and equator.
The thermal expansion properties of pure water are unusual in that water's maximum density is at 39.2°F (4°C), not at its freezing point 32°F (0°C).	• Ice floats. Lakes and shallow seas do not normally freeze solid. Instead a surface layer of ice floats above the cold but unfrozen water where organisms continue to survive.
Water has uniquely powerful solvent properties. Water dissolves more substances than any other common liquid.	• Water is the medium in which life-supporting chemical reactions occur. • Water dissolves minerals from rocks and soil and carries them to the oceans.
Water's surface tension is higher than that of any other liquid.	• Encourages bubble formation below the water surface and droplet formation above it. Both effects enhance the exchange of gases between the oceans and atmosphere. • Surface tension enables some small organisms to anchor in or under the water surface or, in the case of some animals, walk upon it.

© Diagram Visual Information Ltd.

Light in the sea

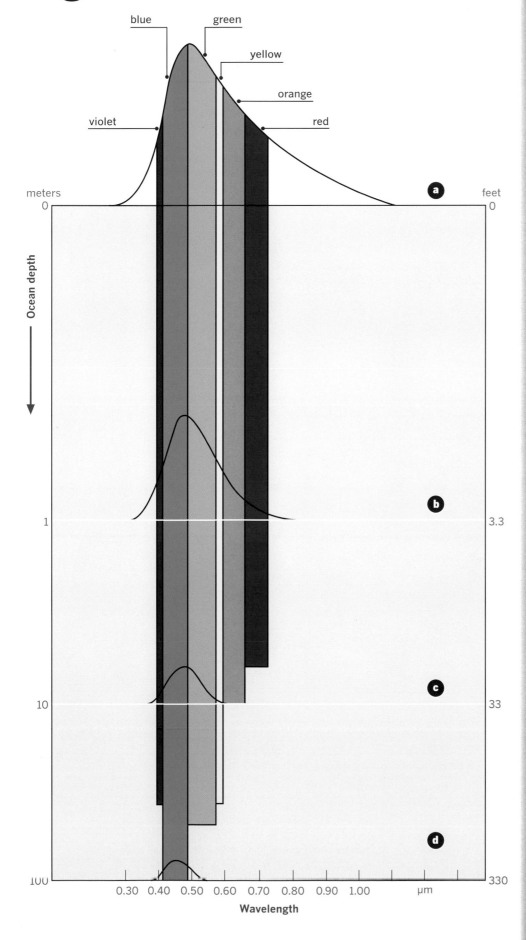

Key words

transparency
turbidity
wavelength

Light transmission properties of water

- Seawater is relatively transparent, but not all wavelengths of visible light are transmitted through it equally well. Blue and green wavelengths penetrate deepest, and violet and yellow penetrate moderately well, but orange and red wavelengths are absorbed within the first 33 feet (10 m).
- Seen with the unaided eye, the colors at depths in excess of 33 feet (10 m) or so have a drab blue or bluish-green cast because the red, orange, and yellow wavelengths of light have been absorbed. Red, orange, or yellow creatures appear black or gray at those depths. Powerful lights that generate the full spectrum of visible light are necessary to reveal the rich variety of colors underwater.
- The transparency of water depends largely on the matter suspended or dissolved in it. This is known as turbidity. Suspended particles—whether living or non-living—tend to color water and to absorb or scatter sunlight, reducing transparency.

a Light energy striking the ocean's surface (energy equals 100 percent).

b Approximately 45 percent of the light energy at the surface remains.

c Approximately 16 percent of the light energy at the surface remains.

d Approximately 1 percent of the light energy at the surface remains.

© Diagram Visual Information Ltd.

Sea surface temperatures

Key words

biogeographical zone	temperate
polar	tropical
subtropical	

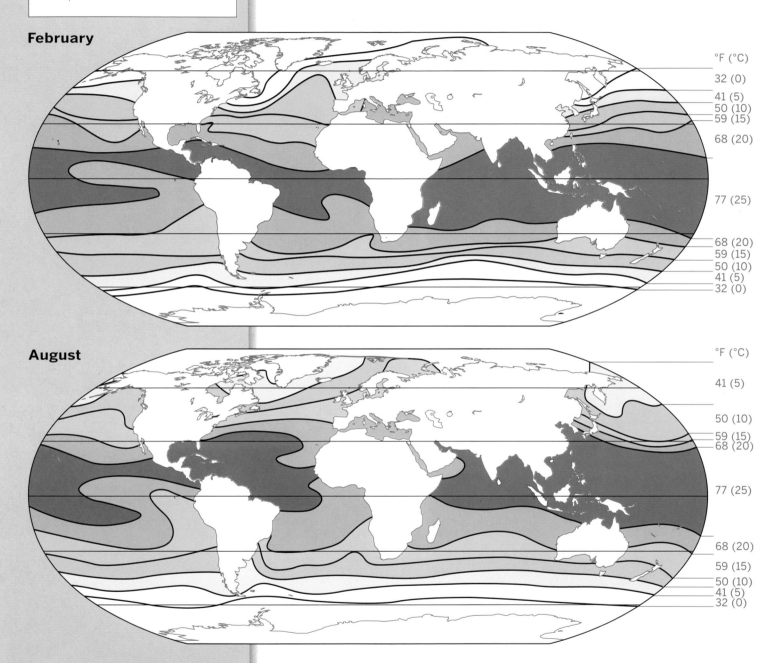

February

°F (°C)
32 (0)
41 (5)
50 (10)
59 (15)
68 (20)
77 (25)
68 (20)
59 (15)
50 (10)
41 (5)
32 (0)

August

°F (°C)
41 (5)
50 (10)
59 (15)
68 (20)
77 (25)
68 (20)
59 (15)
50 (10)
41 (5)
32 (0)

Biogeographic zones based on mean surface temperature		
Designation	**Location**	**Mean surface temperature range °F (°C)**
Polar	Arctic and subarctic Antarctic and subantarctic	28.6–41.0 (–1.9 to 5.0) 28.6–35.6 (–1.9 to 2.0)
Cold temperate	Northern Hemisphere Southern Hemisphere	41.0–50.0 (5.0 to 10.0) 35.6–50.0 (2.0 to 10.0)
Warm temperate	Both hemispheres	50.0–59.0 (10.0 to 15.0)
Subtropical	Both hemispheres	59.0–77.0 (15.0 to 25.0)
Tropical	Both hemispheres	>77.0 (>25.0)

© Diagram Visual Information Ltd.

Temperature gradients

Three-layered ocean

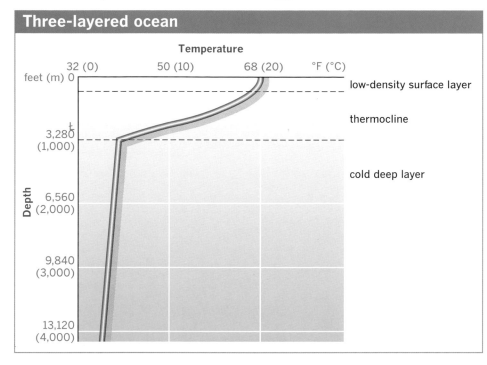

Temperature
32 (0)   50 (10)   68 (20)   °F (°C)

low-density surface layer

thermocline

cold deep layer

Key words

latitude	temperature
polar	gradient
season	thermocline
subtropical	water column
temperate	

The three-layered ocean
- Over most of the open ocean the water column is effectively three-layered throughout the year.
- A warm, low-density surface layer sits on top of a region of rapid temperature transition, the thermocline, below which is a cold deep layer.

Temperature profile at different latitudes
- The three-layered vertical temperature profile exists in tropical, subtropical, and temperate latitudes.
- In polar waters, there is no thermocline and temperature transition between surface and deep water is minimal.

Seasonal change in temperature profile
- In temperate latitudes in spring and summer, a steep thermocline **a** is superimposed on top of the permanent thermocline **b** that exists at moderate depth above the cold deep water.
- In winter, the near-surface thermocline disappears.

Temperature profile at different latitudes

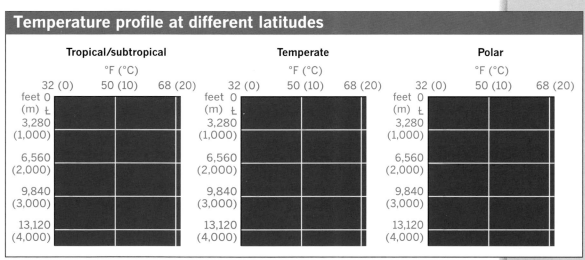

Tropical/subtropical — °F (°C): 32 (0), 50 (10), 68 (20)
Temperate — °F (°C): 32 (0), 50 (10), 68 (20)
Polar — °F (°C): 32 (0), 50 (10), 68 (20)

Seasonal change in temperature profile

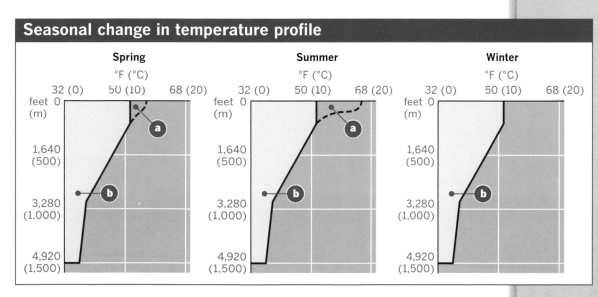

Spring — °F (°C): 32 (0), 50 (10), 68 (20)
Summer — °F (°C): 32 (0), 50 (10), 68 (20)
Winter — °F (°C): 32 (0), 50 (10), 68 (20)

© Diagram Visual Information Ltd.

© Diagram Visual Information Ltd.

Key words

finger rifting	iceberg
floe	nilas
frazil	pancake ice
glacier	polynya
grease ice	sea ice

Sea ice

- There are generally two forms of ice found on the oceans.
- Sea ice is ice that forms when seawater freezes.
- Icebergs are formed from ice originating from glaciers on land.

Formation of sea ice

- In calm, cold seas at surface temperatures of about 28.7°F (–1.9°C), seawater begins to freeze.
- *Frazil* consists of individual ice crystals floating on the ocean's surface.
- *Grease ice* forms when frazil crystals begin to coagulate together.
- *Nilas* is a thin smooth skin of transparent sea ice that flexes with the swell. It forms from grease ice on calm seas.
- In continued cold, calm conditions nilas will thicken to form a smooth-surfaced ice floe.
- *Pancake ice* is an area of unconnected smooth-edged disks of ice that form from grease ice in disturbed waters.
- Pancake ice also eventually coalesces to form a smooth-surfaced ice floe.

Formation of multiyear ice

- During the Arctic winter, newly formed ice thickens to about 6 feet (2 m) if undisturbed.
- Under the action of winds and waves it may override adjacent ice and cause finger-rifting.
- Fresh ice may split to form long, water-filled leads or wide polynya that quickly refreezes.
- Multiyear ice, such as that found in the central Arctic, is thick and immensely strong; it contains layers of ice bonded together by refrozen meltwater.

Sea ice

Formation of sea ice

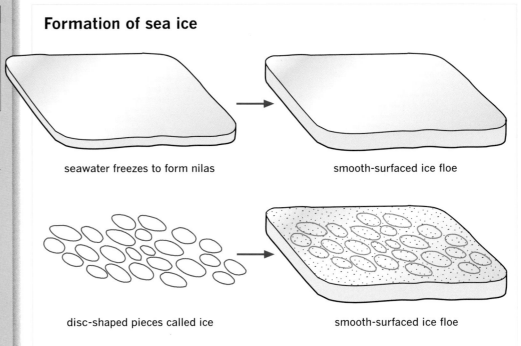

seawater freezes to form nilas

smooth-surfaced ice floe

disc-shaped pieces called ice

smooth-surfaced ice floe

Formation of multiyear ice

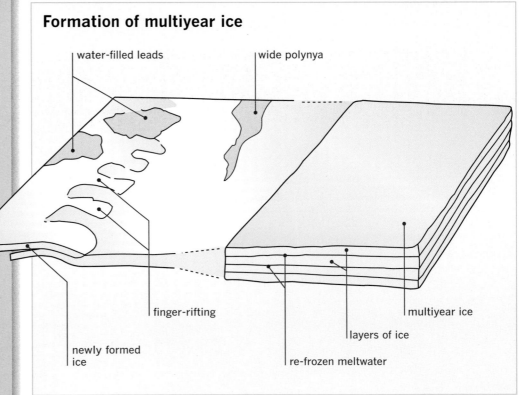

water-filled leads

wide polynya

finger-rifting

newly formed ice

re-frozen meltwater

layers of ice

multiyear ice

Icebergs

Arctic

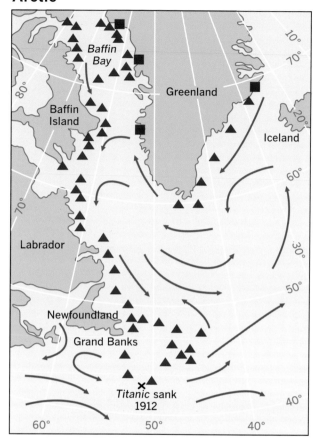

- typical Arctic iceberg calving location
- ▲ iceberg
- → ocean currents

Baffin Bay
Greenland
Baffin Island
Iceland
Labrador
Newfoundland
Grand Banks
✕ *Titanic* sank 1912

10°
70°
80°
20°
60°
70°
30°
50°
40°
60° 50° 40°

Arctic iceberg

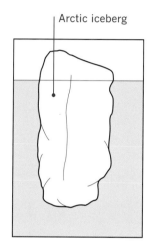

Antarctic

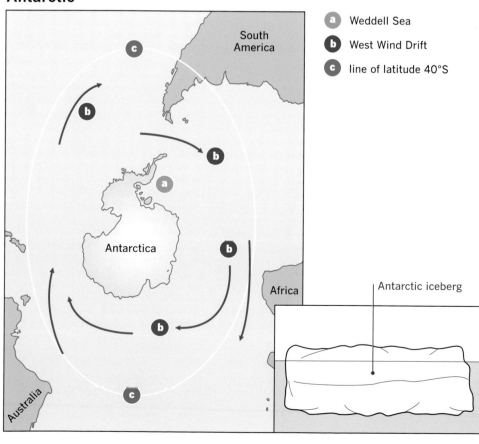

- **a** Weddell Sea
- **b** West Wind Drift
- **c** line of latitude 40°S

South America
Antarctica
Africa
Australia

Antarctic iceberg

Key words
Antarctic
Arctic
calving
iceberg
subarctic

Iceberg origins

- An *iceberg* is a very large chunk of ice floating on an ocean.
- Icebergs are composed of freshwater that has frozen on land.
- When glaciers reach the sea, parts break off the end and float away as icebergs. This is known as "calving."

Arctic icebergs

- A newly calved Arctic iceberg typically weighs 1.65 million tons (1.5 million tonnes) and is more than 1,312 feet (400 m) tall, with less than 20 percent of its mass showing above the waterline.
- More than 10,000 Arctic and subarctic icebergs are calved annually. They drift southward down the coasts of Baffin Island and Labrador.
- In an average year, about 300 icebergs travel far enough south to enter major transatlantic shipping lanes.

Antarctic icebergs

- In the Antarctic, icebergs are calved from land-fringed ice sheets rather than glaciers. Antarctic icebergs tend to be larger than Arctic icebergs and when young they have a flat-topped, tabular shape.
- An iceberg calved from the ice shelf in the Weddell Sea in 1991 covered an area the size of Connecticut: 5,000 square miles (13,000 km²).
- Several thousand Antarctic icebergs are calved annually. The larger ones are carried eastwards on the strong West Wind Drift. Some drift as far north as 40°S before disintegrating.

© Diagram Visual Information Ltd.

© Diagram Visual Information Ltd.

Key words

sound wave
thermocline

Sound transmission properties of water

- Sound waves travel through solids, liquids, or gases as pressure waves that are transmitted from one constituent molecule to the next.
- Sound waves travel more than four times faster in water (mean velocity 4,756 feet per second [1,450 m/s]) than in air (1,096 feet per second [334 m/s] in dry atmosphere at 68°F [20°C]).
- In water, sound waves travel far greater distances than light waves and other forms of electromagnetic radiation.
- In the ocean, sound travels faster with increasing temperature, salinity, and pressure.

SOFAR

- *SOFAR* is an acronym of "Sound Fixing and Ranging." It refers to a narrow layer of the ocean in which temperature and pressure are such that sounds travel the greatest distances.
- When sound waves encounter a thermocline they are refracted downwards toward the region with minimum sound speed. As they travel through deeper water, and therefore a higher-pressure region, the sound waves are refracted back upwards, where they encounter higher temperature water and are refracted downwards again.
- Sound waves are continuously refracted between the higher temperature and higher pressure zones and can travel very long distances—thousands of miles (km)—along this channel, losing very little energy.
- The SOFAR channel is found at a mean depth within the range 1,640 feet (500 m) to 3,280 feet (1,000 m).

Sound in the sea

Effect of temperature and pressure on sound transmission

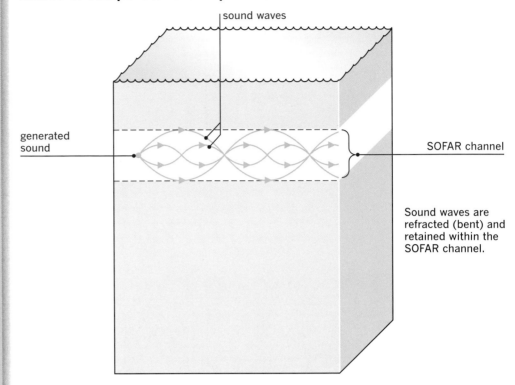

Sound waves are refracted (bent) and retained within the SOFAR channel.

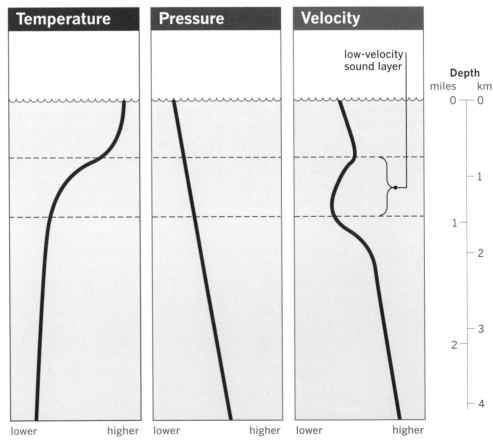

Temperature increases with depth.

Pressure increases with depth.

The effects of temperature and pressure on sound transmission combine to create a low velocity sound layer: the SOFAR channel.

Seawater pressure

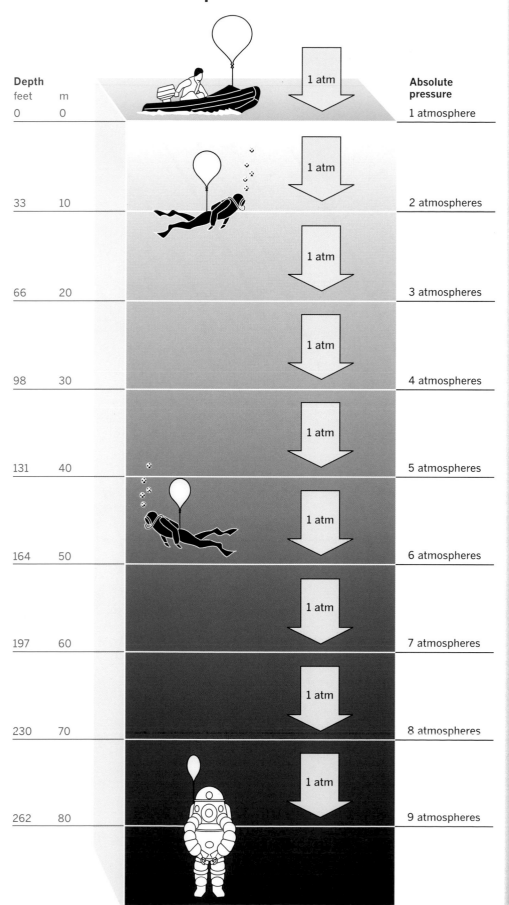

Depth			Absolute pressure
feet	m		
0	0	1 atm	1 atmosphere
33	10	1 atm	2 atmospheres
66	20	1 atm	3 atmospheres
98	30	1 atm	4 atmospheres
131	40	1 atm	5 atmospheres
164	50	1 atm	6 atmospheres
197	60	1 atm	7 atmospheres
230	70	1 atm	8 atmospheres
262	80	1 atm	9 atmospheres

Key words

atmosphere
atmospheric
  pressure

Pressure

● At the sea surface, atmospheric pressure is about one atmosphere (14.7 pounds per square inch [1.03 kg per cm²]). Underwater, pressure increases by one atmosphere for each 33 feet (10 m) of depth.

Gas bladders

● Some fish have gas bladders inside their bodies that allow them to achieve neutral buoyancy.

● Neutral buoyancy is achieved when the buoyancy experienced by a body is the same as the attraction of gravity, so that the body does not rise or sink in the water column. The advantage of neutral buoyancy is that it makes the fish effectively weightless: it therefore requires far less energy to move around.

● By increasing or decreasing the size of its gas bladder, a fish can change the overall density of its body and achieve neutral buoyancy at different depths. This is important because fish need to move up and down in the water column to find food or avoid predators.

● As pressure increases with depth, however, the volume of gas inside a gas bladder decreases, causing the gas bladder to become smaller. This means that a fish must increase the volume of gas in its gas bladder when it goes deeper, and decrease the volume when it rises.

● The same effect would be seen if a diver took a gas-filled balloon beneath the waves:

As the pressure increases with depth, the volume of the gas inside the balloon decreases. The same effect can be observed in the lungs of divers.

© Diagram Visual Information Ltd.

Key words

current	*tropical*
polar	
salinity	
subtropical	
temperate	

Seawater density

Seawater density

- Density is mass per unit volume: the matter in a unit of a given substance, or

  $$d = m/V$$

- The density of seawater is determined by temperature, pressure, and salinity.
- In the open ocean, the density of surface seawater varies between 1.022 and 1.03 grams per cubic centimeter (g/cm³) (**a**).
- In tropical and subtropical regions (**b**) a 9°F (5°C) temperature difference (**c**) produces a density change of 0.0012 grams per cubic centimeter in seawater.
- In polar regions (**d**) a 9°F (5°C) temperature difference (**e**) produces a density change of only 0.0004 grams per cubic centimeter.
- In tropical and subtropical surface waters, temperature change has a greater influence on density, whereas in polar and cold temperate waters, salinity variation is of greater significance.
- In the open ocean, the relative densities of water bodies are of great importance. Relative density determines which will rise and which will fall. These vertical movements in turn influence biological productivity and generate vertical and horizontal currents.

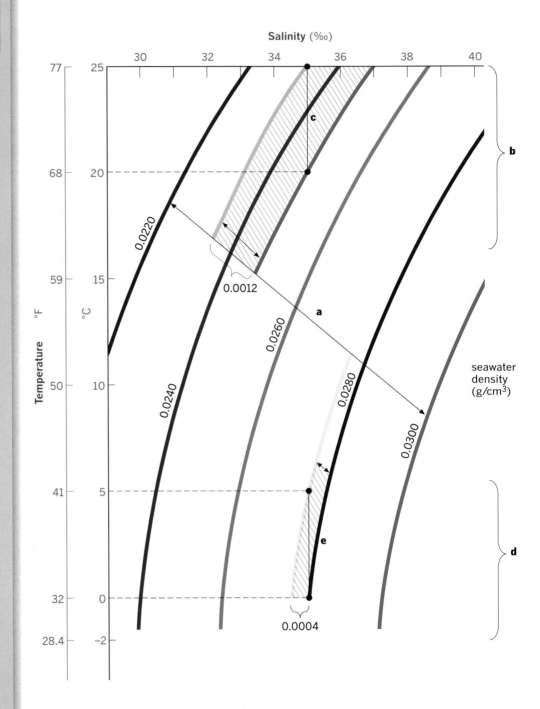

© Diagram Visual Information Ltd.

Water as a solvent

Key words

molecular size
solvent

slightly negatively charged oxygen atoms

water molecules

positively charged sodium ions

negatively charged chloride ions

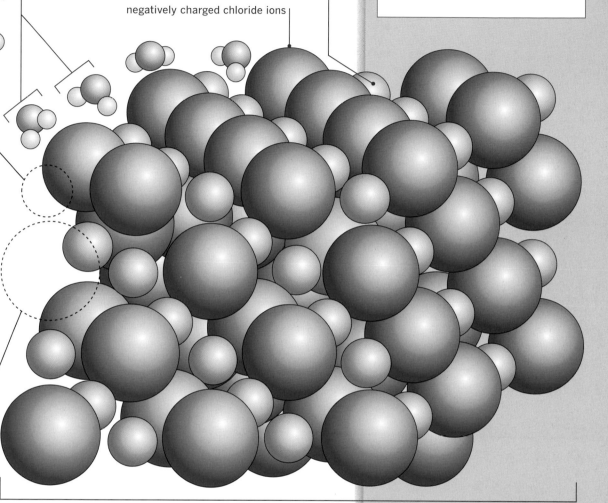

crystal of sodium chloride

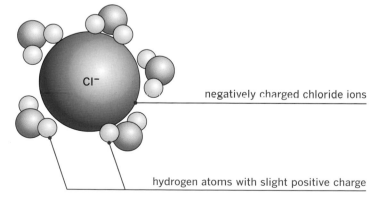

negatively charged chloride ions

hydrogen atoms with slight positive charge

The universal solvent

- Water can dissolve a greater range of substances, in greater amounts, than any other common liquid.
- Water's unique dissolving power is related to its small molecular size and the water molecule's polar nature.
- Polar and ionic substances tend to be soluble in water; covalent substances are generally less soluble in water.
- A crystal of sodium chloride dissolves readily in water because positively charged sodium ions tend to be pulled into solution by the slightly negatively-charged oxygen atoms of water molecules. Negatively charged chloride ions are pulled into solution by the hydrogen atoms in water with a slight positive charge.

© Diagram Visual Information Ltd.

Composition of seawater

© Diagram Visual Information Ltd.

Key words

element
mineral
salinity
seawater
sediment

Seawater composition

- On average, water accounts for 96.53 percent of the chemical composition of seawater. The remaining 3.47 percent is dissolved solids, of which six ions make up more than 99 percent.
- The most common dissolved compound is sodium chloride (salt).
- Although salinity varies from location to location across the ocean, the proportion of salts remains exactly the same everywhere.
- Virtually every other known element can also be found dissolved in seawater, but most are in minute quantities.
- Most minerals are carried into the oceans by riverwater.

Dissolved gases

- Seawater usually contains small amounts of dissolved gases. The most significant of these are nitrogen, oxygen, carbon dioxide, and hydrogen.
- Gases become dissolved in seawater at the ocean's surface. Oxygen and carbon dioxide are also produced and consumed by animal and plant life living in the oceans.
- The amount of gas that a volume of water can dissolve before becoming saturated increases with decreasing temperature.

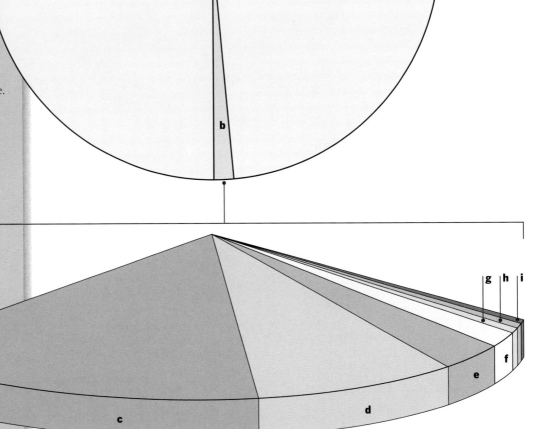

Substance		Amount of substance (parts per thousand)
a	Water	965.31
b	Total dissolved solids	34.69
c	Chloride (Cl^-)	19.10
d	Sodium (Na^+)	10.62
e	Sulfate (SO_4^{2-})	2.66
f	Magnesium (Mg^{2+})	1.28
g	Calcium (Ca^{2+})	0.40
h	Potassium (K^+)	0.38
i	Trace constituents	0.25

Residence times in seawater

Key words

atmospheric fallout	infiltration
	precipitation
biological capture	sea spray
estuary	seawater
hydrothermal vent	volcano

Addition of ions to oceans

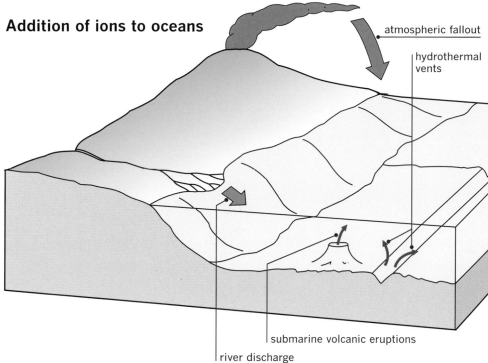

atmospheric fallout

hydrothermal vents

submarine volcanic eruptions

river discharge

Addition of ions to oceans
● Major ions are added to ocean water primarily by: river discharge; atmospheric fallout from land activities such as volcanic eruptions; submarine volcanic activity; and hydrothermal vents.

Removal of ions from oceans

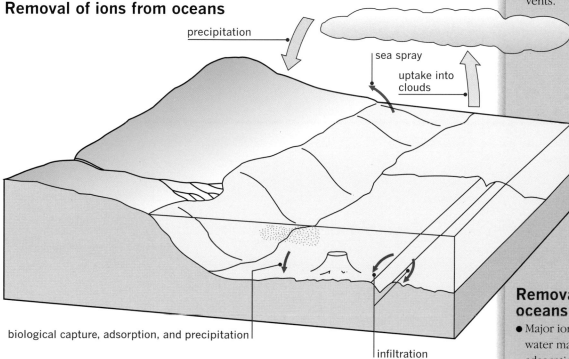

precipitation

sea spray

uptake into clouds

biological capture, adsorption, and precipitation

infiltration

Removal of ions from oceans
● Major ions are removed from ocean water mainly by: biological capture; adsorption and precipitation; sea spray; uptake into clouds and subsequent precipitation over land; and infiltration into ocean ridges.

Residence times for some major ions	
Ion	**Residence time** (years)
Chloride	80,000,000
Sodium	60,000,000
Sulfate	9,000,000
Potassium	6,000,000
Calcium	1,000,000
Iron	100

© Diagram Visual Information Ltd.

Key words

photosynthesis
respiration
seawater

Dissolved gases in seawater

Dissolved gases

- For marine life, oxygen (O_2), carbon dioxide (CO_2), and nitrogen (N_2) are the three most important gases dissolved in seawater.
- The quantity of dissolved gases in seawater can vary widely depending on temperature, agitation of the surface (surface diffusion), and most importantly, the quantity and type of marine life present.

Oxygen

- Oxygen is a product of photosynthesis and is vital for most organisms. It is consumed in respiration.
- Oxygen is replenished by absorption from the air (surface diffusion), and by photosynthesis of surface phytoplankton and seaweed. It is usually poorly replenished at great depth.
- Oxygen concentration generally decreases with depth.

Carbon dioxide

- Carbon dioxide is consumed by photosynthesis and is produced by respiration.
- Carbon dioxide concentration generally increases with depth.

Nitrogen

- Nitrogen is an inert gas.
- The high concentration of nitrogen gas in atmospheric air poses a physiological challenge for diving mammals when the gas dissolves in the bloodstream under pressure.

© Diagram Visual Information Ltd.

Oxygen %	Carbon dioxide %	Nitrogen %
atmosphere	atmosphere	atmosphere
21	0.04	78
surface water	surface water	surface water
36	15	48
total water column	total water column	total water column
6	83	11

Salinity and its measurement

Key words

salinity
salinometer
seawater

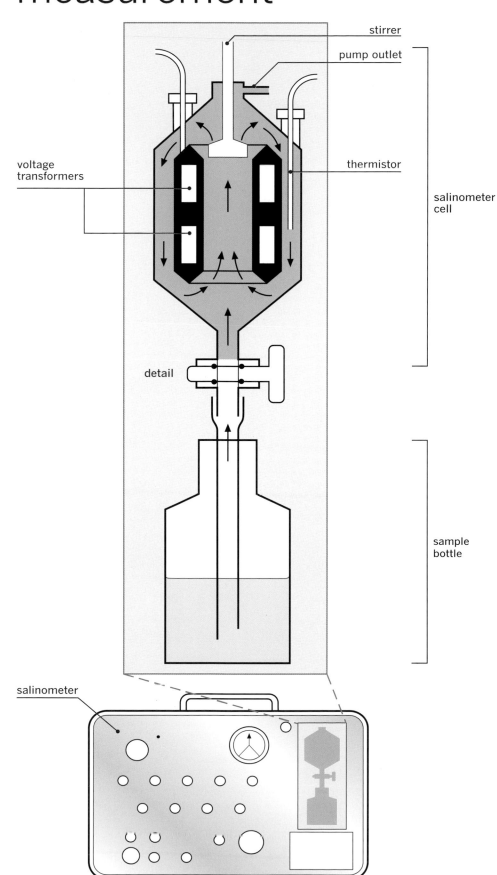

stirrer

pump outlet

thermistor

voltage
transformers

salinometer
cell

detail

sample
bottle

salinometer

Salinity

- Salinity is a measure of the total concentration of dissolved solids in seawater.
- Traditionally, salinity was quoted in parts per thousand, ‰,(grams per kilogram of water; g/kg).
- Salinity is increasingly measured by electrical conductivity and expressed in practical salinity units (PSUs). One PSU is nearly equivalent to one part per thousand.

Measuring salinity

- Salinity used to be measured by evaporating the water from a seawater sample and weighing the salt residue. This method was shown to underestimate the true salinity because some dissolved ions, such as bromide and iodide, decomposed and were not left behind as a residue.
- In 1884, English chemist Willhelm Dittmar established that the relative proportions of major ions in seawater vary very little throughout the open ocean. By finding the concentration of only one major ion, the salinity of seawater could be readily calculated. In practice, the chloride ion (Cl⁻) concentration (chlorinity) is measured because it is the most abundant ion and because a suitable chemical test is easy to carry out.
- Using a salinometer, salinity can be determined to within ± 0.003 parts per thousand (or PSUs) by this method. The conductance of the seawater sample (in ohms) is compared with that of a standard seawater sample at 68°F (20°C). Conductance of the sample is measured across two voltage transformers at a specific temperature, preferably 68°F (20°C).

© Diagram Visual Information Ltd.

Salinity variation

© Diagram Visual Information Ltd.

Key words

estuary	mineral
evaporation	salinity
hypersaline	seawater
hyposaline	tidal pool
lagoon	

Salinity

- The geography of a body of seawater can have a significant effect on its salinity.
- The degree of open access to the rest of the ocean, and the amount of freshwater input from rivers are also major factors.

Hypersalinity

- *Hypersaline* means "having a higher salinity than usual."
- Where a body of water is subject to high rates of evaporation and low rates of freshwater input, seawater is hypersaline.
- Examples are shallow tropical lagoons, tidal pools, and seas with very little freshwater input such as the Red Sea, between northeast Africa and the Arabian peninsula.

Open ocean

- In the open ocean, the salinity of surface water is remarkably uniform, varying within the range 32–37‰ ("‰" means parts per thousand), or 32–37 PSUs, with an average of about 34.7‰, or 34.7 PSUs.

Hyposalinity

- *Hyposaline* means "having a lower salinity than usual."
- Marine environments where seawater is diluted by large amounts of freshwater runoff from land are commonly hyposaline.
- Mostly enclosed seas that do not receive a lot of sunshine also have lower than usual saline levels.
- Seas bordered by ancient and highly-weathered landforms also receive fewer minerals from riverwater because the readily dissolved minerals on land have long since been washed away.
- Examples are estuaries, shallow coastal areas, and semi-enclosed seas such as the Baltic Sea in northern Europe.

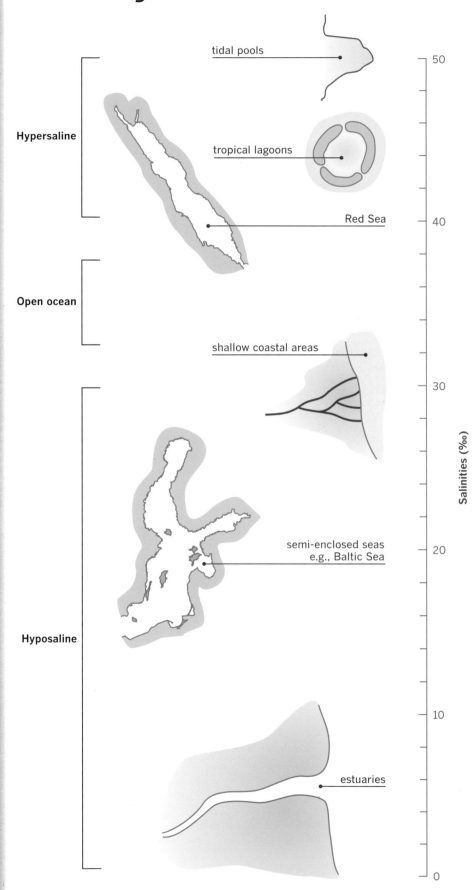

Hypersaline

tidal pools

tropical lagoons

Red Sea

Open ocean

shallow coastal areas

semi-enclosed seas e.g., Baltic Sea

Hyposaline

estuaries

Salinities (‰)

50

40

30

20

10

0

Ocean surface salinity

Geographic distribution of salinity

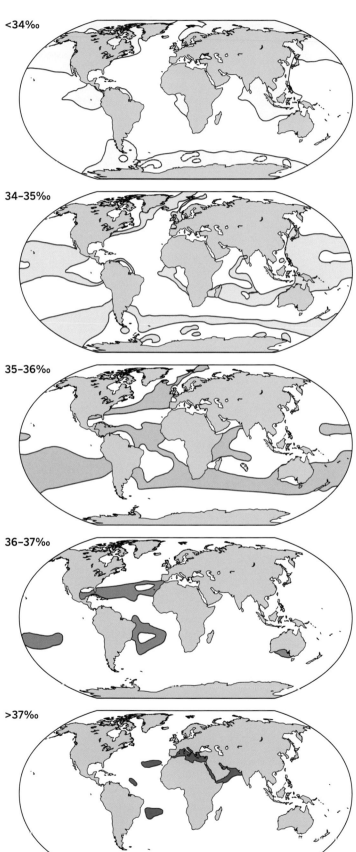

<34‰

34–35‰

35–36‰

36–37‰

>37‰

 figures indicate average salinity in parts per thousand (‰)

Key words

evaporation	seawater
hyposaline	subpolar
polar	subtropical
precipitation	upwelling
runoff	
salinity	

Factors affecting surface salinity

- High local rates of evaporation tend to raise salinity.
- High rates of freshwater input from precipitation or land runoff tend to lower salinity.
- Regions of local upwelling may lower salinity where hyposaline deep water rises to the surface.

Geographic distribution of salinity

- Open ocean salinities are generally greatest in subtropical regions that are closest to very dry land, for example, off the coasts of North Africa and the Arabian peninsula. Here, rates of evaporation exceed rates of precipitation and there is no dilution effect from land runoff.
- Salinities are generally lower in the subpolar and polar regions, the Arctic and Southern oceans. Here, rates of precipitation exceed rates of evaporation. The formation of sea ice however tends to raise salinity in adjacent waters.
- In shallow waters receiving high volumes of freshwater from river systems, salinities are lowered. An example is the the Bay of Bengal off the coast of Bangladesh, where large volumes of freshwater flow into the ocean from the mouth of the River Ganges.
- In marginal seas, salinities may be high where evaporation exceeds precipitation and local runoff. An example is the Arabian Sea. Salinities may be low, where precipitation and local runoff exceed evaporation. An example is the South China Sea.

© Diagram Visual Information Ltd.

© Diagram Visual Information Ltd.

Key words

atmospheric fallout	mantle
biogeochemical cycle	mineral
	precipitation
crust	seawater
erosion	sediment
magma	subduction
	volcano

Biogeochemical cycles

Key stages in marine biogeochemical cycles

1 Chemicals are removed from the oceans by precipitation, adsorption onto particles, and from biological uptake and subsequent deposition of organic material in detritus or in inorganic components, such as shells or skeletons.

2 Some detritus is rapidly decomposed and its constituent elements are dissolved and returned to seawater.

3 Over millions of years, ocean sediments become compacted, water is squeezed out, and minerals precipitate between the grains, cementing the grains together to form sedimentary rock.

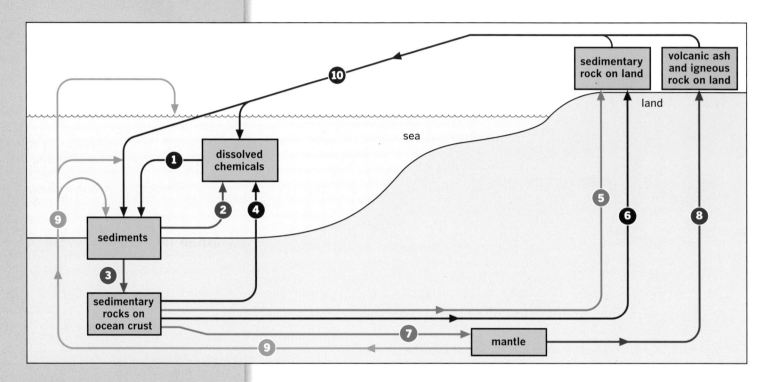

Biogeochemical cycles

- "Biogeochemical" refers to the chemical relationships between the geological and the biological elements and processes of Earth.
- Carbon, nitrogen, and phosphorus are three of the most significant elements that cycle through biogeochemical relationships.
- Elements are absorbed from the environment by living things and incorporated into their structures. These are later released back into the environment—for example, when a creature dies—and may then be incorporated into geological structures, such as sediments.
- The ocean is much greater in volume and area than the land environment and plays a very important role in all of Earth's important biogeochemical cycles.

4 Some chemicals are dissolved out of Earth's crust and enter the sea through hydrothermal vents associated with ocean ridges.

5 Tectonic processes and sea level change expose some sedimentary rocks.

6 Sedimentary rock may enter a subduction zone where it is scraped off and uplifted onto land, or subducted into the mantle where it melts.

7 Magma (molten rock) from the mantle erupts through volcanoes as ash or lava.

8 On landmasses, products of volcanism may form igneous rocks.

9 Products of volcanism may enter the oceans by dissolving out from submerged lava, or from atmospheric fallout.

10 Rocks on land are eroded by wind, water, and ice, and their constituents return to the oceans as dissolved substances or as rock particles that form part of the sediment.

Carbon cycle

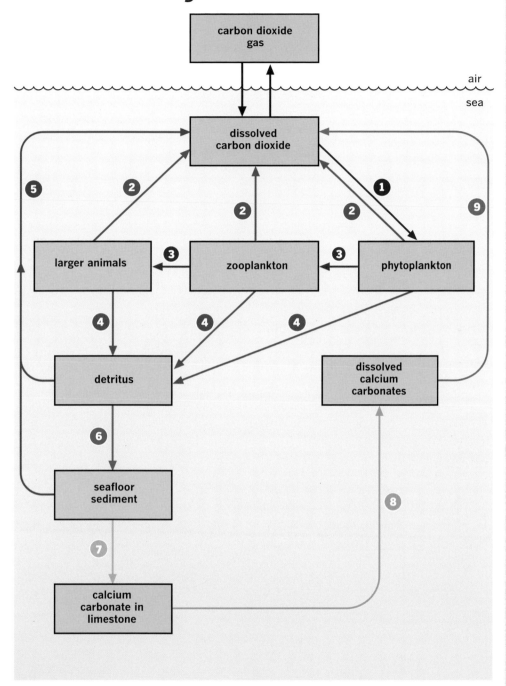

1. Photosynthesis
2. Respiration
3. Consumption
4. Excretion and death
5. Breakdown by decomposers
6. Settlement on seafloor
7. Compaction to form sedimentary rock
8. Under conditions of low carbon dioxide (CO_2) concentration and high pressure, calcium carbonate ($CaCO_3$) dissolves
9. High levels of carbonate ion (CO_3^{2-}) encourage the formation of dissolved carbon dioxide via carbonic acid (H_2CO_3)

Key words

atmosphere
biosphere
carbon cycle
global warming
hydrosphere

lithosphere
photosynthesis
respiration
sediment

Carbon cycle

- The *carbon cycle* refers to the complex process by which carbon passes from Earth's atmosphere to the biosphere, hydrosphere, lithosphere, and then back to the atmosphere.
- For example, plants absorb carbon dioxide from the atmosphere and produce carbohydrates. These carbohydrates are released when a plant (or plant-eater) dies and the carbon enters the lithosphere as calcium carbonate or fossil fuel. These are subject to geological processes that eventually result in the release of the carbon back into the atmosphere.

Human impact on the carbon cycle

- Humans have been burning large quantities of fossil fuels for more than a century.
- This has released a lot of carbon, in the form of carbon dioxide, from the lithosphere that would otherwise have taken millions of years to return to the atmosphere.
- Atmospheric carbon dioxide is known to warm Earth by slowing the rate of heat loss to space. This may be accelerating the general rise in global temperatures that has been occurring since the height of the last ice age.
- The removal of large tracts of forest and ocean pollution that reduces phytoplankton productivity is reducing the capacity of the biosphere to absorb this excess atmospheric carbon dioxide.
- Enhancing phytoplankton productivity may offer a short-term means to help counter rising carbon dioxide levels in the atmosphere.

© Diagram Visual Information Ltd.

© Diagram Visual Information Ltd.

Key words

atmosphere	nitrogen cycle
biosphere	runoff
hydrosphere	
lithosphere	
nitrogen	

Key features of the marine nitrogen cycle

- The *nitrogen cycle* refers to the complex process by which nitrogen passes from Earth's atmosphere, to the biosphere, hydrosphere, lithosphere, and then back to the atmosphere.

- The nitrogen (N) cycle is of particular interest to biological oceanographers because nitrogen in the form of nitrate is a key nutrient that fuels biological productivity.

- The recycling of nitrogen by bacterial decomposition is relatively slow. Coupled with the production of nitrogen gas lost to the air, this may result in the depletion of usable nitrogen in local surface waters.

- Lack of nitrate is quite frequently a limiting factor in the productivity of phytoplankton in the surface waters of the sea.

Nitrogen cycle

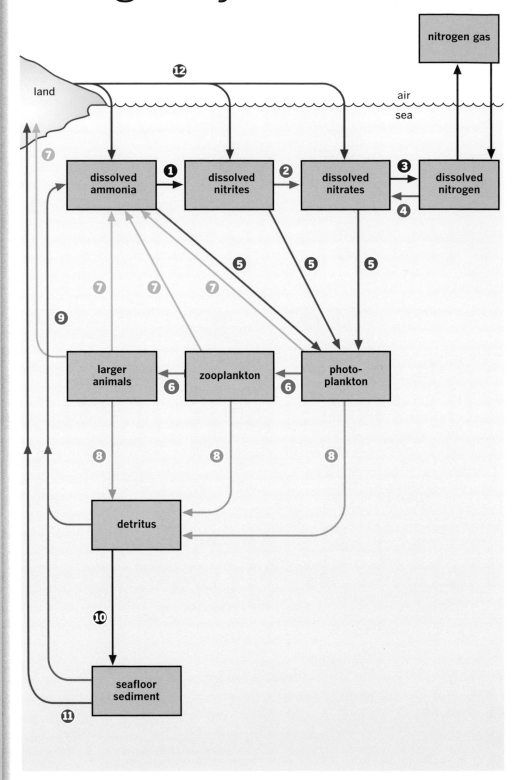

1 Action of nitrite bacteria
2 Action of nitrate bacteria
3 Action of denitrifying bacteria
4 Action of nitrogen-fixing bacteria and cyanobacteria
5 Uptake and assimilation
6 Consumption
7 Excretion
8 Death and excretion
9 Bacterial decomposition
10 Settlement
11 Uplift onto land
12 Weathering and runoff

Phosphorus cycle

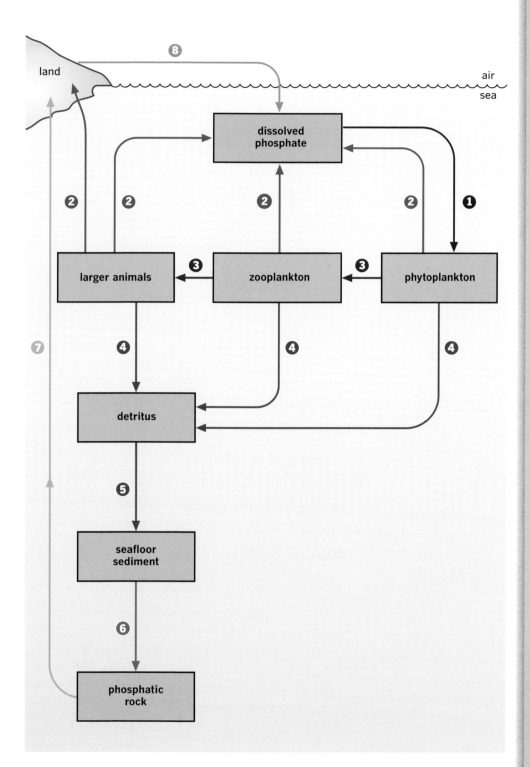

© Diagram Visual Information Ltd.

Key words

biosphere
hydrosphere
lithosphere
phosphorus cycle
runoff

Key features of the marine phosphorus cycle

- The *phosphorus cycle* refers to the complex process by which phosphorus passes from Earth's lithosphere to the biosphere and hydrosphere and then back to the lithosphere.
- The phosphorus (P) cycle is of interest to biological oceanographers because, in the form of dissolved phosphate (PO_4^{3-}), phosphorus is a key nutrient that fuels biological productivity.
- Unlike nitrogen (N), phosphorus is rapidly recycled by bacterial decomposition.
- Phosphate is rarely a limiting factor in the productivity of phytoplankton in the surface waters of the ocean.

---

1 Uptake and assimilation
2 Excretion
3 Consumption
4 Death and excretion

5 Compaction to form sedimentary rock
6 Settlement
7 Uplift onto land
8 Weathering and runoff

© Diagram Visual Information Ltd.

Key words

crust   sediment
hydrocarbon
natural gas
petroleum
plankton

Oil and gas

- Oil, or petroleum, is a complex mixture that mainly consists of hydrocarbons.
- Natural gas is a product of some petroleum deposits. It is a mixture of smaller hydrocarbon molecules: methane (CH_4), ethane (C_2H_6), propane (C_3H_8), and butane (C_4H_{10}).

Oil and gas formation

- The formation of oil and gas deposits requires once-living materials to be buried rapidly so that oxygen is excluded and natural biological decay processes do not take place.
- The biological material, subjected to raised temperatures of 120–250°F (50–129°C) and high pressures within rock strata, is gradually transformed into oil or gas.
- Complex organic substances are changed into simpler, smaller hydrocarbon molecules, producing thick oils, such as asphalt at first, then thinner oils containing "lighter" hydrocarbon fractions, and eventually in some cases, producing natural gas.

Oil locations

1 Productive shallow waters at the ocean margins provide source material for oil and gas deposits. Dead planktonic forms accumulate on the seafloor and are rapidly covered by sediments.

2 Sediments accumulate over tens of thousands of years, forming layers many hundreds of meters thick above the biological remains.

3 At depths of 1.3–2.5 miles (2–4 km) in Earth's crust, and over hundreds of thousands of years, the organic remains may be converted into the hydrocarbons that form oil and gas.

4 Once formed, oil and gas migrate through permeable rock strata, and accumulate under impermeable rock and above water-filled rock.

Oil and gas formation

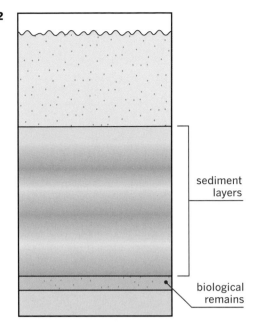

1
shallow
waters

sediment

dead
plankton

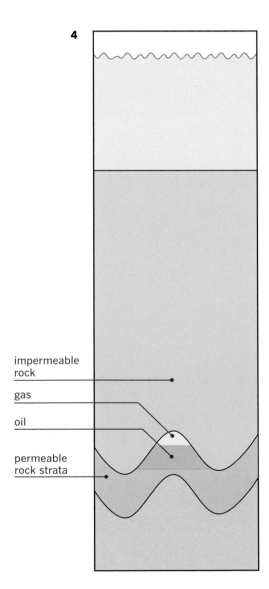

2
sediment
layers

biological
remains

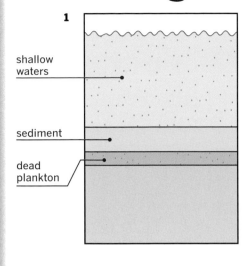

3
Earth's
crust

1.3–2.5 miles
(2–4 km)

gas

oil

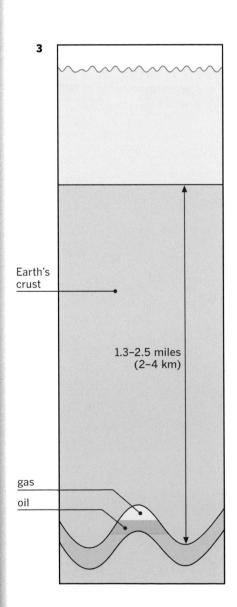

4
impermeable
rock

gas

oil

permeable
rock strata

Coriolis effect

Stationary world
Winds blowing in various directions on a hypothetical nonrotating globe.

Spinning world
The same winds, showing the deflections caused by the Coriolis effect.

Resultant winds
Winds blow from areas of high pressure to areas of low pressure, but the Coriolis effect deflects them and produces the angled paths of Earth's dominant wind systems.

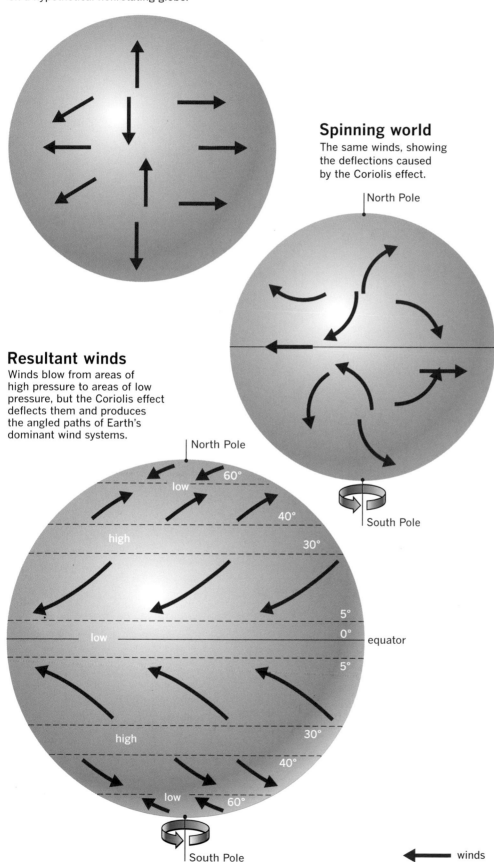

winds

Key words

Coriolis effect
current
hemisphere
prevailing wind

Coriolis effect
- The *Coriolis effect* refers to the deflection of the path of objects moving across Earth's surface caused by Earth's rotation.
- It is because of the Coriolis effect that winds and ocean currents circulate in a clockwise direction in the Northern Hemisphere and a counterclockwise direction in the Southern Hemisphere.

Coriolis effect model
- An imaginary projectile launched from the North Pole toward a point on the equator provides a good example of why the Coriolis effect exists.
- As the projectile travels south, Earth is rotating from west to east underneath it.
- Tracing the ground track of the projectile as it heads toward the equator would produce a line on Earth's surface that curves to the right (with reference to the direction of travel).
- When the projectile arrives at the equator, it will hit a point to the west of the original target point. This is because the target point has moved with Earth's rotation to the east while the projectile was in flight.
- Winds and currents experience the same deflection as the imagined projectile.
- The Coriolis effect only occurs along paths that have a north–south component.

Winds and currents
- Air travels from areas of high pressure to areas of low pressure. Surface ocean currents are propelled by winds or by differences in temperature.
- The Coriolis effect determines the paths that winds or currents take, not their destinations.

© Diagram Visual Information Ltd.

© Diagram Visual Information Ltd.

Key words

Coriolis effect
current
Ekman spiral
Ekman transport
hemisphere

water column

Ekman spiral

- Ocean surface currents move water in the top 330 feet (100 m) of the ocean. They are primarily caused by winds.
- Friction between moving air and the surface of the ocean causes the water to move. However, ocean surface currents do not move in the same direction as the winds that drive them. This is because they are deflected by the Coriolis effect.
- The *Ekman spiral* is a way of visualizing the interaction between winds and the top layer of the ocean.
- At the surface, deflection by the Coriolis effect causes water to move along a path at about 45 degrees to the direction of the wind.
- In the Northern Hemisphere, this deflection is to the right of the wind; in the Southern Hemisphere, it is to the left.
- The amount of energy transmitted to the water from the wind diminishes as depth increases. The water at the very top of the ocean is driven more quickly than the water just beneath it, which is in turn driven more quickly than the water at a still greater depth.
- The more slowly the water is moving, the further it is deflected by the Coriolis effect. By about 330 feet (100 m) depth, the subsurface flow is only about four percent of that at the surface, and the water movement has turned through 180 degrees.

Ekman transport

- *Ekman transport* refers to the net movement of water within the top 330 feet (100 m) of the ocean, and is taken to be at 90 degrees to the wind.
- As water is much denser than air, surface currents generated by Ekman transport reach only two to three percent of the wind speed that generates them.

Ekman transport

The Ekman spiral

Wind-generated water movement in the surface waters of the Northern Hemisphere is depicted.

surface wind direction

direction of surface current

Ekman transport: net water movement within the top 330 feet (100 m)

current rotating through 330 feet (100 m) depth

Depth	
feet	m
0	0
25	10
50	20
75	
100	30
125	40
150	
175	50
200	60
225	70
250	
275	80
300	90
325	100

Geostrophic gyres

Key words

Coriolis effect
current
Ekman transport
geostrophic
  current

geostrophic gyre
gyre
hemisphere

Idealized Northern Hemisphere geostrophic gyre

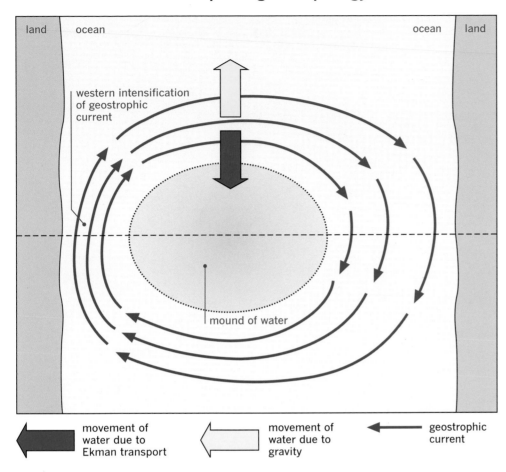

movement of water due to Ekman transport   movement of water due to gravity   geostrophic current

Gyres

- A *gyre* is a large-scale loop of circulation. *Geostrophic gyres* are the large-scale loops of circulating currents that dominate the ocean basins.
- Geostrophic gyres are a result of the deflection of ocean currents by the Coriolis effect.
- In the Northern Hemisphere, surface currents are turned to the right by the Coriolis effect, producing clockwise gyres.
- In the Southern Hemisphere, surface currents are turned to the left, and gyres are counterclockwise.

Features of a Northern Hemisphere gyre

- Ekman transport causes water to accumulate as a large, low-elevation mound at the center of a gyre.
- Water at the peak of the mound tries to flow down the slope under the influence of gravity. At the same time it is deflected to the right by the Coriolis effect. The combination of these two forces results in a current of water that flows in a continuous loop around the outside edge of the ocean basin.
- The Coriolis effect is greater at higher latitudes than at lower latitudes, with the result that water forms a broad equatorwards flow at the eastern boundary of a gyre, and a narrow polewards flow at the western boundary.
- The effect of gravity, and Earth's rotation, cause western boundary currents to be narrower and faster flowing than eastern boundary currents.

Cross section of a Northern Hemisphere geostrophic gyre

Sectioned along broken line above: – – – – – –

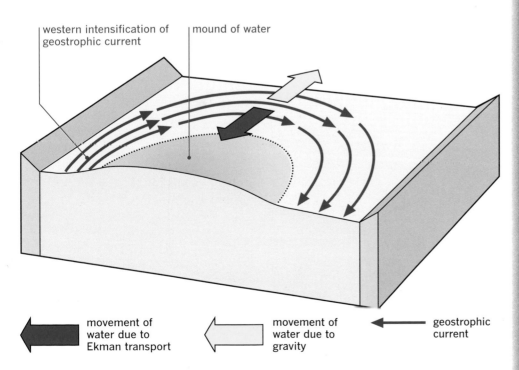

movement of water due to Ekman transport   movement of water due to gravity   geostrophic current

© Diagram Visual Information Ltd.

Surface currents

Key words

cold current   surface current
current   warm current

Principal warm currents

1 North Pacific Current
2 Pacific North Equatorial Current
3 Pacific Equatorial Countercurrent
4 Pacific South Equatorial Current
5 Atlantic North Equatorial Current
6 Florida Current
7 Gulf Stream
8 North Atlantic Current
9 Norway Current
10 Atlantic South Equatorial Current

11 Guinea Current
12 Brazil Current
13 Indian North Equatorial Current
14 Indian Equatorial Countercurrent
15 Indian South Equatorial Current
16 Agulhas Current
17 Kuroshio Current
18 West Australia Current
19 East Australia Current

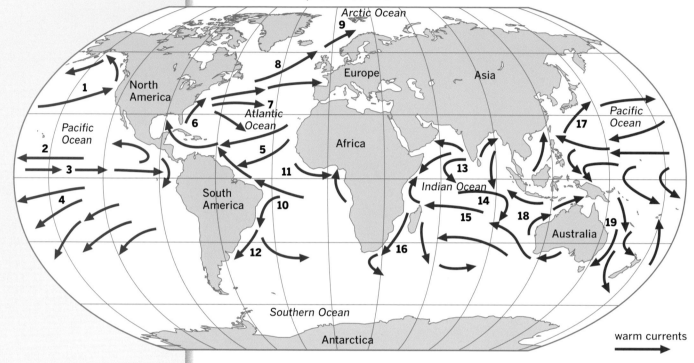

warm currents →

Principal cold currents

a California Current
b Peru Current
c West Wind Drift

d Labrador Current
e Canaries Current
f Benguela Current

g Falkland Current
h Oyashio Current
i Aleutian Current

cold currents →

© Diagram Visual Information Ltd.

Subsurface currents

Thermohaline circulation

Key words

Antarctica	subsurface
bottom water	current
current	surface water
intermediate	thermohaline
water	water column

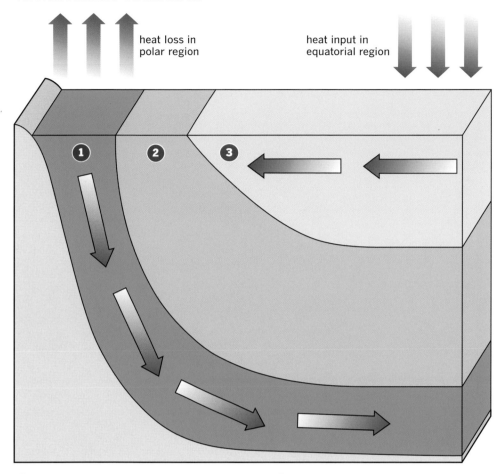

heat loss in polar region

heat input in equatorial region

1 Downwelling
At the poles, water becomes denser as it cools. Its density is also increased as ice is formed. This dense cold water sinks to the ocean floor.

2 Mixing
As the polar water travels across the ocean floor it very gradually mixes with the water above it, becoming warmer and less dense.

3 Upwelling
Water warmed by solar radiation in equatorial regions flows toward the poles to replace downwelling water. Water from the mixing layer wells up to replace it and is in turn heated.

Atlantic water masses

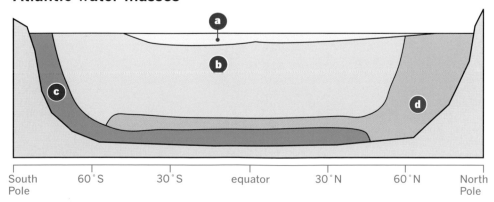

South Pole	60°S	30°S	equator	30°N	60°N	North Pole	

a Surface water

b Intermediate water

c Atlantic Antarctic Bottom Water (AABW)

d North Atlantic Deep Water (NADW)

Thermohaline circulation

- About ten percent of the ocean's water is circulated by surface currents. The other 90 percent is circulated deep beneath the surface by *thermohaline circulation*.
- Thermohaline circulation is driven by variations in temperature and salinity. Thermohaline means "heat-salt."
- Cold, salty seawater is generally denser than warm, less salty seawater. This means that cold, salty seawater tends to sink to the bottom of the oceans.
- At the poles, seawater becomes colder as it loses heat to the atmosphere. It also becomes more salty as ice forms, removing fresh water.
- These processes cause polar seawater to sink and flow along the bottom of the ocean floor toward the equator. This is known as deep or bottom water.
- In equatorial regions, seawater at the surface of the ocean is heated by solar radiation. This warm water flows toward the poles to replace the sinking polar water.
- In between the warm, shallow, surface layer and the cold, deep, bottom water there is a broad band of intermediate water. Bottom water mixes with intermediate water very slowly. Surface water flowing toward the poles is replaced by upwellings of intermediate water.

Atlantic water masses

- In the Atlantic Ocean, seawater from the Arctic sinks to form North Atlantic Deep Water (NADW). In Antarctica it sinks to form Atlantic Antarctic Bottom Water (AABW). AABW is generally denser than NADW and tends to flow underneath it.
- Warm surface water tends to flow toward the Arctic more readily than toward the Antarctic.

© Diagram Visual Information Ltd.

Oceanic conveyor belt

© Diagram Visual Information Ltd.

Key words

bottom water
current
salinity
thermocline
thermohaline

Oceanic circulation

- About 90 percent of the water in the world's oceans circulates beneath the surface. These subsurface currents are driven by thermohaline circulation.
- Cold deep water sinks in polar regions and flows along the bottom of ocean basins. Near Greenland and Iceland, ice formation and winter cooling generates North Atlantic deep water that flows southwards. Deep water also forms off the coast of Antarctica.
- Differences in the salinity of deep water in the Atlantic and Pacific ocean basins drives a flow of bottom water from one to the other.
- Warm water at intermediate and surface levels follows a path from the Pacific and Indian oceans through the South Atlantic to the North Atlantic.
- This "oceanic conveyor belt" transfers warm water from tropical regions to polar regions and cold water from polar to tropical regions. Without this flow, temperature differences between the equatorial regions and the poles would be much greater.
- It is estimated that water takes between 1,000 and 2,000 years to make one complete circuit of this global system.

Oceanic circulation

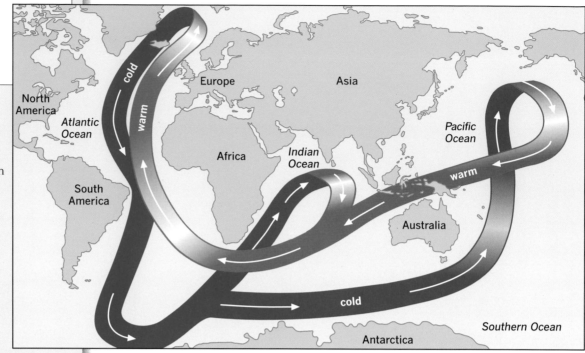

warm, low salinity surface and intermediate water

cold, high salinity deep and bottom water

Sites of deep water formation

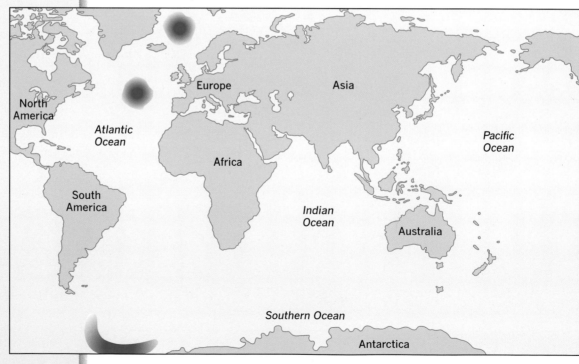

zones where deep and bottom waters form and sink

Downwellings

Key words

bottom water	surface water
downwelling	
Ekman transport	
nutrient	
reef	

Coastal downwelling in the Southern Hemisphere

General features
- A *downwelling* is a sinking of water from the surface to deeper layers.
- Downwellings are associated with comparatively clear, nutrient-sparse surface waters. The downwelled water is warm and oxygen-rich but nutrient-poor.
- In tropical and subtropical waters downwellings are commonly associated with coral reefs.

Types
- Coastal downwellings are found where persistent winds blow onshore or parallel with the shore, in such a way that Ekman transport causes surface water to move onshore. Surface water displaces deeper water. Such downwellings occur on the western boundaries of the Pacific and Atlantic oceans.
- Open-ocean downwellings occur where surface water currents converge.
- At the Antarctic convergence, Antarctic intermediate water sinks below subantarctic surface water where the two water masses converge.
- Off Greenland and Iceland, ice formation encourages downwelling that leads to the formation of North Atlantic deep water.

1 Prevailing wind
Persistent winds blow parallel to the coastline pushing water downwind and creating an ocean surface current.

2 Ekman transport
The Coriolis effect deflects the wind-driven surface current to the right. Ekman transport results in a net movement of water onshore.

3 Downwelling
Water moving onshore is forced to sink.

© Diagram Visual Information Ltd.

© Diagram Visual Information Ltd.

Key words

bottom water   upwelling
current
Ekman transport
nutrient
surface water

General features

- An *upwelling* is a rise of water from deeper to surface layers.
- Upwellings are commonly associated with raised productivity. The upwelled water is normally cool and rich in nutrients and fertilizes the surface layers, raising phytoplankton productivity.
- Upwellings are often associated with rich fisheries. In the 1990s, between a third and a half of the oceanic fish and squid catch came from areas of upwelling.

Types

- Coastal upwellings are found where persistent winds blow offshore or parallel to the shore, in such a way that Ekman transport causes surface water to move offshore. Water from below rises up to take its place. Such upwellings occur on the eastern boundaries of the Pacific and Atlantic oceans.
- Open ocean upwelling occurs at the equator where surface water currents diverge.
- Near Antarctica, North Atlantic deep water wells up to fuel productivity in the Southern Ocean.
- Smaller-scale upwellings occur where seabed topography causes vertical mixing of water, such as on the downstream side of headlands, sea mounts, or offshore islands.

Upwellings

Coastal upwelling in the Southern Hemisphere

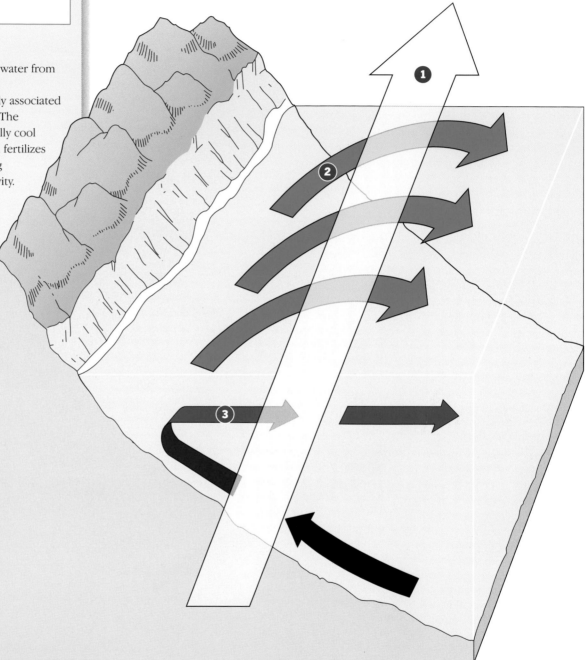

1 **Prevailing wind**
Persistent winds blow parallel to the coastline pushing water downwind and creating an ocean surface current.

2 **Ekman transport**
The Coriolis effect deflects the wind-driven surface current to the right. Ekman transport results in a net movement of water offshore.

3 **Upwelling**
Water rises along the coastline to replace water moving offshore.

El Niño

Key words

bottom water
El Niño
nutrient
surface water
upwelling

Normal conditions

A tongue of cold surface water **a**, indicating upwelling, extends from the Peruvian coast in January 1984.

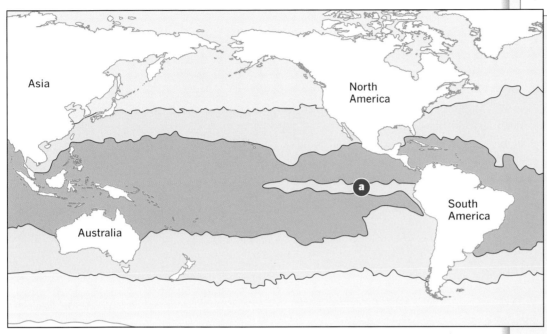

El Niño

- *El Niño* refers to the condition of higher-than-normal temperatures in the surface waters of the equatorial Pacific off South America.
- *El Niño* means "boy child" or "Christ child" in Spanish. It usually occurs in December, when a slackening in trade winds causes the upwelling of cold water off the Peruvian coast to slow or stop.
- The upwelling of nutrient-rich water is associated with high phytoplankton productivity, and supports a rich Peruvian anchovy fishery. The occurrence of El Niño conditions marks the end of the peak fishing season, and the anchovies disperse.
- An El Niño event is a year in which the suppression of the upwelling is much more pronounced than usual. The anchovy fishery is poor in that year.
- El Niño events are associated with much wider-scale climatic events that impact upon at least half the globe.

El Niño conditions

At the height of an El Niño event, as here in January 1983, the upwelling is suppressed and the tongue of cold surface water is absent **b**.

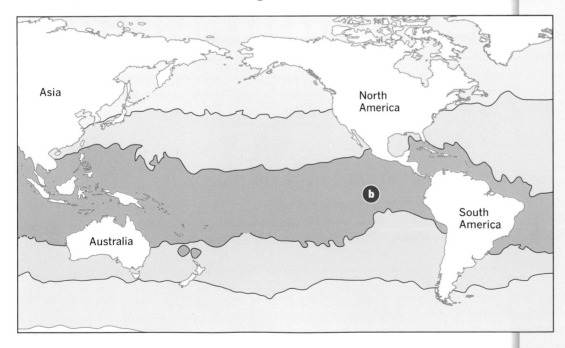

Sea surface temperatures

 32–54°F (0–12°C)   55–76°F (13–24°C) 77–86°F (25–30°C)

© Diagram Visual Information Ltd.

© Diagram Visual Information Ltd.

Key words

equator	*sea level*
high tide	*tide*
low tide	

Tides

- A *tide* is a periodic rise and fall of the sea surface caused by the gravitational attraction of the Moon, and to a lesser extent, the Sun.

Simple equilibrium model

- This model assumes that Earth is covered in water to a uniform depth. The effect of the gravitational attraction of the Sun is ignored.
- The Moon's gravitational attraction draws Earth's water toward it on the side nearest the Moon, forming a bulge. On Earth's opposite side, the Moon's gravitational attraction is correspondingly less and an opposite bulge forms.
- The locations of tidal bulges are regions of high tide. The troughs in between are regions of low tide.
- Earth spins on its axis once every 24 hours, so that tidal bulges (and the troughs in between) travel around Earth in a 24-hour period.
- The Moon advances slowly in its own orbit around Earth, so that a full tidal cycle is not 24 hours, but slightly longer—24 hours 50 minutes. Any point on Earth should experience two tidal crests (high tides) and two tidal troughs (low tides) within a 24-hour 50-minute period.
- The Moon does not simply remain overhead at the equator. Its overhead position gradually shifts between 28.5°N and 28.5°S. Because of this, the two tidal bulges (high tides) and troughs (low tides) per tidal cycle are rarely of exactly equal size.

Limitations of the model

- In practice, the presence of landmasses and variation in the shape and depth of ocean basins markedly alters this simple pattern.
- The gravitational attraction of the Sun also influences the tides, giving rise to spring and neap tides.

Tides

Gravitational effect of the Moon on Earth's surface waters

Moon overhead at the equator

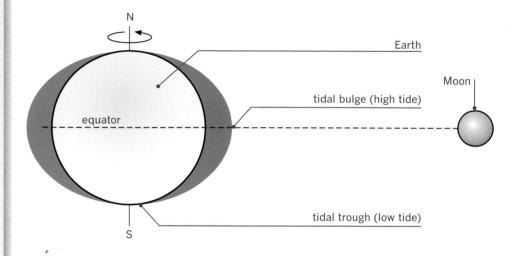

Moon overhead at 28.5°N

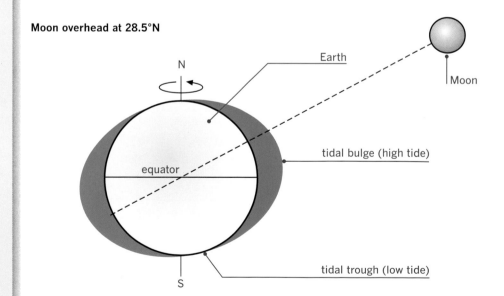

Spring and neap tides

Generation of spring and neap tides

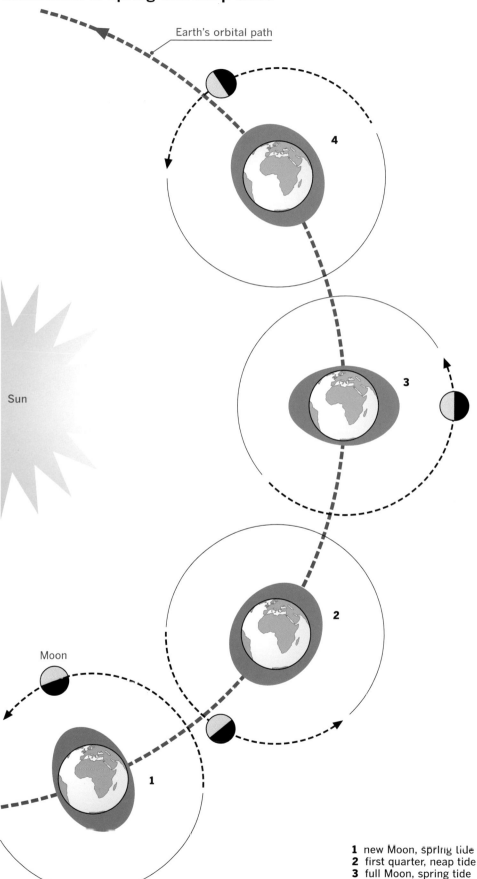

Earth's orbital path

Sun

Moon

4

3

2

1

1 new Moon, spring tide
2 first quarter, neap tide
3 full Moon, spring tide
4 third quarter, neap tide

Key words

high tide   perigee
low tide   spring tide
neap tide   tide

Generation of spring and neap tides

- *Spring* and *neap tides* are generated by the gravitational attraction of the Sun adding to or counteracting the effect of the Moon's gravitational attraction.

- A spring tide occurs when the Sun and Moon are aligned so that their gravitational attractions are added. A larger-than-normal high tide and a correspondingly lower-than-normal low tide results. Spring tides occur at the full Moon and the new Moon.

- A neap tide occurs when the Sun and the Moon are at right angles (90°) relative to Earth so that their gravitational attractions have opposing effects. This creates smaller-than-normal high tides and higher-than-normal low tides. Neap tides occur when the Moon is at one-quarter and three-quarters.

- In every lunar month (29.5 days) there are two sets of spring tides and two sets of neap tides, with tides of intermediate size in between.

Exceptional tides

- Spring tides occur every month, but the largest spring tides occur when it is actually spring in the Northern Hemisphere.

- These tides occur when the Moon is at its closest to Earth (perigee) and the Sun is directly overhead at the equator. Under these conditions the gravitational effects of the Sun and the Moon on Earth's oceans are at their greatest.

- Such spring tides may have a 20 percent greater tidal range than regular spring tides.

© Diagram Visual Information Ltd.

Tide types

Key words

Coriolis effect   semidiurnal tide
diurnal tide   tide
mixed tide

Variations in tide

- When viewed from above, Earth spins counterclockwise and the tidal bulge generated by the Moon's gravitational attraction progresses westwards. It is constrained by landmasses and deflected by the Coriolis effect.
- In some basins, the tidal bulge behaves as a progressive (traveling) wave. In other situations, the tidal bulge behaves as a standing wave. The complex interactions between tidal bulge, landmasses, and ocean floor topography generate at least three types of tide.

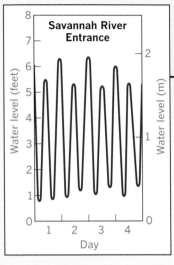

Semidiurnal (semidaily) tides

These are tides of the conventional form, with two tides, both of similar tidal range, within a lunar day (24 hours 50 minutes), e.g., Savannah River Entrance, Georgia.

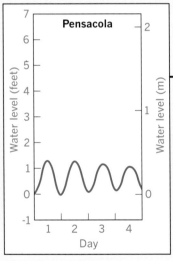

Diurnal (daily) tides

A single tide once within a lunar day, e.g., Pensacola, Alabama.

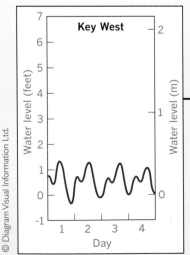

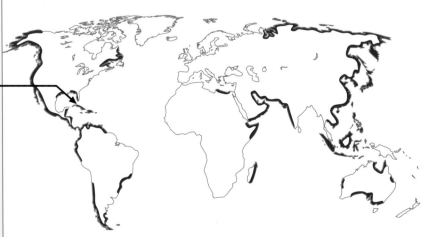

Mixed semidiurnal tides

Two tides of markedly different tidal range within a lunar day, e.g., Key West, Florida.

© Diagram Visual Information Ltd.

Internal waves and standing waves

Key words

internal wave	stationary wave
pycnocline	thermocline
seiche	wave
standing wave	

Internal waves

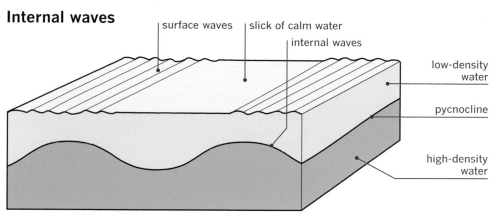

Motion of a standing wave

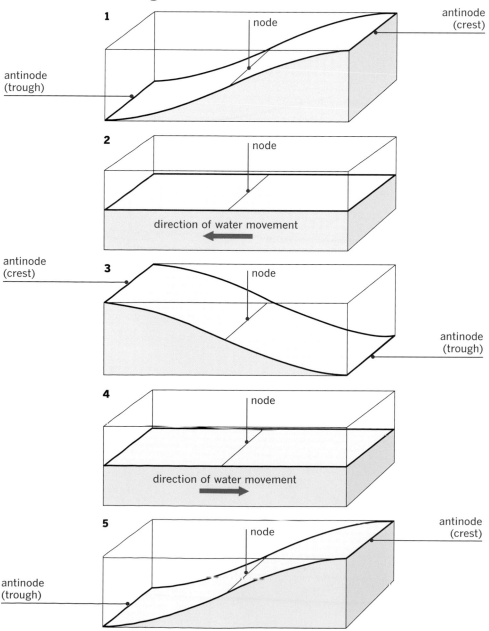

Internal waves

- An *internal wave* is a form of wave that occurs, usually beneath the surface, at the boundary between two layers of water with different densities.
- A *pycnocline* is a narrow boundary layer separating two thicker layers with different densities.
- A *thermocline* is a boundary separating two layers with different temperatures (and usually therefore different densities).
- Internal waves may form at thermoclines or pycnoclines.
- Internal waves are generated by various forces: tidal surges, wind stress, seismic displacements, and even the wake from a moving vessel.
- Internal waves are barely visible at the surface (the wave trough may be associated with calm surface water), but they can be important in mixing layers of the water column and they have been implicated as a cause of submarine accidents.

Standing waves

- A *standing wave* is a form of wave that occurs when two traveling waves with equal amplitudes that are moving in opposite directions interfere with one another.
- The result is a wave with peaks and troughs that move vertically but not horizontally (**1–5**). The peaks and troughs are known as *antinodes* and the points where the water neither rises or falls are known as *nodes*.
- Standing waves are also known as *stationary waves* or *seiches*. They do not progress through the water but instead oscillate about a point or axis (the node).
- Stationary waves are found in all oceans. They can be generated by sudden changes in meteorological conditions, such as intense storms and marked drops in atmospheric pressure.

© Diagram Visual Information Ltd.

Ocean waves

Key words

crest
fetch
orbital
swell

trochoidal wave
trough
wave

Wind-generated ocean waves

- Most ocean waves are generated by wind.
- With a wind blowing at a constant speed in the same direction, the size of the wave it generates is a function of its speed, and the extent of open ocean that it affects is known as the *fetch*.

Seas and swells

- At sea, winds rarely blow at a constant speed in the same direction for very long. As a result, where wind-generated waves are forming there is often a jumbled mix of waves of different heights, wavelengths, and directions. This is known as a *sea*. Waves in a sea are often trochoidal (with pointed crests and rounded troughs).
- As waves travel away from an area of wave-generation they may sort themselves so that waves of similar height and wavelength are traveling in the same direction. Here, the waves are smoother and more rounded. This is known as a *swell*.

Movement in a wave

- Wind-driven waves in deep water transfer energy and form horizontally, but cause little net movement of water.
- An object on the surface caught by a wave tends to roll, turn in a circle, and return to its starting point. It is not swept along with the passing wave.
- Such waves generate orbital motions in the top layer of the water column.
- The orbitals gradually diminish in size and disappear at a depth of about half the wave's wavelength.

© Diagram Visual Information Ltd.

Wave features

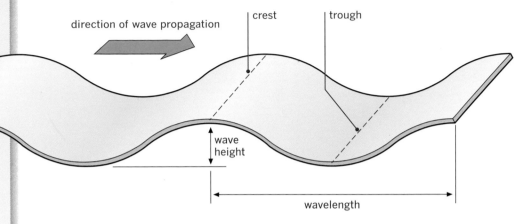

Sea

Swell

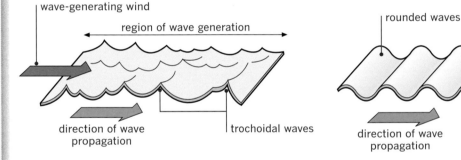

Movement in a wave

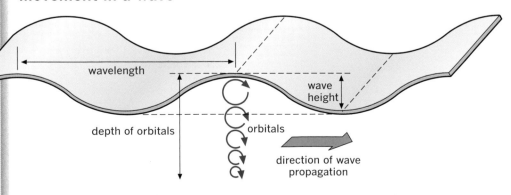

Shore waves

Waves approaching a shore

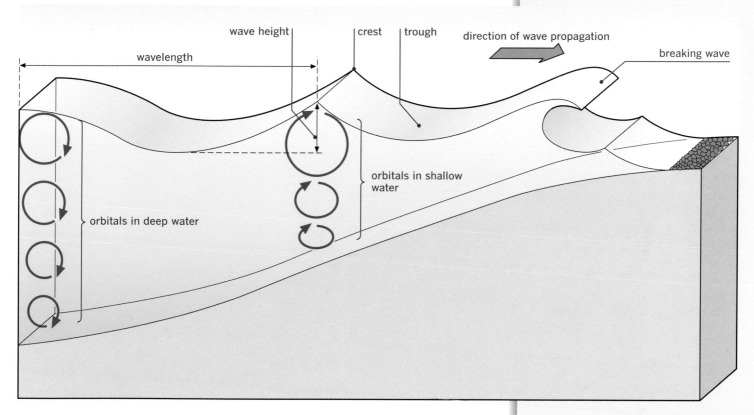

wave height — crest — trough — direction of wave propagation — breaking wave

wavelength

orbitals in shallow water

orbitals in deep water

Water particle motion

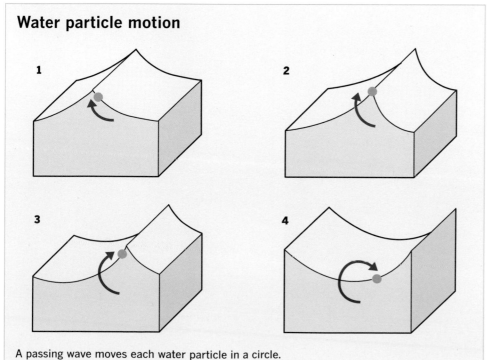

1 **2** **3** **4**

A passing wave moves each water particle in a circle.

Shallow-water waves

- In shallow water (depths less than half a wave's wavelength) the seabed interferes with the downward progression of an ocean wave's orbitals.
- Lower orbitals become flattened.
- Friction with the sea bottom slows the advance of the wave.
- Wave height increases and the wave crest becomes more peaked.
- When wave steepness (wave height:wavelength) reaches the critical ratio of 1:7, the wave breaks.
- Approaching a shore, waves usually break when water depth is about 1.3 times wave height; a five-foot (1.5 m) high wave breaks in about 6.5 feet (2 m) depth of water.
- Surfers choose gently sloping shores where waves crash gradually, rather than steeply sloping shores where waves crash abruptly.

© Diagram Visual Information Ltd.

© Diagram Visual Information Ltd.

Key words

crest	tsunami
earthquake	volcano
shore	wave
tidal wave	
trough	

Tsunami

- A *tsunami* is a large wave produced by a seismic event that causes a sudden, massive displacement of water.
- Tsunamis are sometimes called "tidal waves" although tides do not form them.

General features

- Tsunamis are most commonly generated by earthquakes or volcanoes. They can also be generated when landslides deposit large quantities of material into the ocean.
- Tsunamis have long wavelengths, typically in the range of 65–130 miles (100–200 km).
- The wave height of a tsunami in the open ocean is small, often less than 3 feet (1 m).
- On reaching shallow water, the forward motion of the wave is slowed by friction. The wave may reach a dangerously high level, sweeping ashore and carrying boats, seashore structures, and people with it.
- Tsunamis can cause great loss of life and destruction. On December 26, 2004, a series of tsunamis caused by a large earthquake on the seafloor off the coast of Sumatra, Indonesia spread across the Indian Ocean. At least 310,000 people were killed in coastal regions from Indonesia to the east coast of Africa.

Tsunamis

Tsunami progression

1

Generation
A section of seafloor has subsided, creating a wave trough.

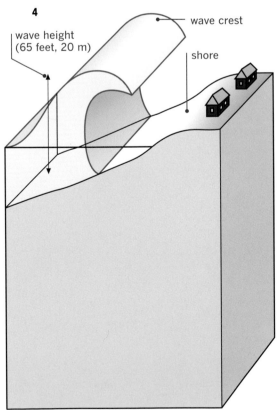

2

Propagation in deep water
The tsunami has low wave height but very long wavelength. In water 2.5 miles (4 km) deep the tsunami travels at 450 miles per hour (720 kmph).

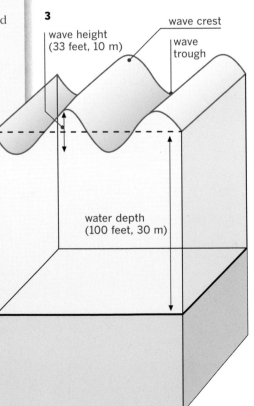

3

Propagation in shallow water
The tsunami slows and builds.

4

Inundation
As the wave breaks on the shore, large volumes of seawater are carried inland.

Coastal breezes

Sea breezes

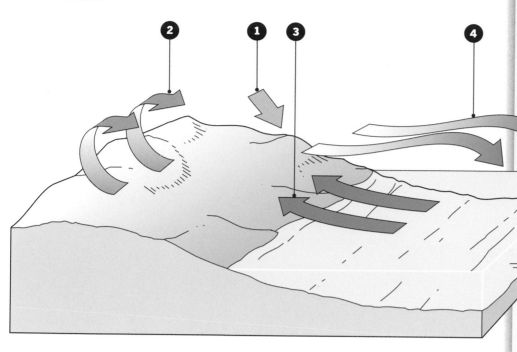

1. Solar radiation is absorbed by both sea and land, but the heat capacity of the land is less and it warms up more quickly.

2. Dry air close to the land surface warms quickly and rises.

3. Cool moist air close to the sea surface moves ashore to replace the rising air. A cool onshore sea breeze is thus generated during the day.

4. Aloft, an offshore airflow descends to complete the cycle.

Land breezes

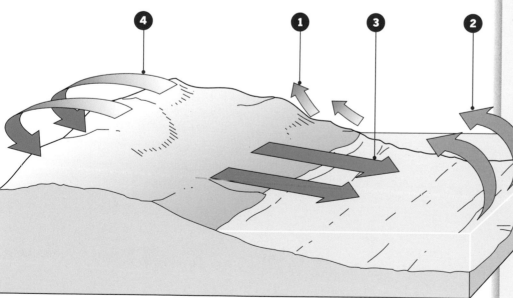

1. Radiant heat energy is lost more rapidly from the land than the sea.

2. Warm, moist air close to the sea surface rises.

3. Cool air from the land moves offshore to replace the rising air. A cool offshore land breeze is generated at night.

4. Aloft an onshore airflow descends to complete the cycle.

Key words

coast	temperate
offshore breeze	tropical
onshore breeze	

Coastal breezes

- Seawater has a higher heat capacity than land. Given the same conditions of solar irradiation, seawater both gains and loses heat more slowly than adjacent land. This difference in thermal characteristics gives rise to coastal breezes.

- In a typical 24-hour period coastal breezes change direction from onshore breezes to offshore breezes.

- Coastal breezes vary markedly in intensity and regularity, depending on location and time of year. They are most pronounced in the tropics and subtropics, and in temperate latitudes during the summer.

Sea breezes

- *Sea breezes* are cool onshore breezes that usually occur during daylight hours.

- During the day, air above the land is heated more quickly than air above the sea and begins to rise. Air above the sea flows onshore to replace the rising warm air. This flow of air is a sea breeze.

Land breezes

- *Land breezes* are offshore breezes that usually occur during the hours of darkness.

- During the night, air above the sea is warmed by heat escaping from the water. This air rises and is replaced by air flowing offshore from the land. This flow of air is a land breeze.

© Diagram Visual Information Ltd.

© Diagram Visual Information Ltd.

Key words

fair-weather
* waterspout*   *waterspout*
tornadic
* waterspout*

Waterspout

- A *waterspout* is a funnel-shaped vortex of rising air occurring over water. There are two main types: *tornadic waterspouts* and *fair-weather waterspouts*.
- Waterspouts can occur over seas, lakes, or any large body of water. They most frequently occur in areas where tornadoes are also common.

Tornadic waterspouts

- A tornadic waterspout is formed when a tornado—an intense, rotating column of air extending from the base of a thunder-storm cloud to the ground—travels over water.
- Tornadic waterspouts can be highly destructive.

Fair-weather waterspouts

- A fair-weather waterspout forms over warm water where rotating moist air rises rapidly in a highly humid atmosphere.
- Fair-weather waterspouts only form over water.
- They are most likely to form when the water is at its warmest and cooler air passes over it.
- Fair-weather waterspouts are smaller and less destructive than the tornadic variety. They are also far more common than tornadic waterspouts.

Waterspouts

Features of a waterspout

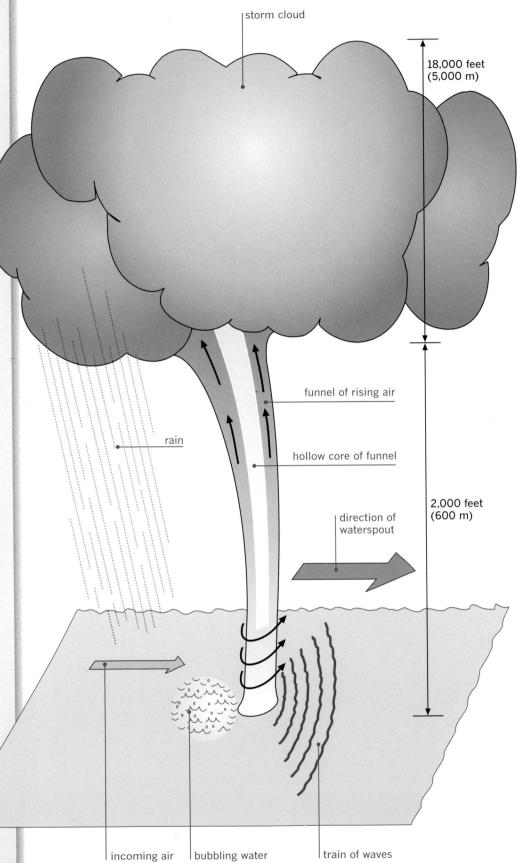

storm cloud

18,000 feet
(5,000 m)

funnel of rising air

rain

hollow core of funnel

direction of
waterspout

2,000 feet
(600 m)

incoming air   bubbling water   train of waves

Ocean surface topography

Jason 1

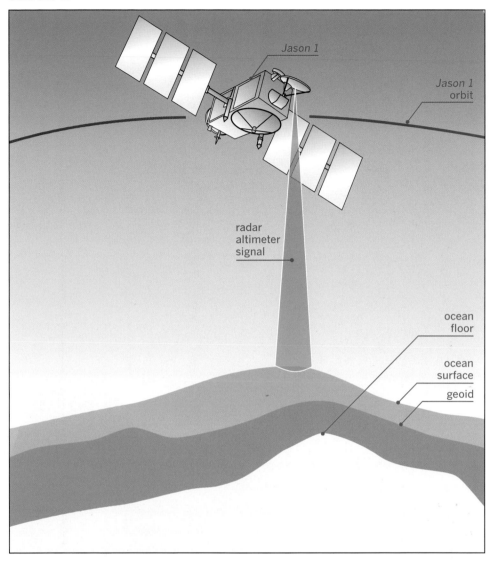

Key words

geoid
Ocean

Ocean surface variation

- The distance between the surface of the Ocean and the center of Earth varies widely from place to place.
- Several factors account for this variation. Local differences in the gravitational attraction of Earth can cause variations in the height of the ocean's surface of up to 300 feet (100 m). Ocean currents can cause changes of about 3 feet (1 m). Local solar heating causes water to expand in some areas, raising the ocean's surface by 10 to 40 inches (30–100 cm)
- *Jason 1* is a joint U.S.-French satellite carrying instruments (radar altimeters) that enable it to measure ocean surface topography with an accuracy of 1.7 inches (4.2 cm).
- Scientists are able to subtract the influences of gravity variation (using a reference altitude known as the "geoid") and currents from *Jason 1*'s data to reveal small variations due to temperature change. The results can be used to predict the onset of El Niño conditions and to understand the behavior of the Ocean better.

Jason 1 ocean surface height data

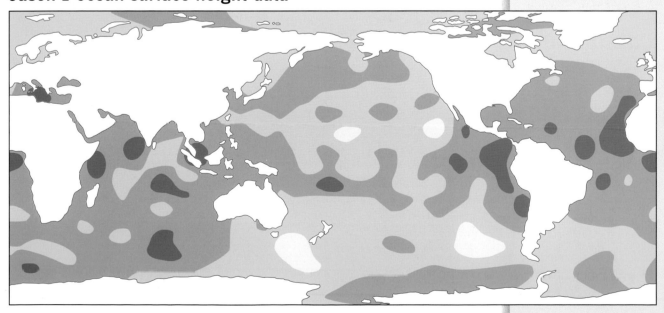

Variation in altitude inches (cm)

-4 to -8
(-10 to -20)

0 to -4
(0 to -10)

0 to 4
(0 to 10)

4 to 8
(10 to 20)

© Diagram Visual Information Ltd.

© Diagram Visual Information Ltd.

Key words

evolution
radiation
seawater

First life

- Modern evolutionary theory suggests that life on Earth has evolved from non-life within the last four billion years.
- The first known fossils of life-forms on Earth date from about 3.6 billion years ago.

Life in the oceans

- Life probably first arose in the Ocean. There are three important reasons why this is thought to be the case:
- Most organisms are at least two-thirds water. Water is sparse on land but superabundant in the Ocean.
- Water absorbs harmful ultraviolet radiation. Most UV radiation is absorbed within the top few meters of seawater. Surface levels of UV radiation have probably only fallen from dangerously high levels within the last billion years (after the formation of the atmosphere's ozone layer)—long after life had first evolved;
- Most freshwater contains relatively low concentrations of dissolved substances. Seawater, on the other hand, has high concentrations of dissolved substances, and their total concentration is similar to that found in many simple life-forms, such as microbes, animals, and plants.

Origins of life

Stanley Miller's apparatus

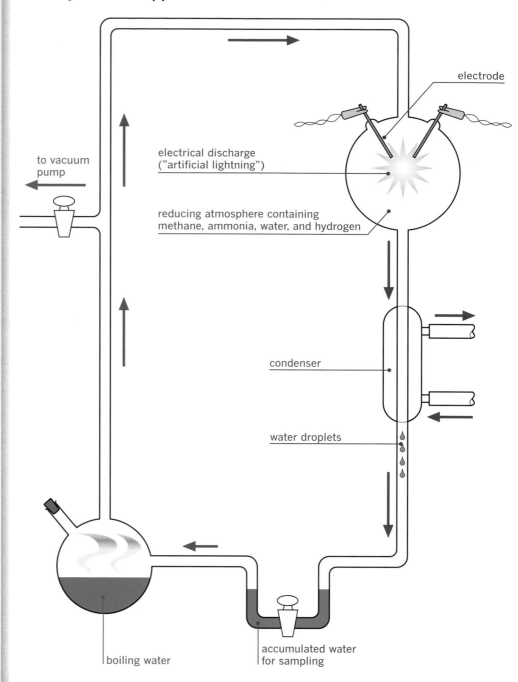

electrode

electrical discharge ("artificial lightning")

to vacuum pump

reducing atmosphere containing methane, ammonia, water, and hydrogen

condenser

water droplets

boiling water

accumulated water for sampling

Testing a scenario

- In the 1950s, U.S. chemist Stanley Miller (b. 1930) was able to synthesize simple molecular building blocks of life by passing electrical sparks ("artificial lightning") through a "reducing atmosphere" of methane, ammonia, water, and hydrogen—mimicking conditions believed to exist on the early Earth. His experiment is shown above.
- Among the chemicals Miller collected were amino acids (building blocks of proteins), purines, and pyrimidines (organic bases found in RNA, DNA, ATP, and other key biomolecules).
- Stanley Miller's experiments helped suggest how some of the molecular building blocks of life might have arisen.

Other scenarios

- Until recently the best candidate for the evolution of life began with the notion of a "biochemical soup" that accumulated in oceans or chemical-rich lakes. There are other possibilities:
- Simple life-forms might have arrived "ready made" in cosmic debris falling to Earth.
- Some scientists have suggested the first terrestrial life-forms were silicon-based and evolved in clays.
- With the recent discovery of archaebacteria that thrive in high-temperature hydrothermal vents and granite rock hundreds of feet below ground, alternatives for a non-oceanic origin of life are becoming increasingly plausible.

History of life

The procession of life on Earth

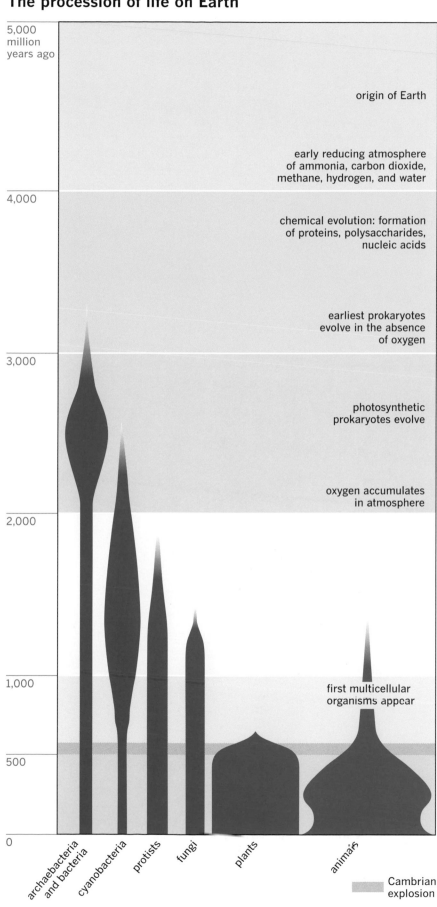

- 5,000 million years ago — origin of Earth
- early reducing atmosphere of ammonia, carbon dioxide, methane, hydrogen, and water
- 4,000 — chemical evolution: formation of proteins, polysaccharides, nucleic acids
- earliest prokaryotes evolve in the absence of oxygen
- 3,000 — photosynthetic prokaryotes evolve
- oxygen accumulates in atmosphere
- 2,000
- 1,000 — first multicellular organisms appear
- 500
- 0

archaebacteria and bacteria · cyanobacteria · protists · fungi · plants · animals

Cambrian explosion

Key words

atmosphere
evolution

- Current best estimates suggest that Earth is about 4,600 million (4.6 billion) years old.
- For more than three-quarters of that time (about 3.5 billion years) it has been inhabited by life-forms.
- For about 3 billion years, organisms living in the sea have dominated life on Earth. It is only in the last 500 million years that terrestrial forms have evolved and proliferated.

3,500–4,000 million years ago
- Chemical evolution during this period probably gave rise to the chemical building blocks of life, such as proteins, polysaccharides (complex sugars), and nucleic acids (DNA and RNA).
- The first life-forms on Earth were probably bacteria-like. They evolved in an oxygen-free environment.

2,000–2,500 million years ago
- Photosynthesis—an organism's capacity to manufacture organic compounds by utilizing sunlight energy—had evolved by about 2,500 million years ago. Oxygen was excreted as a byproduct of photosynthesis.
- By about 2,000 million years ago oxygen began to accumulate in the atmosphere.

800–1,000 million years ago
- Eukaryote organisms (those with complex cells containing a nucleus and membrane-bound organelles) had evolved by this time.
- Fossils of multicellular forms date back to 850 million years ago.

500–600 million years ago
- As Earth cooled, perhaps creating a richer variety of habitats, an explosive diversification of life took place (the Cambrian explosion).
- By 500 million years ago, most of the major body plans of animals had evolved in the sea.

Since 500 million years ago
- Oxygen levels in the atmosphere were sufficient to create a substantial ozone layer that absorbed dangerous ultraviolet light. This made it possible for organisms to colonize the land.
- Algae, invertebrates (animals without backbones), and then vertebrates (animals with backbones) colonized the land.
- Major extinction events occurred five times between 500 and 65 million years ago.
- Some scientists consider that Earth is currently undergoing a major extinction event as a result of modification of the environment by human activities.

© Diagram Visual Information Ltd.

Key words

atmosphere
climate
photosynthesis
sea level

Environmental change

- Environmental conditions on Earth have changed over timescales ranging from decades to eons.
- Some changes, such as atmospheric oxygen levels, have been progressive and constant (oxygen levels have only risen, never fallen).
- Most physical and chemical changes oscillate in an irregular fashion in response to numerous variables such as levels of volcanism, the drift of continents, changes in Earth's orbit, and meteorite impacts.
- The presence of life on Earth, as in the production of oxygen gas by photosynthesis, has had a profound influence on the physical and chemical environment.

1 Atmospheric oxygen levels have gradually increased as photosynthetic organisms have flourished.

2 Sea levels have changed markedly, partly in response to changing climate but also as a result of tectonic changes such as continental drift. Alterations in ocean currents have, in turn, had widespread effects on climate.

3 The global climate has alternated between icehouse and hothouse conditions. Such changes probably stem from shifts in Earth's orbit around the Sun. Major meteorite impacts may have played a role too.

© Diagram Visual Information Ltd.

Environmental change

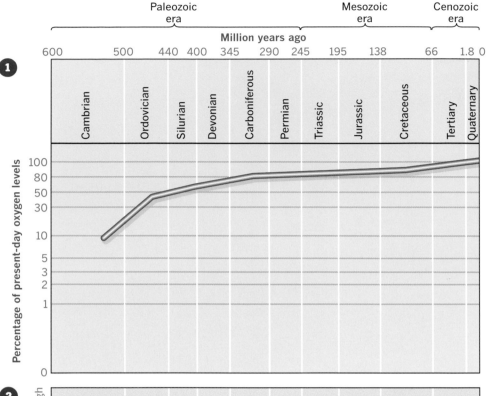

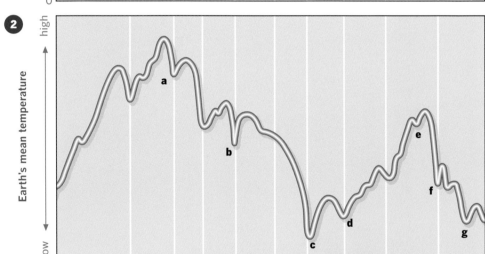

a–g Major marine extinction events. These have usually coincided with falls in sea level.

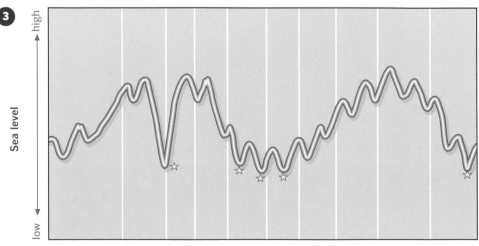

☆ major glaciations

Food chains

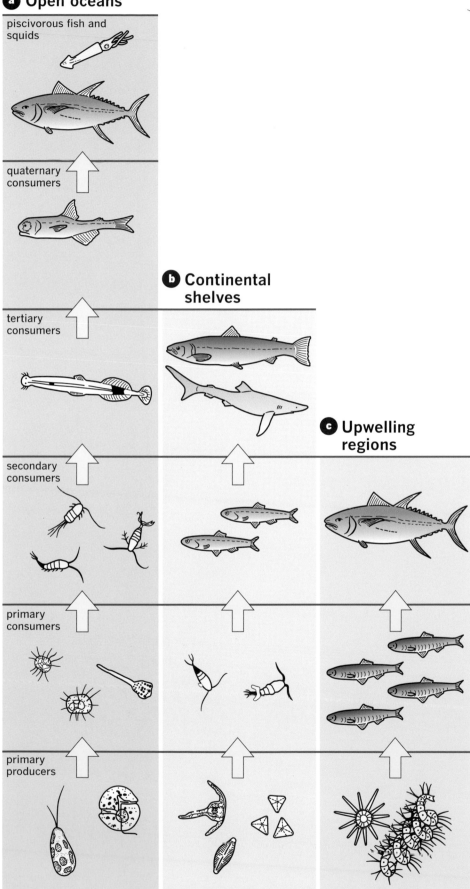

a Open oceans

piscivorous fish and squids

quaternary consumers

tertiary consumers

b Continental shelves

secondary consumers

c Upwelling regions

primary consumers

primary producers

Key words

food chain
plankton
primary producer
trophic level

Food chains

- A *food chain* is a set of organisms that pass energy from one member to another. The organisms at the bottom of the food chain are eaten by the next organism in the food chain, which is in turn eaten by the next.
- Often, more than one species occupies the same position in the hierarchy of the food chain. These levels are known as *trophic levels*.
- At the bottom of a food chain there are always organisms that harvest energy directly from the Sun. In the oceans these are phytoplankton. They are known as *primary producers*.
- The trophic levels above the primary producers are referred to as primary, secondary, tertiary (and so on) consumers.
- The number of trophic levels in a food chain depends on the local environment. For example, open ocean food chains tend to be longer than coastal water food chains because there are more species in the former than in the latter.

a In the open oceans, where the dominant primary producers are of very small size, food chains are long.

b On continental shelves in temperate waters, dominant primary producers are of intermediate size and food chains are of intermediate length.

c In upwelling regions, where primary producers are much larger, food chains are short.

© Diagram Visual Information Ltd.

Key words

food chain
plankton
respiration
trophic level

Efficiency of energy transfer

- The diagram shows energy flow through a North Atlantic food chain. It assumes that ten percent of the energy at one trophic level is passed on to the next. In a food chain, the efficiency of energy transfer between trophic levels is typically 6–15 percent.
- Within a trophic level, a large amount of energy is lost through respiration to maintain the organism. Of the remainder only a proportion is consumed by organisms at the next trophic level.
- In ideal conditions, for each 500,000 units of radiant energy, only one unit is available to be consumed by humans.

Features of the food chain

1. **Sunlight**: radiant energy striking the sea surface: 500,000 energy units.
2. **Phytoplankton**: of sunlight energy striking the sea surface, two percent is utilized by phytoplankton: 10,000 energy units.
3. **Copepods**: ten percent of the energy in phytoplankton is passed on to copepods (dominant members of the zooplankton community) when they consume phytoplankton: 1,000 energy units.
4. **Herring**: ten percent of the energy in copepods is passed on to herring—a dominant plankton-feeding fish: 100 energy units.
5. **Atlantic cod**: ten percent of the energy in herring is passed on to cod—a dominant predatory fish: ten energy units.
6. **Fish caught by fishermen**: only 0.0002% of the radiant energy striking the sea surface is available to be harvested by fishermen. In practice, overfishing and the negative effects of climate change on reproduction have drastically lowered the stocks of cod in the North Atlantic: one energy unit.

© Diagram Visual Information Ltd.

North Atlantic food chain

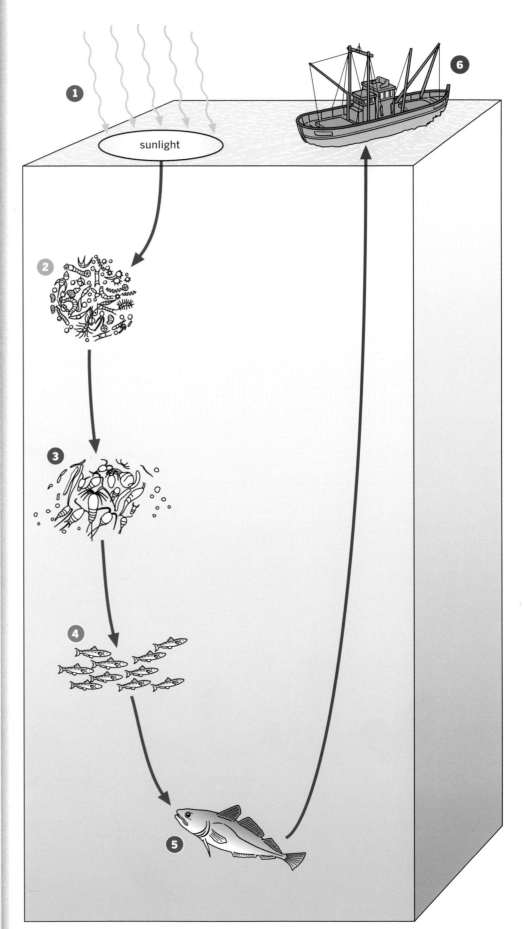

sunlight

Antarctic food web

Examples of consumers and producers

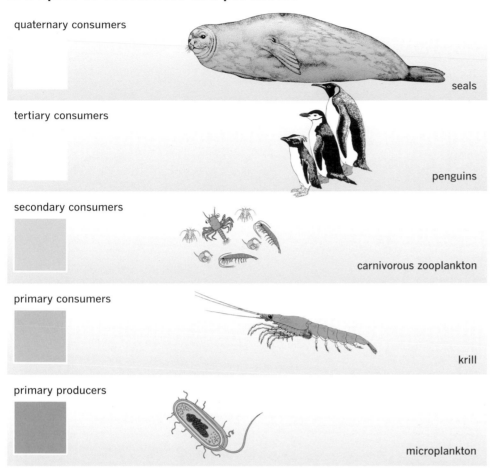

quaternary consumers

seals

tertiary consumers

penguins

secondary consumers

carnivorous zooplankton

primary consumers

krill

primary producers

microplankton

Key words

Antarctic	plankton
food chain	trophic level
food web	

Food webs

- A *food web* refers to the interrelated food chains that exist in nature.
- The food-chain model has organisms at one trophic level feeding exclusively on organisms at a lower trophic level. In reality, organisms consume other organisms at several different trophic levels and feeding preferences may change during a life cycle.

Antarctic food web

- The shrimplike krill, *Euphausia superba*, plays a central role in the Antarctic food web.
- Krill are the dominant primary consumers of microplankton. They are in turn eaten by creatures from whales to seabirds.
- Should krill be harvested on a large scale by humans, this could have a devastating effect on other animal populations that feed on krill.
- In the diagram, organisms have been allocated to a trophic level on the basis of their major food source.

Antarctic food web

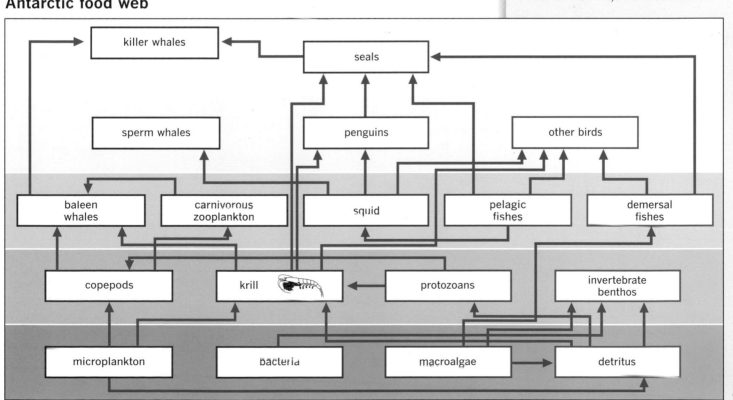

© Diagram Visual Information Ltd.

© Diagram Visual Information Ltd.

Key words

bacteria   protozoa
dissolved organic
  material (DOM)
microbial loop
plankton

Microbial loops

- The *microbial loop* refers to the activities of marine bacteria and protozoa in breaking down detritus and *dissolved organic material (DOM)*.
- Energy and nutrients from dead organisms are returned to the main food web through the microbial loop. DOM cannot be directly ingested and absorbed by larger organisms.

The microbial loop

Microbial loop in the main food chain

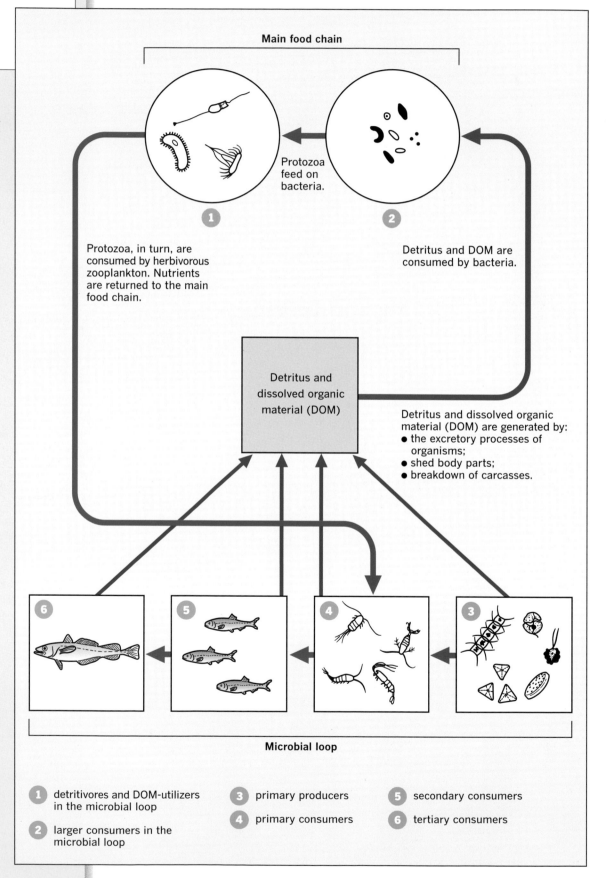

Main food chain

Protozoa feed on bacteria.

Protozoa, in turn, are consumed by herbivorous zooplankton. Nutrients are returned to the main food chain.

Detritus and DOM are consumed by bacteria.

Detritus and dissolved organic material (DOM)

Detritus and dissolved organic material (DOM) are generated by:
- the excretory processes of organisms;
- shed body parts;
- breakdown of carcasses.

Microbial loop

1. detritivores and DOM-utilizers in the microbial loop
2. larger consumers in the microbial loop
3. primary producers
4. primary consumers
5. secondary consumers
6. tertiary consumers

Primary productivity of organic carbon

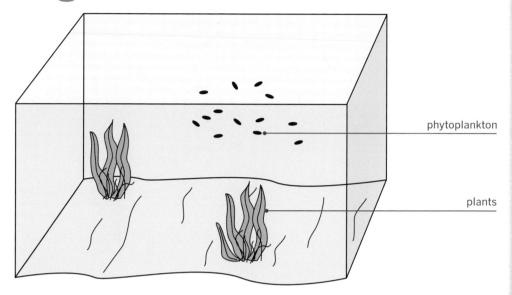

phytoplankton

plants

Key words

chemosynthesis
photosynthesis
plankton
primary producer
water column

Primary productivity

- *Primary productivity* is the rate at which inorganic carbon is converted into organic carbon by photosynthetic or chemosynthetic organisms.
- In communities where photosynthetic producers predominate (almost all marine communities), primary productivity refers to the production of both phytoplankton in the water column and plants that grow on the sunlit seafloor.

Rates of net primary production* (ocean regions)

Mean net primary productivity (gC/m²/year)

Region	
coral reefs	1,500
seagrass beds	1,000
estuaries and saltmarshes	800
continental upwelling (e.g., Peru Current)	400
continental shelf-break (e.g., Grand Banks, east coast of Canada)	200
temperate or subarctic open ocean (e.g., North Pacific)	150
tropical or subtropical open ocean (e.g., Sargasso Sea)	100
ice-covered polar waters	25

● = 25 gC/m²/year

Measuring primary productivity

- Measuring primary productivity gives an indication of the energy available to the rest of the community.
- Primary productivity— the rate of primary production—is measured in metric units: the amount of carbon (in grams) fixed under a square meter of sea surface in a day (gC/m²/day) or in a year (gC/m²/year).

Comparing rates of primary production

- Rates of primary production vary enormously in different parts of the ocean system, depending largely on nutrient availability, sunlight penetration, and temperature.

Rates of net primary production* (terrestrial regions)

Mean net primary productivity (gC/m²/year)

Region	
tropical rain forest	1,200
temperate farmland	600
extreme desert	2

● = 25 gC/m²/year

* Net primary production = gross primary production – respiration by producers

© Diagram Visual Information Ltd.

© Diagram Visual Information Ltd.

Key words

secondary
  producer
trophic level

Secondary productivity

- Production by secondary producers is the total amount of animal biomass (wet weight of tissue) produced per unit area per unit time.
- Secondary productivity is measured in metric units as the amount of carbon incorporated by animals under a square meter of sea surface in a year (gC/m²/year).

Assessment of secondary productivity

- Typically, only certain aspects of secondary productivity are estimated.
- It is difficult and time-consuming to identify and monitor all the consumers in a system, from microscopic protozoa to the largest predators.
- Levels of secondary production can be inferred from levels of primary production.
- Catch statistics for commercially fished species at the top of the food chain offer a measure of secondary productivity.

Comparison of rates of secondary production

- Rates of secondary production vary enormously in different parts of the ocean system. They depend largely on primary productivity, the length of the food chain (number of trophic levels), and ecological efficiency (the proportion of energy passed on from one trophic level to the next).

Secondary production

Fish production for different ocean regions

Region	Upwelling	Continental shelf	Open ocean
Mean primary productivity ● = 25 gC/m²/year	500	300	75
Number of trophic levels	2–3	4	6
Mean ecological efficiency	20%	15%	10%
Mean fish production (gC/m²/year)	45	1	0.00075

Food chains for different ocean regions

Upwelling

fish-eating fish

plankton-eating fish

large phytoplankton

Continental shelf

fish-eating fish

plankton-eating fish

medium-sized zooplankton

medium-sized phytoplankton

Open ocean

fish-eating fish

plankton-eating fish

large zooplankton

medium-sized zooplankton

small zooplankton

small phytoplankton

Rocky shore: intertidal zone

Key words

high tide
intertidal zone
low tide
shore

Intertidal zone

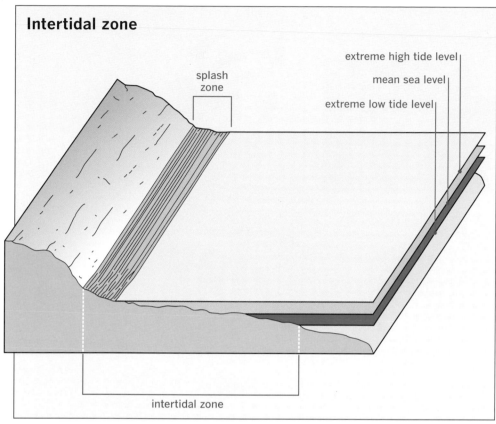

splash zone

extreme high tide level

mean sea level

extreme low tide level

intertidal zone

Parts of the intertidal zone

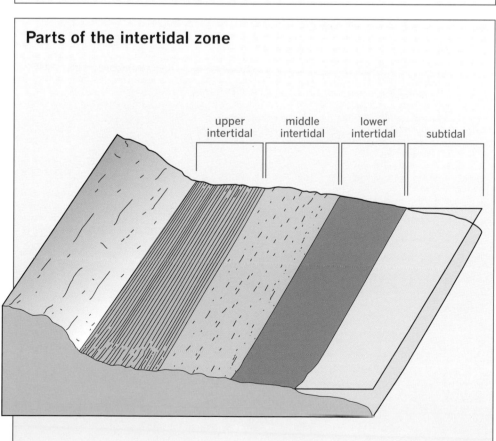

upper intertidal

middle intertidal

lower intertidal

subtidal

Intertidal zone

- The *intertidal zone* is the region of the shore lying between extreme low tides and extreme high tides, plus that region of the upper shore strongly affected by wave splash and spray.
- The nature of the animal and plant communities in the intertidal zone varies with the nature of the substrate and ambient temperature.
- On a given shore, the nature of the plant and animal community varies with height on the shore.

Environmental conditions

- A great variety of environmental conditions exists in the intertidal zone.
- This is due, in large part, to various levels on the shore being exposed to the air and submerged in seawater for different periods of time during the tidal cycle.

Parts of the intertidal zone

- The *upper intertidal zone* is submerged only by the highest spring tides and, at its upper limit, is only ever wetted by wave splash and spray.
- The *middle intertidal zone* is regularly submerged and uncovered by tides.
- The *lower intertidal zone* is submerged most of the time.
- The *subtidal zone* consists of the shallow water just below the intertidal zone. Here, the combination of total immersion, good light penetration, and abundant nutrients supports rich plant life—whether phytoplankton or attached seaweeds. Marine life is abundant here.

© Diagram Visual Information Ltd.

© Diagram Visual Information Ltd.

Rocky shore: vertical zonation

Key words

intertidal zone
shore
temperate
vertical zonation

Vertical zonation

- *Vertical zonation* is the banding pattern of a rocky shore produced by the various communities of organisms that live at its different levels.
- Some form of vertical zonation is characteristic of most rocky shores, particularly temperate ones that have an evenly sloping rock face.
- A given species is usually found only within a particular vertical range, rather than throughout the intertidal zone. This gives rise to a series of distinct bands, or zones, at different levels on the shore.
- A zone is sometimes named after the dominant organism in the community, for example, a "barnacle zone" or "mussel zone."

Factors in vertical zonation

- Physiological investigations and transplantation experiments suggest that the upper limit at which a species lives on the shore is usually determined by physical factors.
- Experiments in which an organism is excluded from an area of shore suggest that biological factors—especially predation or competition—determine the lower limit of a species on the shore.

Lichens from the upper intertidal zone

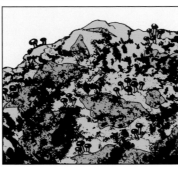

Fucus distichus **from the middle intertidal zone**

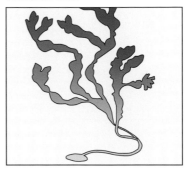

Chondrus crispus **from the lower intertidal zone**

Laminaria **from the extreme lower intertidal zone**

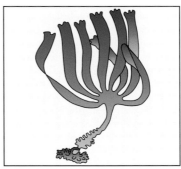

Vertical zonation on a temperate rocky shore of the U.S. Atlantic coast

1

Upper intertidal zone
Marine organisms that live here are well adapted to withstand exposure to the air: typically lichens, small snails (periwinkles), limpets, and mats of cyanobacteria.

2

Middle intertidal zone
A gradation in environmental conditions often produces a distinctive vertical zonation with:
a a barnacle zone;
b a mussel zone. Here, mussels and seaweed (especially *Fucus*, *Ascophyllum* and *Pelvetia*) predominate.

3

Lower intertidal zone
Characterized by the red algae, called Irish moss (*Chondrus crispus*), and green algae (*Enteromorpha*).

4

Extreme lower intertidal zone
Characterized by kelps (*Laminaria*, *Egregia*).

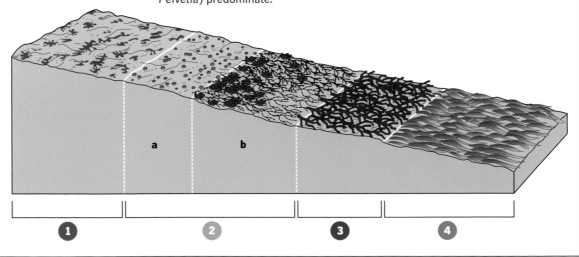

Rocky shore: competition and predation

Key words

intertidal zone
keystone
predator
shore
tide

Organisms of the intertidal zone

 Ocher sea star
(*Pisaster ochraceous*)

 Mussel
(*Mytilus californianus*)

Rockweeds
(e.g. *Fucus*)

 Acorn barnacles
(*Balanus glandula* and *B. cariosus*)

 Gooseneck barnacle
(*Pollicipes*)

A rich intertidal community where sea stars are present

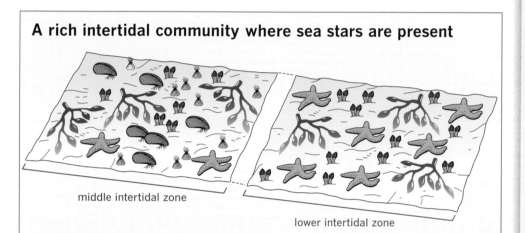

middle intertidal zone

lower intertidal zone

Mussels dominate when sea stars are removed

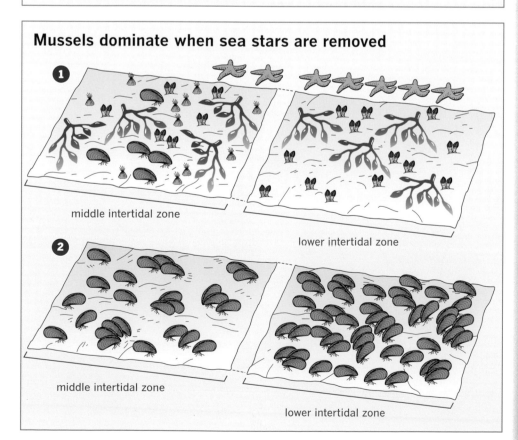

❶

middle intertidal zone

lower intertidal zone

❷

middle intertidal zone

lower intertidal zone

Predation and competition

- On temperate rocky shores of the northwest Pacific coast of North America, the ocher sea star, *Pisaster ochraceous*, is a major predator of mussels and, to a lesser extent, barnacles.
- Sea stars hunt underwater. In the *middle intertidal zone*, sea stars have limited time to find and consume barnacles and mussels.
- The *lower intertidal zone* is submerged for most of the tidal cycle. Sea stars have abundant opportunity to find and consume mussels and barnacles here. Mussels, the sea stars' favorite prey, tend to be consumed before they reach adulthood.
- Sea stars are classed as a *keystone predator,* because their presence or absence is a major determinant of community structure.

Intertidal community where sea stars are present

- The consumption of mussels by sea stars creates openings for other species to colonize the intertidal zone.
- Acorn barnacles, goose barnacles, and seaweed colonize the shore.
- Sea stars also feed on dog whelks—one of the barnacle's major predators—thus giving barnacles a greater opportunity to colonize.

Mussels dominate when sea stars are removed

- In experiments, when sea stars are removed regularly by hand ❶ (or are excluded from areas by the use of cages) mussels eventually dominate the exclusion area.
- The mussels outcompete other organisms and form dense beds on the shore ❷

© Diagram Visual Information Ltd.

Sandy shore fauna

© Diagram Visual Information Ltd.

Key words

fauna	*vertical zonation*
sandy shore	
shore	
temperate	
tide	

Characteristics of sandy shores

- Sandy shores contain a high proportion of particles in the size range 0.0025–0.08 inches (0.063–2.0 mm).
- Many of the organisms live below the sand surface.
- Upper shore sand is drier than that on the lower shore.
- Vertical zonation occurs on sandy shores but is less obvious than on rocky shores.

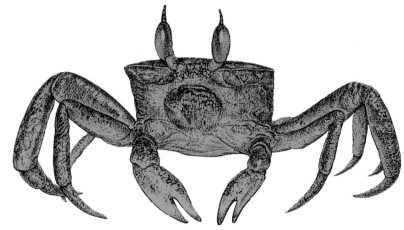

binocular vision crab

sand dollar (*Mellita*)

scallop

Sandy shore community members on a temperate U.S. Atlantic shore

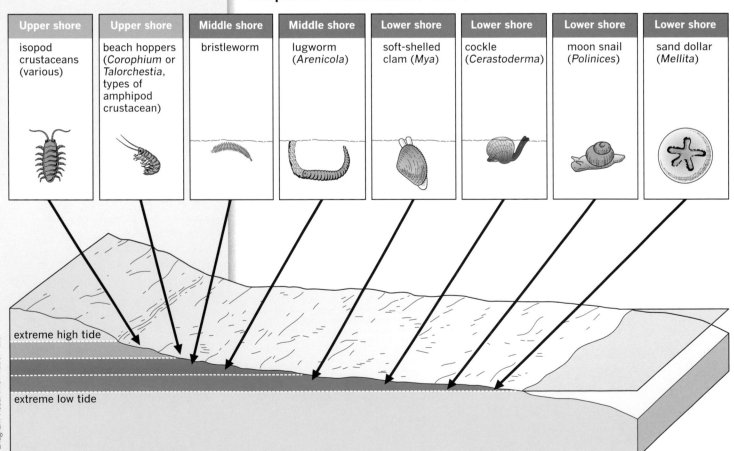

Upper shore	Upper shore	Middle shore	Middle shore	Lower shore	Lower shore	Lower shore	Lower shore
isopod crustaceans (various)	beach hoppers (*Corophium* or *Talorchestia*, types of amphipod crustacean)	bristleworm	lugworm (*Arenicola*)	soft-shelled clam (*Mya*)	cockle (*Cerastoderma*)	moon snail (*Polinices*)	sand dollar (*Mellita*)

extreme high tide

extreme low tide

Muddy shore fauna

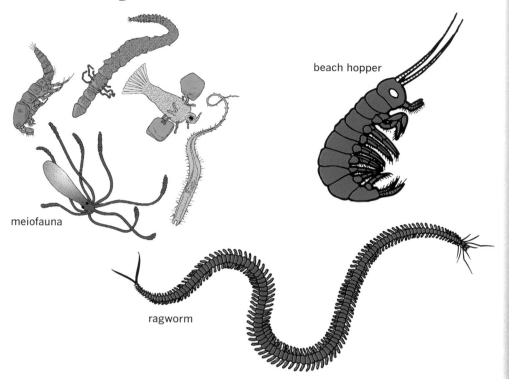

meiofauna

beach hopper

ragworm

Key words

anaerobic
fauna
muddy shore
respiration
vertical zonation

Characteristics of muddy shores

- Muddy shores contain a high proportion of particles in the size range 0.00016–0.0025 inches (0.004–0.062 mm).
- Many of the organisms live below the mud surface.
- Oxygen penetration is poor and organisms living below the top few inches respire anaerobically or must ventilate their burrows with oxygenated water.
- Vertical zonation is not apparent on muddy shores. The shore slope is less than one degree and all levels of the shore retain large volumes of water.

Mud flat community members on a temperate U.S. Atlantic shore

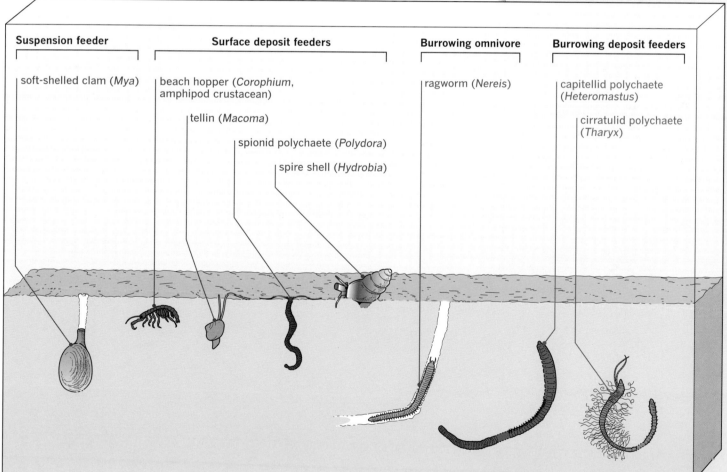

Suspension feeder

soft-shelled clam (*Mya*)

Surface deposit feeders

beach hopper (*Corophium*, amphipod crustacean)

tellin (*Macoma*)

spionid polychaete (*Polydora*)

spire shell (*Hydrobia*)

Burrowing omnivore

ragworm (*Nereis*)

Burrowing deposit feeders

capitellid polychaete (*Heteromastus*)

cirratulid polychaete (*Tharyx*)

© Diagram Visual Information Ltd.

© Diagram Visual Information Ltd.

Key words

adaptation   sandy shore
exoskeleton   sediment
interstitial space shore
meiofauna
muddy shore

Meiofauna

- *Meiofauna* are small animals in the size range 0.004–0.08 inches (0.1–2.0 mm).
- They inhabit the sandy and muddy sediments living in the spaces between particles known as "interstitial spaces."
- Meiofauna are common on shorelines and are thought to be the most abundant group of animals on the seafloor.
- They are very abundant with up to a million individuals present in every cubic meter of surface sediment.
- The meiofauna form a miniature community, with herbivores (**a**), omnivores (**b–d**), and carnivores (**e**).

Meiofauna adaptations

- Regardless of their evolutionary origins, most forms in the meiofauna are wormlike or flattened, enabling movement between sediment particles.
- They have well-developed exoskeletons (**a**) or strengthened body walls to resist crushing.
- They have the ability to contract (**e**) or move away from potential mechanical damage.
- They have adhesive organs (**b** and **e**) to attach to sand particles. These enable them to remain attached to sediment particles when the sediment is stirred up and moved by currents or waves.
- They have hooks or claws (**a** and **c**) to maintain position in the sand and to move around.

Sandy and muddy shore meiofauna

a Harpacticoid copepod; grazes on benthic diatoms and dinoflagellates.

b Bryozoan, *Monobryozoon*; a suspension feeder.

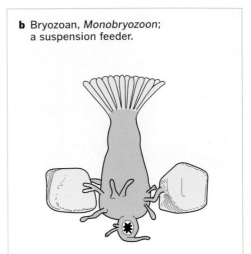

c Gastrotrich, *Urodasys*; a detritus feeder.

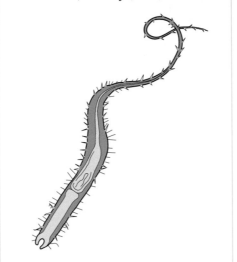

d Polychaete, *Psammodrilus*; a detritus feeder.

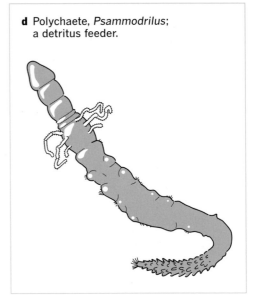

e Hydroid cnidarian, *Halammohydra*; a predator.

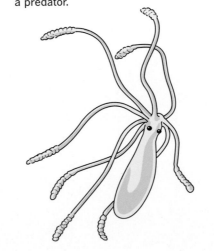

Plankton

Types of plankton

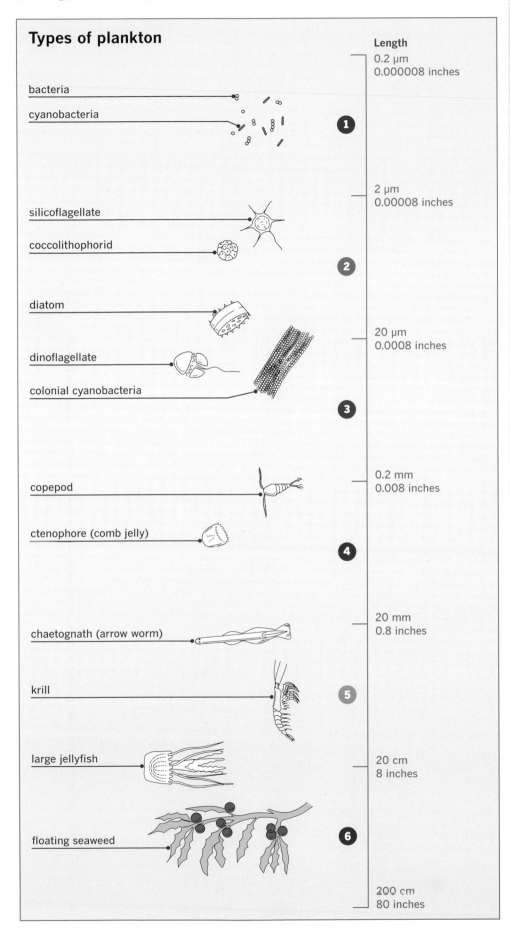

	Length
	0.2 µm
	0.000008 inches

bacteria

cyanobacteria

1

silicoflagellate

coccolithophorid

2

diatom

dinoflagellate

colonial cyanobacteria

3

copepod

ctenophore (comb jelly)

4

chaetognath (arrow worm)

krill

5

large jellyfish

floating seaweed

6

2 µm
0.00008 inches

20 µm
0.0008 inches

0.2 mm
0.008 inches

20 mm
0.8 inches

20 cm
8 inches

200 cm
80 inches

Key words

bacterioplankton	photosynthesis
current	phytoplankton
food chain	plankton
holoplankton	surface water
larva	trophic level
mereoplankton	zooplankton

Plankton

- *Plankton* are organisms that float in the surface waters and drift with the ocean currents. They form the first few trophic levels of most ocean food chains.

Types of plankton

- *Bacterioplankton* are planktonic bacteria and cyanobacteria. They are prokaryotic organisms that have simple cellular organization and are less than 0.00008 inches (2 µm) long.
- *Phytoplankton* are photosynthetic plankton. They range in size from single cells about 0.00008 inches (2 µm) long to chain cells of up to 0.08 inches (2 mm) long.
- *Zooplankton* are animal plankton that feed on phytoplankton (herbivorous zooplankton) or other zooplankton (carnivorous zooplankton).
- *Mereoplankton* are zooplankton that are the larval stages of nonplanktonic creatures.
- *Holoplankton* are zooplankton that remain as zooplankton throughout their life cycles. They range in size from heterotrophic protists about 0.00008 inches (2 µm) long to jellyfish about 39 inches (1 m) across.

Classification based on size

1 **Picoplankton**
0.000008–0.00008 inches (0.2–2 µm)

2 **Nanoplankton**
0.00008–0.0008 inches (2–20 µm)

3 **Microplankton**
0.0008–0.008 inches (20–200 µm)

4 **Mesoplankton**
0.008–0.8 inches (0.2–20 mm)

5 **Macroplankton**
0.8–8 inches (2–20 cm)

6 **Megaplankton**
8–80 inches (20–200 cm)

© Diagram Visual Information Ltd.

© Diagram Visual Information Ltd.

Key words

euphotic layer	plankton
food chain	sediment
nutrient	upwelling
photosynthesis	
phytoplankton	

Phytoplankton

- *Phytoplankton* are plankton that photosynthesize. They are essentially free-floating, water-dwelling plant life.
- Like most plant life, phytoplankton absorb atmospheric carbon dioxide and produce oxygen.
- Because phytoplankton need light, they only live in the well-lit surface layers of the ocean (or lakes). This is known as the *euphotic layer*.
- Phytoplankton are thought to produce about 98 percent of the oxygen in the atmosphere.
- They also produce dimethyl sulfide (DMS) which is converted to sulfate in the atmosphere, where it reflects solar radiation and acts as condensation nuclei for cloud formation.

Phytoplankton nutrients

- As well as sunlight, phytoplankton also need carbon dioxide and nutrients, such as iron, to grow.
- Large quantities of carbon dioxide from the atmosphere diffuse into the oceans at the ocean surface.
- Carbon is locked into the bodies of phytoplankton, which sink to the bottom of the ocean when they die.
- Up to 90 percent of the world's carbon is thought to be locked in ocean-floor sediments formed mostly from the bodies of phytoplankton.
- Other nutrients are brought to the surface by upwellings. Where upwellings fail, phytoplankton levels crash and the rest of the food chain starves.

Phytoplankton

Major divisions of phytoplankton

Division	Chrysophyta				Dinophyta
Subgroup	Cryptomonads	Cocco-lithophores	Silico-flagellates	Diatoms	Dinophytes (Dino-flagellates)
No. of marine species	>100	200	>100	>3,000	>1,000
Size and structure	Small unicellular, lacking a skeleton. Two flagella.	Small unicellular, with calcareous plates (coccoliths) on outer surface.	Small unicellular, with an internal skeleton of silica and a single flagellum.	Large unicellular, sometimes in chains. Cell wall of silica, in two tightly fitting halves.	Large unicellular, sometimes in chains. Cell wall sometimes strengthened with cellulose. Two flagella of unequal length.
Example	*Chroomonas*	*Coccolithus*	*Dictyocha speculum*	*Skeletonema* / *Chaetocerus*	*Gonyaulax* / *Ceratium*

Holoplankton

Protist holoplankton

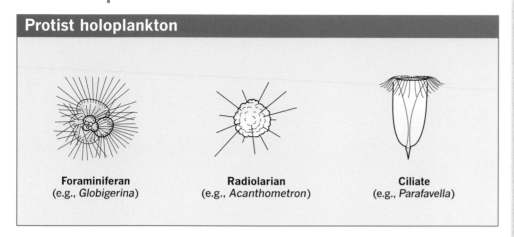

Foraminiferan
(e.g., *Globigerina*)

Radiolarian
(e.g., *Acanthometron*)

Ciliate
(e.g., *Parafavella*)

Crustacean holoplankton

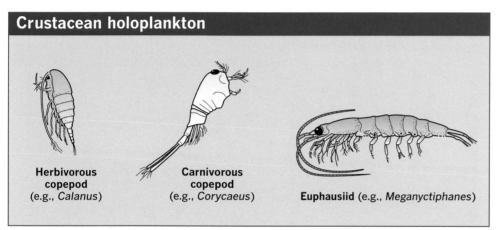

Herbivorous copepod
(e.g., *Calanus*)

Carnivorous copepod
(e.g., *Corycaeus*)

Euphausiid (e.g., *Meganyctiphanes*)

Larger non-crustacean holoplankton

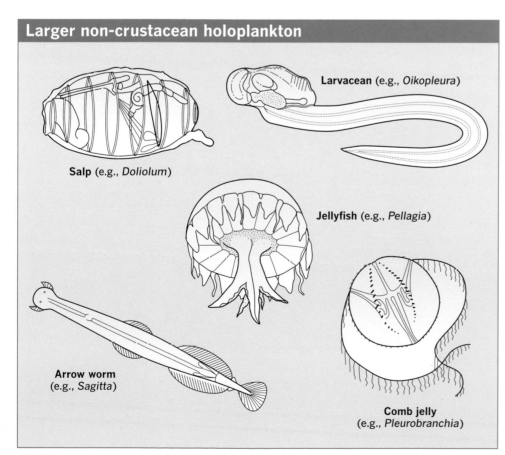

Salp (e.g., *Doliolum*)

Larvacean (e.g., *Oikopleura*)

Jellyfish (e.g., *Pellagia*)

Arrow worm
(e.g., *Sagitta*)

Comb jelly
(e.g., *Pleurobranchia*)

Key words

crustacean	trophic level
holoplankton	zooplankton
larvae	
phytoplankton	
plankton	

Holoplankton

- Some organisms are plankton for only part of their life cycle. The larval stages and young of many species are classified as plankton only until they reach their adult stages.
- The permanent members of animal plankton (*zooplankton*) are called *holoplankton*.

Protist holoplankton

- Protist holoplankton play a vital role as herbivores, consuming phytoplankton and making this energy available to higher trophic levels.

Crustacean holoplankton

- Larger zooplankton, especially copepods and euphausiids, are dominant members of the holoplankton community. Some are herbivores, some omnivores, and others carnivores.
- Crustacean holoplankton are the most abundant animals on Earth.

Noncrustacean holoplankton

- Noncrustacean zooplankton include a group known as predatory gelatinous organisms. These are jellyfish and similar organisms such as comb jellies and colonial medusa. These organisms typically capture prey with stinging cells or sticky mucus deposits.
- Other noncrustacean zooplankton include arrow worms and wormlike tunicates such as salps and larvaceans.
- These organisms are typically much larger than crustacean or protist holoplankton. Some qualify as megaplankton since they are at least 8 inches (20 cm) in diameter.

© Diagram Visual Information Ltd.

Key words

coral reef	plankton
estuary	rocky shore
kelp bed	subtidal zone
larva	zooplankton
meroplankton	

Meroplankton

- Meroplankton are temporary members of the zooplankton. They are organisms that live as plankton for only part of their life cycle.
- Meroplankton are the planktonic larvae of animals from a wide variety of habitats: rocky shores, subtidal communities such as kelp beds, and coral reefs, estuaries, and the deep ocean floor.
- While living as meroplankton these organisms feed on yolk sacs retained from the eggs they hatched from or on other plankton.
- These larvae often bear almost no resemblance to their adult forms and have entirely different lifestyles.
- The larvae play a vital role in the dispersal phase of the life cycle.
- Meroplankton are seasonally abundant, particularly in coastal waters.

Crustacean meroplankton

- Crustaceans are by far the most abundant members of the zooplankton (including meroplankton) in both species and number of individuals.
- Common crustacean meroplankton include the larvae of lobsters, crabs, prawns, barnacles, brine shrimp, and copepods.

Non-crustacean meroplankton

- Common noncrustacean meroplankton include the larvae of starfish, sea urchins, snails, polycheate worms, and fish.

© Diagram Visual Information Ltd.

Meroplankton

Crustacean meroplankton

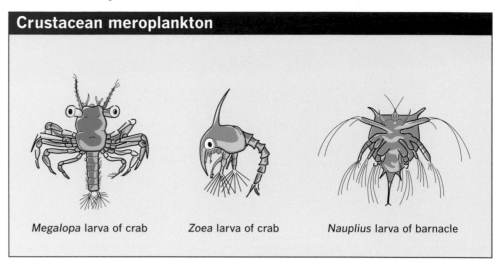

Megalopa larva of crab   *Zoea* larva of crab   *Nauplius* larva of barnacle

Noncrustacean meroplankton

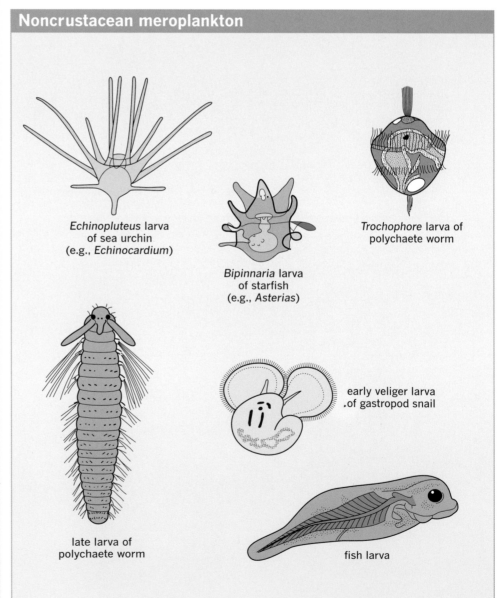

Echinopluteus larva of sea urchin (e.g., *Echinocardium*)

Bipinnaria larva of starfish (e.g., *Asterias*)

Trochophore larva of polychaete worm

early veliger larva of gastropod snail

late larva of polychaete worm

fish larva

Planktonic adaptations

Key words

adaptation   zooplankton
larva
nutrient
phytoplankton
plankton

Increased buoyancy

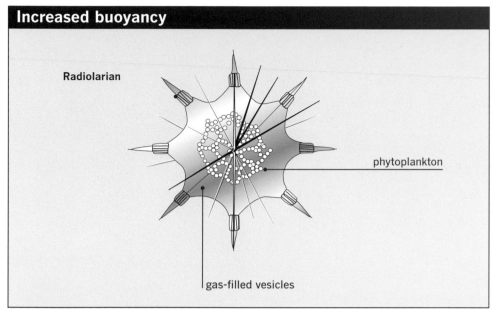

Radiolarian

phytoplankton

gas-filled vesicles

Body shape increases resistance to sinking

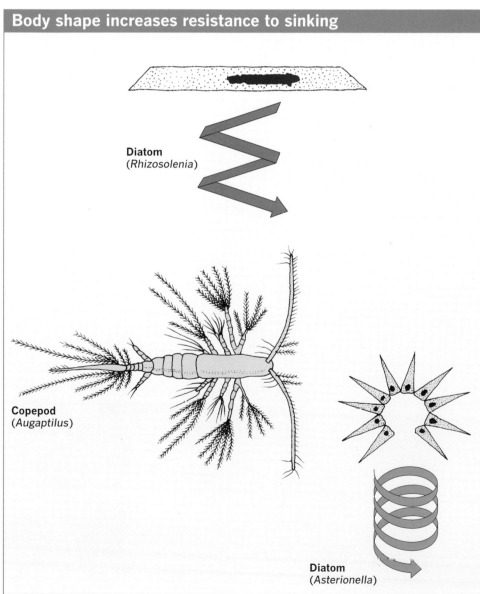

Diatom
(*Rhizosolenia*)

Copepod
(*Augaptilus*)

Diatom
(*Asterionella*)

Surface area and volume

- All phytoplankton and many zooplankton are microscopic in size.
- Their small size and complex shapes produce a high surface area-to-volume ratio.
- A high surface area-to-volume ratio favors the rapid exchange of gases by diffusion and creates a high frictional resistance, which means they sink slowly.
- It also facilitates the rapid excretion of wastes across the body surface, light trapping, and nutrient absorption.

Increased buoyancy

- Many plankton have buoyancy aids. For example, phytoplankton, notably diatoms, and zooplankton such as copepods, fish eggs, and larvae, contain bouyant oil droplets that also act as food stores.
- Some planktonic cyanobacteria and radiolaria contain gas-filled vesicles.
- Certain dinoflagellates, and various zooplankton, including salps and comb jellies, exclude or excrete heavy ions (e.g., Mg^{2+}, SO_4^{2-}) and retain less dense ones (e.g., NH_4^+, Cl^-).

Body shape

- Many plankton have body shapes that tend to make them sink more slowly.
- Some plankton are flattened. They sink slowly, moving back-and-forth in a "falling-leaf" pattern.
- Long projections and spines increase surface area and slow sinking. They may also deter potential grazers or predators from consuming the individual.
- Chains of individuals can assume shapes that encourage sinking in a slow spiral or zigzag path.

© Diagram Visual Information Ltd.

© Diagram Visual Information Ltd.

Key words

bacteria	pollution
downwelling	red tide
phytoplankton	
plankton	

Red tide

- A *red tide* is a dense phytoplankton bloom that colors surface seawater.
- Red tides are usually reddish brown but they can be any color within the range blue to yellow, depending on the main constituent species.

Causes

- The factors that trigger the explosive growth of red-tide forming phytoplankton species are not known precisely.
- Downwellings, where currents converge, may cause dinoflagellates to congregate as they swim up against the current and toward the light.
- Organic pollution by sewage discharge and/or fertilizers rich in nitrates and phosphates have been implicated in some incidences of red tide.

Oxygen depletion

1 The phytoplankton in a red tide eventually die.
2 Bacteria feed on the decaying remains of the phytoplankton and multiply.
3 The huge numbers of bacteria consume so much oxygen that many other organisms suffocate.

Poisoning

Some phytoplankton species that produce red tides contain toxic chemicals. These chemicals may be intended to deter herbivores.

1 Saxitoxin, produced by some red-tide forming phytoplankton, attacks the nervous system of vertebrates but not most invertebrates. Zooplankton and filter-feeding shellfish can accumulate saxitoxin, but remain unharmed.
2 Vertebrates—including fish, birds, marine mammals, and humans—that consume the zooplankton or shellfish are poisoned.

Red tides

Oxygen depletion

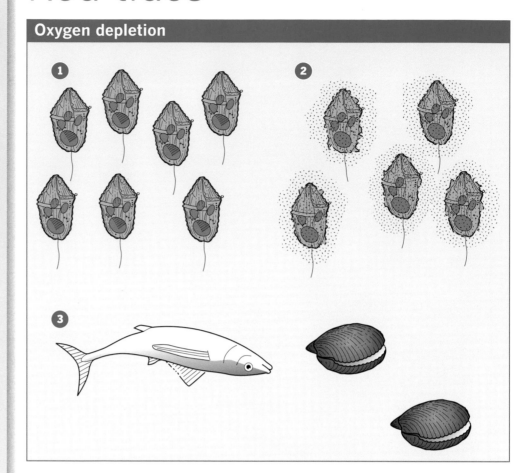

Poisoning

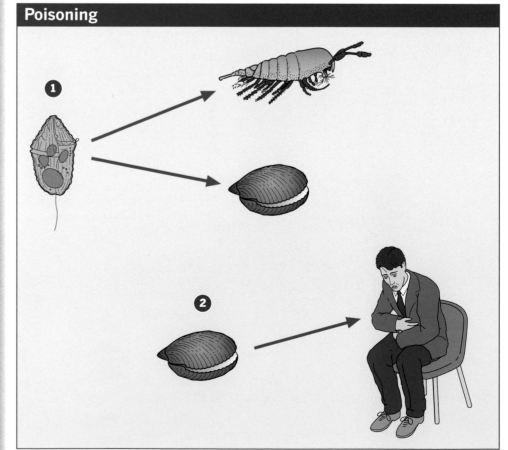

Major subdivisions of the marine environment

Organisms of the marine environment

nekton

plankton

benthos

Key words

abyssal zone	nekton
bathyal zone	pelagic realm
benthic realm	plankton
benthos	realm
hadal zone	subtidal zone
intertidal zone	

Realms

- The *pelagic realm* includes those organisms that live in the water column away from the sea bed.
- The *benthic realm* includes those organisms that live on or close to the sea bed.
- *Nekton* are strongly swimming organisms.
- *Plankton* are those organisms that predominantly drift on currents.

Realms of the marine environment

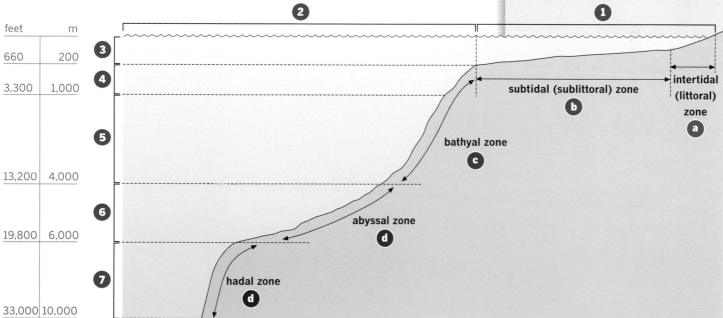

feet	m
660	200
3,300	1,000
13,200	4,000
19,800	6,000
33,000	10,000

subtidal (sublittoral) zone

intertidal (littoral) zone

bathyal zone

abyssal zone

hadal zone

Subdivisions of the pelagic realm

1 **Neritic zone:** the water mass overlying a continental shelf

2 **Oceanic zone:** open ocean waters beyond the continental shelf

3 **Epipelagic zone** (euphotic or sunlit zone): 0–660 feet (0–200 m) depth

4 **Mesopelagic zone** (twilight zone): 660–3,300 feet (200–1,000 m) depth

5 **Bathypelagic zone:** 3,300–13,200 feet (1,000–4,000 m) depth

6 **Abyssopelagic zone:** 13,200–19,800 feet (4,000–6,000 m) depth

7 **Hadopelagic zone:** 19,800–33,000 feet (6,000–10,000 m) depth

Subdivisions of the benthic realm

a **Intertidal (littoral) zone** The region of the shore between extreme high and low tide levels affected by wave splash.

b **Subtidal (sublittoral) zone** The benthic zone underlying the waters of the continental shelf.

c **Bathyal zone** The benthic zone from the shelf break to about 13,200 feet (4,000 m).

d **Abyssal zone** The benthic zone between 13,200 and 19,800 feet (4,000 and 6,000 m).

e **Hadal zone** The benthic zone between 19,800 and 33,000 feet (6,000 and 10,000 m).

© Diagram Visual Information Ltd.

© Diagram Visual Information Ltd.

Key words

adaptation	turbidity
epipelagic zone	zooplankton
euphotic zone	
photosynthesis	
phytoplankton	

Epipelagic zone

- The *epipelagic zone* is also known as the "euphotic" or "sunlit" zone. It is the zone that receives sufficient sunlight for photosynthesis to occur.
- The depth of the euphotic zone depends on climate and the turbidity of the sea water. In tropical seas, the maximum depth is about 660 feet (200 m).
- Phytoplankton is the main source of primary productivity in this zone.
- Phytoplankton form the basis of nearly all oceanic food chains.
- Zooplankton graze on the phytoplankton. Some zooplankton remain in the epipelagic zone. Others migrate vertically from the mesopelagic zone.
- Zooplankton are food for other zooplankton and for pelagic life-forms such as fish, squid, and marine mammals.
- About 90 percent of humankind's seafood is caught in the epipelagic zone.

Epipelagic adaptations

- Many zooplankton are effectively transparent. In sunlit waters, this lessens their visibility to predators.
- Many epipelagic fish are countershaded. This makes them appear dark from above and light from below, which provides additional protection from predators by blending them into the background.

Epipelagic zone

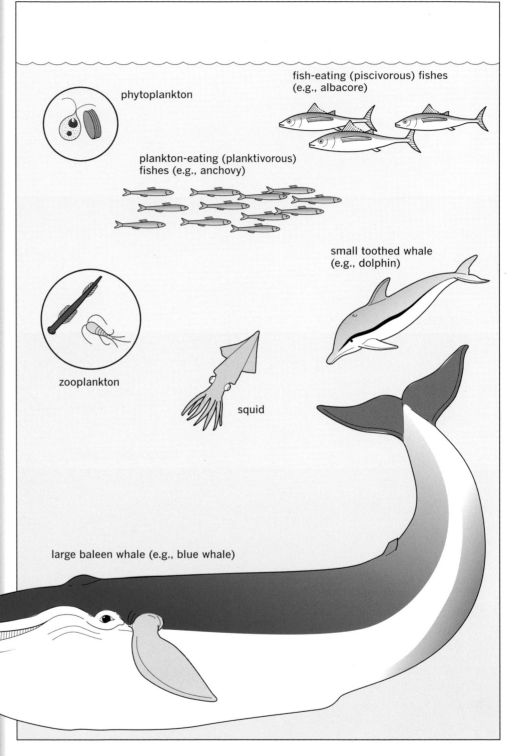

phytoplankton

fish-eating (piscivorous) fishes (e.g., albacore)

plankton-eating (planktivorous) fishes (e.g., anchovy)

zooplankton

squid

small toothed whale (e.g., dolphin)

large baleen whale (e.g., blue whale)

semitransparent larvacean

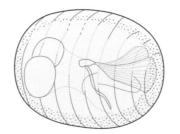

countershaded epipelagic fish

Mesopelagic zone

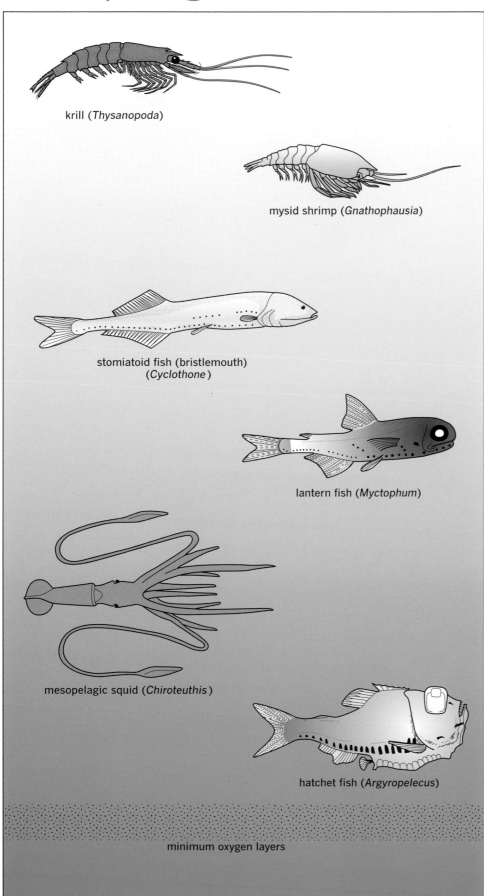

krill (*Thysanopoda*)

mysid shrimp (*Gnathophausia*)

stomiatoid fish (bristlemouth)
(*Cyclothone*)

lantern fish (*Myctophum*)

mesopelagic squid (*Chiroteuthis*)

hatchet fish (*Argyropelecus*)

minimum oxygen layers

Key words

disphotic zone	vertical migration
mesopelagic	zooplankton
zone	
turbidity	
twilight zone	

Mesopelagic zone

- The *mesopelagic zone* is also called the "disphotic zone" or the "twilight zone." It receives a small amount of diffuse sunlight, but not enough to support photosynthesis.
- The depth of the mesopelagic zone varies depending on climate and the turbidity of the seawater. In tropical seas it lies between about 660 and 3,300 feet (200 and 1,000 m).
- The diffuse light is predominantly of blue and blue-green wavelengths.
- In some fish and squid, light-producing organs (photophores) disrupt the animal's outline. In some species, the arrangement of photophores serves as a means of identification.
- Many mesopelagic zooplankton and fish make daily vertical migrations to feed on phytoplankton and each other in the epipelagic zone.
- Others stay in the mesopelagic zone. They are predators, ambushing prey, or are detritus feeders, consuming carcasses or fecal matter that descend from the epipelagic.
- Most members of the fish community are only 1–10 inches (2–25 cm) in length.

Features

- There is a steep temperature gradient across the mesopelagic zone. Large-scale density changes across this layer result in particulate material—especially fecal pellets—accumulating in layers where oxygen is depleted.
- At depths in the range 1,300–2,650 feet (400–800 m) respiration by bacteria and animals that feed on particulate material causes the water to become depleted of oxygen locally.

© Diagram Visual Information Ltd.

© Diagram Visual Information Ltd.

Key words

adaptation
bioluminescence
mesopelagic
zone
vertical migration

Small size and large jaws

- Most mesopelagic fish are 1–10 inches (2–25 cm) long with only a very few species reaching 6 feet (2 m).
- Food is sparse in the mesopelagic. Predatory fish that remain in the mesopelagic are opportunistic feeders, consuming whatever potential prey they encounter.
- Many species have long curved teeth and cavernous mouths to ensure prey do not escape once grasped.
- Some species have jaws that unhinge and a gut that distends, which means they can consume prey larger than themselves.

Dark lining

- Many carnivorous mesopelagic fishes have a pigmented lining (peritoneum) to their abdominal cavity. This prevents the bioluminescence from ingested prey shining out through the body wall and attracting other predators.

Vertical migration

- Fish and zooplankton that migrate to the epipelagic zone must withstand great temperature and pressure changes.
- Fish that are vertical migrators have a skeleton and musculature well-developed for swimming. They possess a functional swim bladder to regulate buoyancy during ascent and descent.

Mesopelagic adaptations

Small size, large jaws

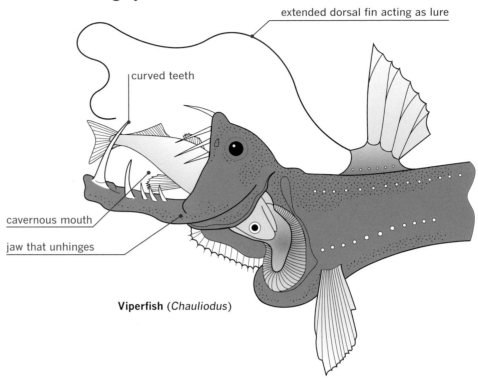

extended dorsal fin acting as lure

curved teeth

cavernous mouth

jaw that unhinges

Viperfish (*Chauliodus*)

Dark lining

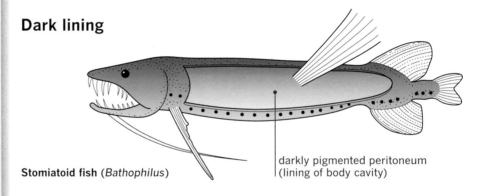

Stomiatoid fish (*Bathophilus*)

darkly pigmented peritoneum (lining of body cavity)

Vertical migration

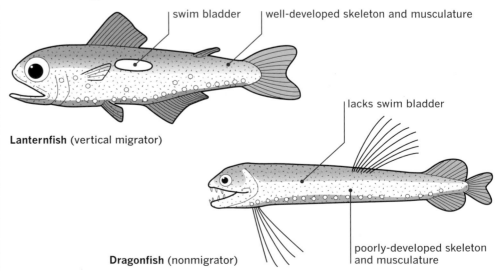

swim bladder

well-developed skeleton and musculature

Lanternfish (vertical migrator)

lacks swim bladder

Dragonfish (nonmigrator)

poorly-developed skeleton and musculature

Mesopelagic coloration

Coloration and body shape

laterally compressed body

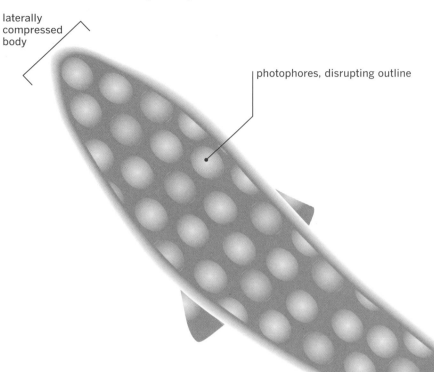

photophores, disrupting outline

Vision

field of acute vision

field of acute vision

large, upwardly directed eyes

Midwater fish (*Scopelarchus*)

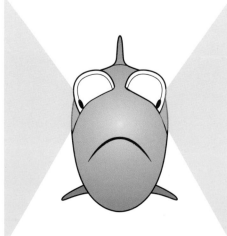

wide, lateral field of vision

wide, lateral field of vision

Key words

adaptation
bioluminescence
mesopelagic
zone
photophore

Coloration and body shape

- Inhabitants of the lower mesopelagic are often red or near-black to blend in against the background of diffuse blue-green light.
- Mesopelagic fish are commonly countershaded, with dark backs and silvery sides.
- Some midwater shrimps and fish can control the light-emitting intensity of their photophores to blend in with the prevailing light conditions.
- Many mesopelagic fish are laterally compressed and/or have photophores on their ventral surface to reduce and disrupt their body outline as seen from below.

Vision

- Many midwater shrimps, squid, and fish have unusually large, sensitive eyes.
- Some fish species have upwardly directed eyes to locate prey items against the diffuse light filtering from above.
- Some mesopelagic fish, octopuses, and krill have eyes with a central region for acute vision in brighter light (whether natural or bioluminescent) and a peripheral region that gives a wide lateral field but with poor acuity.
- Some fish eyes have yellow filters that help distinguish between bioluminescent and background light.

© Diagram Visual Information Ltd.

Bioluminescence

- *Bioluminescence* is the production of light by living organisms.
- The enzyme luciferase catalyzes the conversion of luciferin to a product with the emission of light rather than heat. Different forms of luciferin are found in different animal groups.
- Bioluminescence is common among organisms of the mesopelagic and upper bathypelagic.
- Some fish and squid manufacture their own luciferin. Others harbor light-emitting symbiotic bacteria.
- Bioluminescence is commonly associated with photophores (light-emitting organs).

The functions of bioluminescence

- **Attracting prey**
  In anglerfish, a bioluminescent lure (esca) on the end of a modified dorsal fin (illicium) attracts prey to the vicinity of the predator's mouth.

- **Defense**
  Some deep-sea squids (e.g., *Histioteuthis*) eject a cloud of luminescent fluid when threatened. This distracts a potential predator and masks the squid's escape.

- **Communication**
  Among myctophids (lantern fish) the elaborate arrangement of light-organs is species-specific. The light patterns may serve as identifiers for schooling or for finding potential mates.

© Diagram Visual Information Ltd.

Bioluminescence in the deep sea

Attracting prey

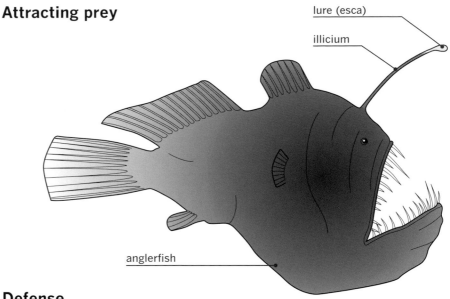

lure (esca)

illicium

anglerfish

Defense

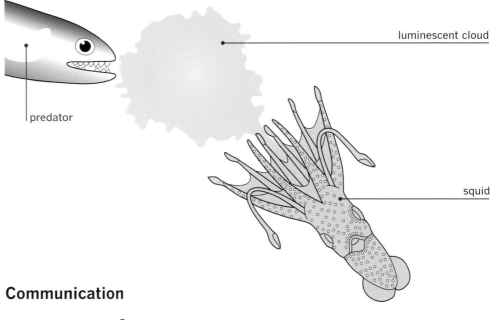

predator

luminescent cloud

squid

Communication

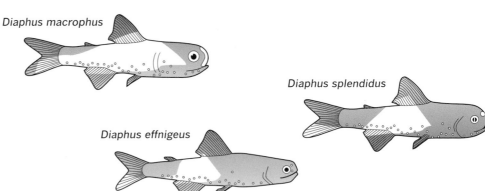

Diaphus macrophus

Diaphus splendidus

Diaphus effnigeus

The differing arrangement of photophores is shown by light patches and small pale circles on the body, excluding the eye.

The pelagic deep sea

Key words

abyssopelagic
    zone
aphotic zone
bathypelagic
    zone

Gulper eel
(*Eurypharynx pelecanoides*)

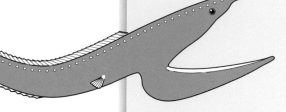

Deep-sea zones

- The *bathypelagic zone* is the region of the water column from about 3,300–13,200 feet (1,000–4,000 m).
- The *abyssopelagic zone* is the region of the water column from about 13,200–19,800 feet (4,000–6,000 m) depth.

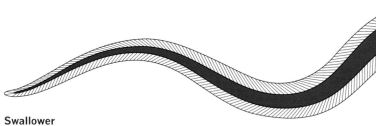

Swallower
(*Saccopharynx ampullaceus*)

- Both are also referred to as the *aphotic zone* or the "midnight zone" because no sunlight reaches them.

Features

- The aphotic zone encompasses 90 percent of the ocean environment. It represents the largest near-uniform biological volume on Earth.
- Pressures are very high, ranging from about 100 to 600 atmospheres with increasing depth.
- Ambient temperatures are in the range 30–39°F (−1° to +4°C).

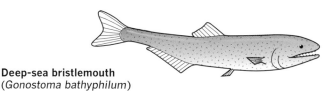

Deep-sea bristlemouth
(*Gonostoma bathyphilum*)

Pelagic deep-sea fishes

- More than 2,000 species of fish have been identified in the aphotic zone. More than one third of these are anglerfish.
- Deep-sea fish have reduced skeletons and musculature, and lack swim bladders.
- Most pelagic deep-sea fish are small carnivores, much shorter than 6 feet (1 m) long, with giant stomachs.

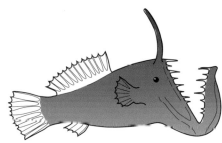

Anglerfish
(*Melanocetus johnsoni*)

© Diagram Visual Information Ltd.

© Diagram Visual Information Ltd.

Key words	
abyssopelagic zone	bathypelagic zone
adaptation	bioluminescence
aphotic zone	

Senses

- Light is absent or, where present, is bioluminescent and intermittent.
- Eyes, where present, are usually reduced in size.
- Some bathy- and abyssopelagic fish species are eel-like, perhaps an adaptation to increase the length of the vibration-sensitive lateral line that extends along the flank of the fish.
- Many deep-sea fish probably have a highly developed sense of smell.

Reproduction

- Finding a mate in the dark, sparsely-populated abyss is problematic.
- Many species probably secrete specific chemical attractants (pheromones) to find a mate.
- Both bioluminescent and vibratory signals are probably used as attractants by some fish and invertebrate species.
- In some deep-water anglerfish, the male attaches to, and becomes parasitic on, the female once he has found her.
- A few fish and crustacean species are hermaphroditic (contain both male and female sex organs). Potentially, any mature individual can mate and exchange sperm with any other individual.

Large mouth and stomach

- Food is even sparser in the deep sea than it is in the mesopelagic realm.
- A predatory fish that can consume any prey it meets, regardless of size, will be at an advantage.
- Some species have very large jaws and a gut that distends, which means they can consume prey larger than themselves.

Adaptions of pelagic deep-sea fish

Female anglerfish (*Ceratias holboelli*) with an attached parasitic male

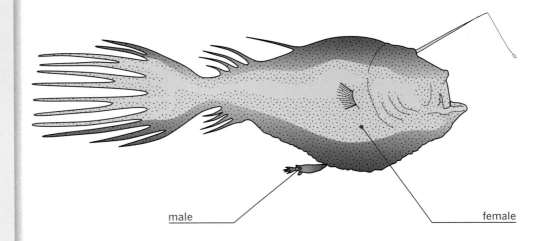

male   female

Great swallower (*Chiasmodon*)

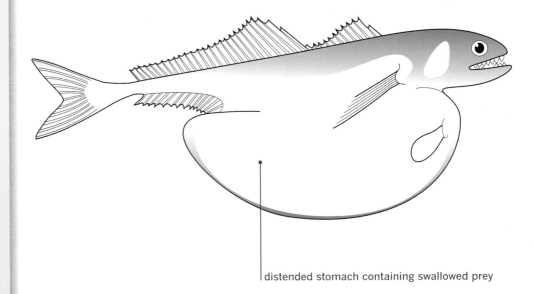

distended stomach containing swallowed prey

Fish of the deep-sea floor

Tripod fish
(*Bathypterois*)

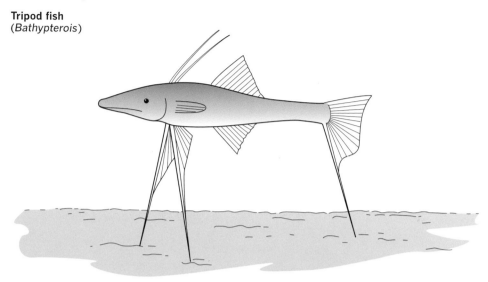

Hagfish
(*Eptatretus*)

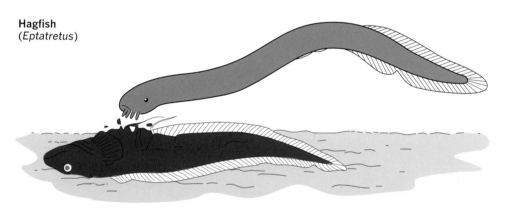

Grenadier
(*Lionurus*)

Brotulid
(*Bassogigas*)

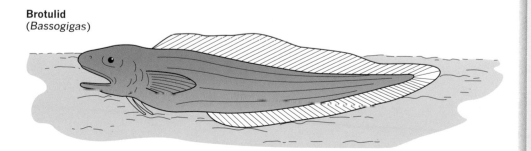

Key words

abyssopelagic zone	bathypelagic zone
adaptation	
aphotic zone	

Deep-sea floor fish

- Fish of the deep-sea floor, beyond 6,600 feet (2,000 m) depth, tend to be larger and more muscular than fish of the bathy- and abyssopelagic zones.
- Fish associated with these abyssal and lower bathyal communities probably have a highly developed sense of smell. Most are scavengers.
- Some of the fish living on or close to the deep-sea floor—hagfish and grenadiers (rattail fish), for example—belong to some of the most ancient groups of fish. They have probably become marginalized to this zone after being outcompeted elsewhere by more recently evolved forms.

Typical examples

- Tripod fish settle on the seafloor, resting on their elongated fins. They face the current to snap up edible particles that drift past.
- Hagfish scavenge on the carcasses of creatures that have sunk to the ocean floor. They also eat marine worms and other invertebrates that live on or close to the ocean floor.
- Hagfish have the ability to form knots with bodies. These muscular convulsions help them to escape predators. They are also able to produce large quantities of thick slime as a defense mechanism.
- Rattail fish, also known as grenadiers, are thought to inhabit all deep ocean regions. They feed on carcasses and prey on marine worms and small crustaceans living on or close to the ocean floor. They have been observed feeding on tube worms close to hydrothermal vents.
- Brotulids of the genus *Bassogigas* are thought to be the deepest living fish. An example was caught at a depth of about 27,200 feet (8,300 m) in the Atlantic Ocean's Puerto Rico Trench. Very little is known about them because they are so rarely observed.

© Diagram Visual Information Ltd.

© Diagram Visual Information Ltd.

Key words

continental shelf	subtidal zone
intertidal zone	
shelf break	
sublittoral zone	
substrate	

Subtidal zone

- The *subtidal zone* is the seabed between the intertidal zone and the shelf break of the continental shelf. It is also known as the "sublittoral zone."
- The *inner subtidal zone* is the region of the subtidal zone where there is sufficient sunlight for plants to grow on the seabed.
- The *outer subtidal zone* is the region where there is insufficient sunlight for seaweed to grow on the seabed.

Subtidal communities

- The type of biological community that develops in the inner subtidal zone is largely determined by: the nature of the substrate (for example, whether it is soft- or hard-bottomed); ambient seawater temperatures; other physical factors, such as current speed and water turbidity; chemical features, such as nutrient availability, salinity, and the presence or absence of pollutants.
- Hard coral, seagrass meadows, or kelp forests are three common subtidal communities. Each provides food and shelter to a large range of other organisms.

Subtidal zone

Tidal zones

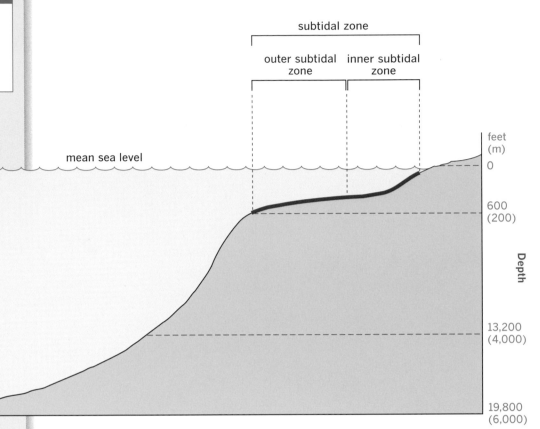

Hard coral communities Found on hard-bottomed subtidal zones in subtropical and tropical waters where water is clear, of near-normal salinity, and free of pollutants.

Seagrass communities Found on soft-bottomed subtidal zones of temperate, subtropical, and tropical waters.

Kelp communities Found on hard-bottomed subtidal zones of temperate and polar waters in areas of upwelling, heavy surf, or strong currents.

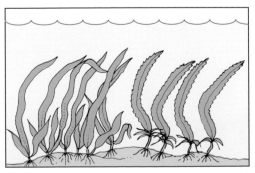

Bathyal zone

Animal communities of the bathyal zone

Suspension feeders
sea pen (*Pennatula*)
soft coral on a rocky outcrop
sponge (*Crateromorpha*)
stalked crinoid
(*Anachalypsicrinus*)

Predator
sea spider (or pycnogonid)

Deposit feeder
sea cucumber
(*Scotoplanes*)

feet (m)

mean sea level

0

600
(200)

Depth

13,200
(4,000)

19,800
(6,000)

Key words

adaptation   meiofauna
bathyal zone
continental slope
hydrothermal
  vent

Bathyal zone

- The *bathyal zone* is the seabed from depths of 660 to 13,200 feet (200–4,000 m).
  - It includes most of the continental slope.
  - Most of the hydrothermal vents discovered so far have been found in this zone.

Bathyal communities

- A steady drizzle of material settles on the seabed in this zone. Some of this detritus is biological in origin and forms a food source for many of the organisms of the bathyal zone.
- The waters above the bathyal seafloor are some of the most biologically productive regions of the oceans. Consequently, the rain of biological detritus that they produce is particularly rich in nutrients.
- Much of the seabed is covered in fine sediment that harbors an abundance of microscopic animals (*meiofauna*).
- Suspension feeders are common in the shallower parts of this zone, particularly where there is a hard bottom.
- No sunlight reaches the seabed at this depth, so no corals or plant life can survive.
- Deposit feeders often predominate in the deeper parts of the zone.
- Those animals that walk on the soft seabed often have adaptations to raise their bodies clear of the sediment.

Sea pen
(*Pennatula*)

Soft coral

Sponge
(*Crateromorpha*)

Stalked crinoid
(*Anachalypsicrinus*)

Sea spider
or pycnogonid

Sea cucumber
(*Scotoplanes*)

© Diagram Visual Information Ltd.

© Diagram Visual Information Ltd.

Key words

abyssal plain
abyssal zone
adaptation
continental shelf

Definition

- The *abyssal zone* is the seabed from depths of about 13,200 to 19,800 feet (4,000– 6,000 m).
- It extends from the bottom of the continental shelf across the abyssal plain.

Key features

- As in the bathyal zone the food supply is sparse but may be seasonal, with a heavier fall of detrital material from the epipelagic and mesopelagic regions during the most productive seasons.
- Occasionally, large carcasses, such as whale or giant squid, may descend to the ocean floor. Scavengers may live off such carcasses for months.

Abyssal gigantism

- Some deep-sea crustaceans are slow-growing, long-lived, and late-maturing. The amphipod, *Alicella gigantea* (6 inches; 15 cm long) and the isopod *Bathynomus giganteus* (15 inches; 42 cm long) reach much larger sizes than their shallower water relatives.
- Slow growth and enlarged size could be a side effect of metabolism at low temperatures and high pressure.
- There may be a selective advantage in producing large eggs and larvae. Large, deep-sea crustaceans do not produce planktonic larvae. The larvae remain at depth instead.
- Larger young are able to range over longer distances and consume a wider variety of food than smaller larvae. This could be an advantage in a food-scarce environment.

Abyssal zone

Animal communities of the abyssal zone

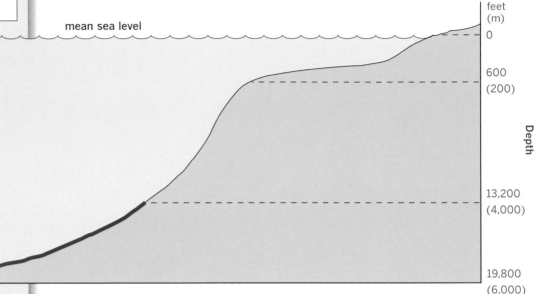

mean sea level

feet (m)

0

600 (200)

13,200 (4,000)

19,800 (6,000)

Depth

Invertebrate scavengers and predators

Galatheid crab (*Munidopsis*)
also bathypelagic

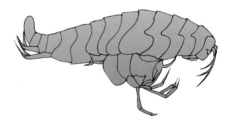

Deep-sea amphipod (*Alicella*)
also bathypelagic

Isopod (*Bathynomus*)
also bathypelagic

Deposit feeders

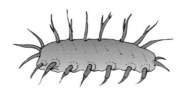

Sea cucumber
(*Oneirophanta*)

Sea cucumber
(*Psychropotes*)

Deep scattering layers

Echograms
The echograms show deep scattering layers by day and night.

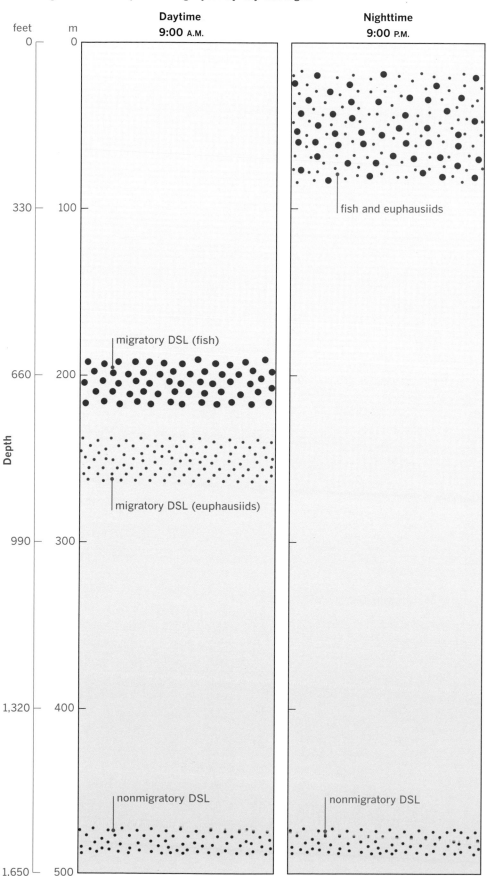

Daytime
9:00 A.M.

Nighttime
9:00 P.M.

fish and euphausiids

migratory DSL (fish)

migratory DSL (euphausiids)

nonmigratory DSL

nonmigratory DSL

Depth

feet	m
0	0
330	100
660	200
990	300
1,320	400
1,650	500

Key words

deep scattering layer (DSL)
epipelagic zone
mesopelagic zone

sonar
vertical migration

Definition and key features

- When sonar equipment was first used by oceanographers several mysterious "layers" were found at different depths in the water column.
- Sonar works by emitting sound waves that are reflected by objects. These layers were reflecting some of these sound waves.
- Layers that appeared on sonar readings in this way came to be known as *Deep scattering layers* (DSLs).
- Further investigation showed that DSLs are caused by the scattering and reflection of sound waves from groups of organisms—particularly fish, euphausiids, and shrimps—congregating at specific depths.
- Euphausiids and shrimps have hard exoskeletons made of chitin. This characteristic makes them very effective at reflecting sonar.
- A group of small fish (myctophids) are also common elements in DSLs. These fish have gas-filled swim bladders, which gives them a lower overall density than the water around them—another characteristic that is highly reflective to sonar.
- Sometimes as many as five DSLs can be present during the daytime. These often change depth through the course of a day and may merge.
- The vertical movement of DSLs are often associated with the vertical migration of organisms through the water column.
- Many organisms migrate from deeper to shallower waters and back again every 24 hours. These are known as "diel vertical migrations."

© Diagram Visual Information Ltd.

© Diagram Visual Information Ltd.

Key words

diel vertical
 migration (DVM)
phytoplankton
plankton
vertical migration

water column
zooplankton

Diel vertical migration

- A *diel vertical migration* (DVM) is a migration pattern through the water column that is repeated at 24-hour intervals.

- Many marine species carry out DVMs moving from shallower, sunlit waters during the day, to deeper waters during the night.

- Although, by definition, plankton cannot freely move horizontally, they are capable of moving vertically through the water column.

- Considering their small size, many plankton migrate large distances through the water column. The smallest species can migrate 1,000–1,300 feet (300–400 m). Some larger species migrate more than 2,600 feet (800 m). Both of these journeys are undertaken twice a day.

- Phytoplankton may migrate through the water column to maximize their exposure to sunlight during the day, and minimize their exposure to predators at night.

- Zooplankton often migrate with phytoplankton in order to feed off them or to hunt other plant-eating zooplankton.

- Changes in light levels provide the signal for migrations to begin. It is thought that migrating plankton sense the ambient light in the water around them and rise or fall through the water column to keep it at a constant level. These regions of constant light conditions are known as "isolumes." Evidence for this theory is provided by observations that show that plankton migrate different distances depending on how cloudy the sky is, and that a solar eclipse can trigger migrations at the wrong time of day.

Diel vertical migrations

Migration types

Nocturnal migration
Many midwater zooplankton and fish rise from the mesopelagic to the epipelagic zone at dusk and descend to their previous level at sunrise. These vertical migrations can be detected through the movement of deep scattering layers revealed by sonar.

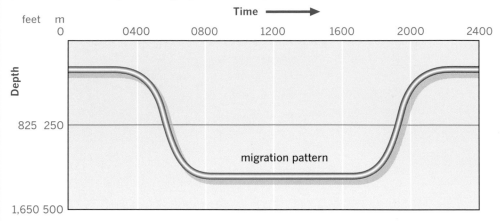

Reverse migration
In some epipelagic communities, phytoplankton and/or zooplankton descend through the epipelagic zone at night and ascend during the day.

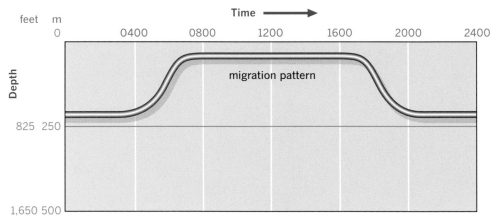

Twilight (double) migration
Some mesopelagic zooplankton rise to the epipelagic zone at dusk, descend during the night, rise again near dawn, and then descend to their daytime position.

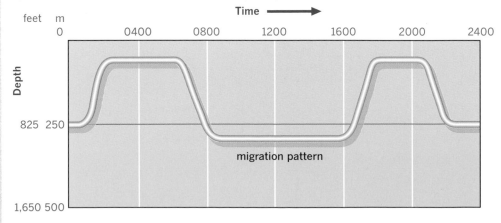

Seasonal vertical migrations

Seasonal vertical migration of a North Pacific copepod

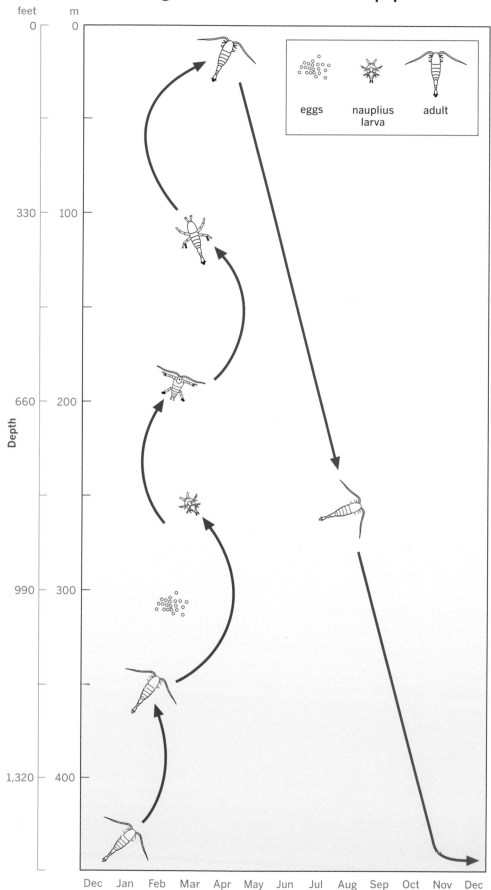

Key words

larva
plankton
polar
season
seasonal vertical
  migration

(SVM)
temperate
vertical migration
zooplankton

Seasonal vertical migration

- A *seasonal vertical migration* (*SVM*) is a migration pattern through the water column that is triggered by a change in the season
- SVMs are most common in polar or temperate waters where there is a large variation in climate between seasons.

Polar zooplankton

- In polar regions, phytoplankton production is highly seasonal, being greatest in spring and summer.
- The zooplankton that feed on them are only found in surface waters during spring and summer.
- In autumn and winter they remain at cooler depths to conserve energy.

Life cycle migrations

- Some species migrate to different depths in the water column at different stages of their life cycle.
- These life cycle stages often correspond to seasons.
- For example, among free-living copepods, different stages of the life cycle are commonly found at different depths, and are associated with different seasons of the year.

© Diagram Visual Information Ltd.

© Diagram Visual Information Ltd.

Key words

algae	holdfast
brown algae	phaeophyte
chlorophyte	red algae
frond	rhodophyte
green algae	

Seaweed

- *Seaweed* are a large and vaguely defined group of marine algae.
- They are distinct from phytoplankton (many of which are also algae) because they spend at least a part of their lives attached to the seabed.
- They also differ from most other algae in that they are generally multicellular and not microscopic in size.
- Seaweed are not "higher" plants like most of the plants on land because they do not have roots, shoots, or flowers. They are a simpler and much older group of organisms.
- Seaweed have "holdfasts" instead of roots that attach them to the seabed and "fronds" instead of leaves.
- Some seaweeds have gas-filled bladders that help them to float.
- There are about 10,000 species of seaweed compared to about 235,000 species of flowering plant.
- Seaweed are either red, green, or brown. *Chlorophyta* (green algae) include green seaweed, *phaeophyta* (brown algae) include brown seaweed, and *rhodophyta* (red algae) include red seaweed.
- Most phaeophyta and rhodophyta are marine organisms, but many chlorophyta are freshwater or terrestrial organisms.

Seaweed

Types of seaweed

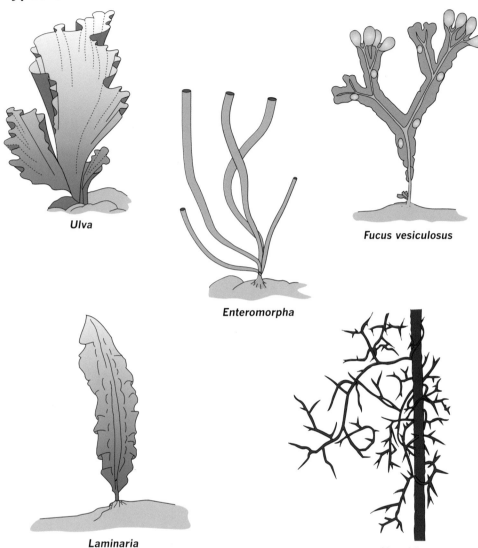

Ulva

Enteromorpha

Fucus vesiculosus

Laminaria

Chondria

Division (common name)	Approx. no. living marine species	Structure and size	Photosynthetic pigments	Storage products
Chlorophyta (green algae) Examples: *Ulva, Enteromorpha*	900	Unicellular and multicellular Ranging from microscopic 0.0004 inches (10 μm) to 3 feet (1 m) long.	Chlorophyll Carotenes	Starch
Phaeophyta (brown algae) Examples: *Fucus vesiculosus, Laminaria*	1,500	Multicellular. 4 inches (10 cm) to 30 feet (9 m) long.	Chlorophyll Xanthophylls Carotenoids	Laminarin and others (e.g. fucox-anthin)
Rhodophyta (red algae) Examples: *Chondria*	4,000	Unicellular and multicellular. Microscopic 0.0008 inches	Chlorophyll Carotenes Phycobilins (20 μm) to 6 feet (2 m) long.	Starch and others

Sponges and cnidaria

Sponges
Phylum Porifera

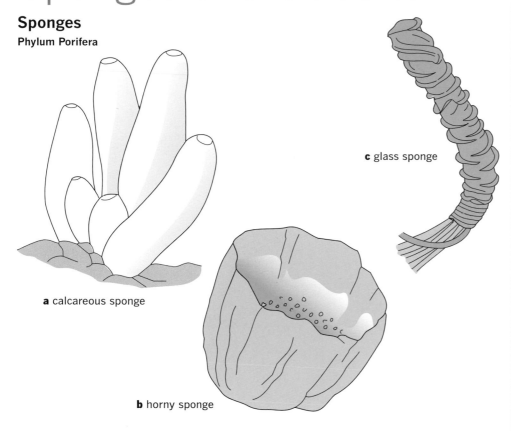

c glass sponge

a calcareous sponge

b horny sponge

Cnidarians
Phylum Cnidaria

d jellyfish

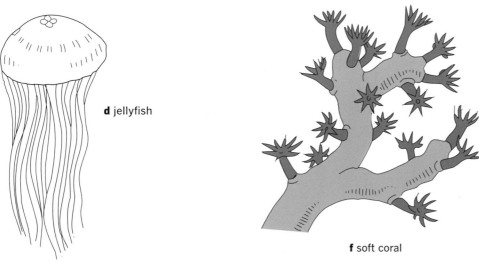

f soft coral

e sea anemone

Key words

cnidarian
poriferan
soft coral
sponge

Sponges (Phylum Porifera)

- *Sponges* are a group of very simple animals. They are also known as poriferans after their phylum Porifera. There are about 10,000 species, most of which are marine, though a few are freshwater.
- They range in size from a fraction of an inch (a few mm) to 6 feet (2 m).
- They have no nerves, muscles, or internal organs, and consist essentially of a body cavity connected to the exterior by pores.
- Sponges are filter feeders: flagellated collar cells line the body cavity and are used to create water currents that draw in oxygen and food particles.
- Four classes of sponge are recognized, based on structure and composition of the skeleton:
   class Calcare (**a**);
   class Demospongiae (**b**);
   class Hexactinellida (**c**);
   class Sclerospongiae (rare).

Cnidarians (Phylum Cnidaria)

- *Cnidarians* are a group of simple animals that include sea anemones, jellyfish, hydras, and corals.
- There are about 9,400 species: most are marine, but a few live in freshwater.
- They are radially symmetrical with a mouth, simple sensory organs, and a nervous system.
- They have one of two basic body patterns: polyp (hydroid) or medusa.
- They capture prey items using tentacles and nematocysts (stinging cells).
- There are four classes of cnidarians:
   class Hydrozoa (hydroids);
   class Scyphozoa (true jellyfish) (**d**);
   class Anthozoa (sea anemones, **e**, and corals, **f**);
   class Cubozoa (sea wasps and box jellyfish).

© Diagram Visual Information Ltd.

© Diagram Visual Information Ltd.

Key words

annelid	nemertean
chaetognathan	platyhelminth
nematode	

Flatworms (Platyhelminths)

- There are about 15,000 species of flatworm, most of which are parasitic.
- One class—Turbellaria—has free-living marine representatives: small flatworms with a simple gut and ciliated underside.

Ribbonworms (Nemerteans)

- There are about 650 species of ribbonworm, most of which are marine, with a few living in freshwater or soil.
- They are small ribbonlike benthic worms with a ciliated body surface and a long proboscis used for capturing prey.

Roundworms (Nematodes)

- There are about 80,000 species, living in all habitats.
- Roundworms have a through gut.
- Many are free-living and some are parasitic. Most free-living roundworms are less than 0.5 inches (6 mm) long. One parasite species living inside a sperm whale's gut reaches 30 feet (9 m) in length.

Segmented worms (Annelids)

- There are about 15,000 species, living in all habitats.
- The body is divided into many clearly visible segments.
- Two classes contain marine representatives: Class Polychaeta (polychaetes or bristleworms), e.g., sandworm, *Nereis*; and Class Hirudinea (leeches).

Arrow worms (Chaetognathans)

- There are only about 60 species, all of which are marine.
- Arrow worms are important zooplankton, with almost transparent bodies.

Marine worms

Turbellarian flatworm

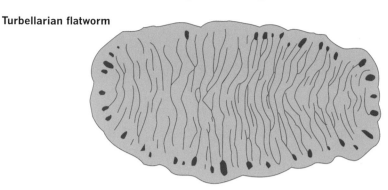

Ribbonworm

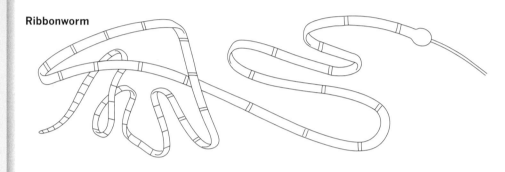

Roundworm (nematode)

Sandworm (polychaete)

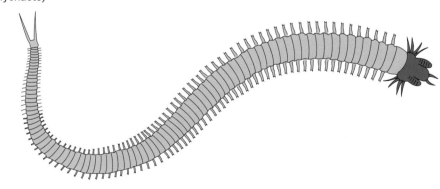

Arrow worm (chaetognath)

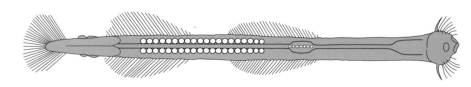

Mollusks

Chiton

Whelk

Tusk shell

Mussel

Octopus

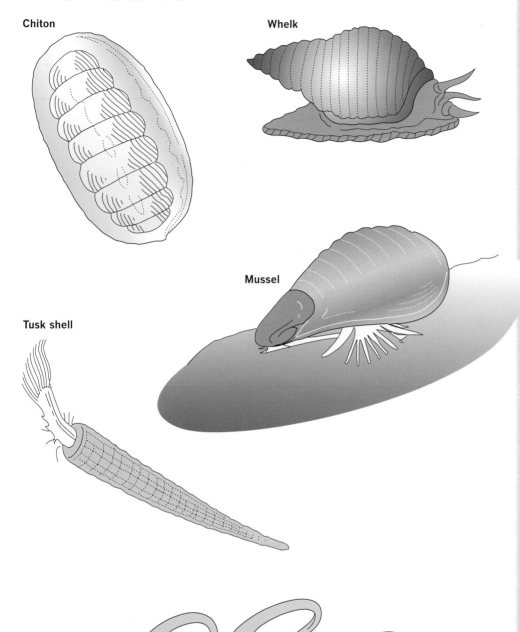

Key words

mollusk

Mollusks (Phylum Mollusca)

- *Mollusks* are a large and diverse group of animals.
- There are about 65,000 living species of mollusk. Most are marine, but some are freshwater or terrestrial.
- They range in size from a fraction of an inch (a few mm) to the giant squid at 60 feet (18 m).
- They have unsegmented bodies, usually with an external shell (sometimes internal).
- Despite their great variety of forms, all mollusk bodies have a similar plan: head (with tentacles and eyes); a muscular foot; a visceral mass containing the major internal organs; and a mantle that secretes the shell, where present.
- There are seven classes of mollusk, five of which have common marine representatives:

  class Amphineura (chitons);
  class Gastropoda (gastropods—includes snails and limpets);
  class Scaphopoda (tusk shells);
  class Bivalvia (bivalves, including clams, oysters, and mussels);
  class Cephalopoda (cephalopods, including octopus, cuttlefish, and squid).

© Diagram Visual Information Ltd.

© Diagram Visual Information Ltd.

Key words

arthropod
exoskeleton

Arthropods (Phylum Arthropoda)

- *Arthropods* are the largest group of animals. About 80 percent of species alive today belong to the phylum Arthropoda.
- There are about one million known living species. Most are terrestrial, but about 50,000 are marine.
- Some modern classifications consider the phylum Arthropoda to be three separate phyla: the Chelicerata (chelicerates); the Mandibulata (mandibulate arthropods); and the Crustacea (crustaceans).
- The name "Arthropoda" refers to the jointed legs characteristic of this phylum.
- All have bodies covered by an exoskeleton containing chitin and/or calcium carbonate.
- They range in size from a fraction of an inch (less than 1 mm) to the spider crab at 6 feet (2 m) across.
- There are several classes, three of which have common marine representatives:
  class Merostomata (horseshoe crabs);
  class Pycnogonida (sea spiders);
  class Crustacea (crustaceans):
      subclass Branchiopoda (brine shrimps),
      subclass Ostracoda (ostracods),
      subclass Copepoda (copepods),
      subclass Cirripedia (barnacles),
      subclass Malacostraca.
- There are several orders, including:
  order Isopoda (isopods);
  order Amphipoda (amphipods);
  order Eupausiacea (euphausiids, including krill);
  order Decapoda (decapods, including crabs, lobsters, and shrimps).

Arthropods

Class Merostomata

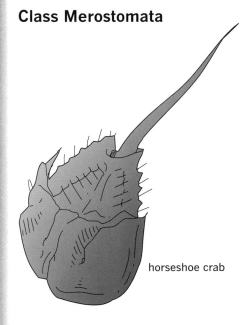

horseshoe crab

Class Pycnogonida

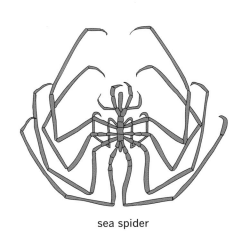

sea spider

Subclass Branchiopoda

brine shrimp

Subclass Ostracoda

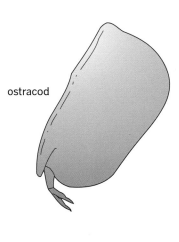

ostracod

Subclass Copepoda

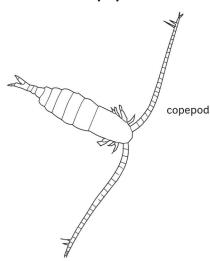

copepod

Subclass Cirripedia

barnacle

Echinoderms

Class Echinoidea

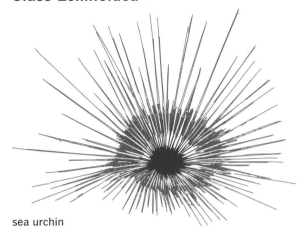

sea urchin

Class Opiuroidea

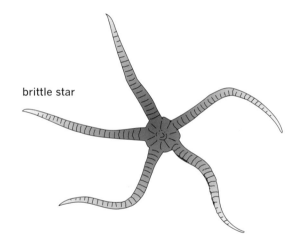

brittle star

Class Holothuroidea

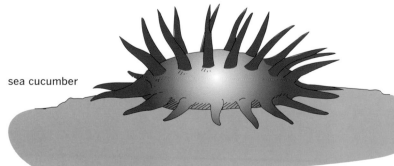

sea cucumber

Class Asteroidea

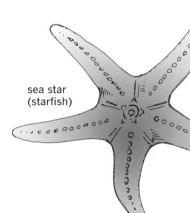

sea star
(starfish)

Class Crinoidea

sea lily
(feather star)

Key words

echinoderm
echinodermata

Echinoderms (Phylum Echinodermata)

- *Echinoderms* are a group of exclusively marine animals. It is the largest phylum with no freshwater or terrestrial representatives.
  - There are about 70,000 living species.
- They range in size from less than an inch (20 mm) to the tiger's tail sea cucumber at 6 feet (2 m) long.
- The name *echinoderm*, meaning "spiny-skinned," derives from the spines embedded in the body wall of most forms.
  - Most echinoderms have radial symmetry, with components distributed to a five-part plan.
- Many echinoderms are able to regrow large parts of their bodies. A starfish cut radially into several parts (like cutting a cake) can eventually regenerate into the same number of individual starfish.
- The water vascular system, a hydraulic system used to extend and withdraw tubed feet or tentacles, is unique to echinoderms.
- There are six classes, five of which have common marine representatives:
  - class Echinoidea (sea urchins, sand dollars);
  - class Asteroidea (sea stars or starfish);
  - class Opiuroidea (brittle stars);
  - class Crinoidea (feather stars, sea lilies);
  - class Holothuroidea (sea cucumbers);
  - class Concentricycloidea (sea daisies)—only two species are known.

© Diagram Visual Information Ltd.

© Diagram Visual Information Ltd.

Key words

agnathan
jawless fish

Ancient jawless fish

- Early jawless fish had evolved by the Cambrian period (543–490 mya) and were the forerunners of today's fish.
- One group, the ostracoderms, diversified into a variety of forms, most of which became extinct by the end of the Devonian period (354 mya).
- One group of ostracoderms, the anaspids, had features similar to those of modern lampreys.

Modern jawless fish

- Modern jawless fish (agnathans) have specialized lifestyles as external parasites (lampreys) or as deep-sea scavengers (hagfish).
- Agnathans lack the vertebral column (spine) and jaws of other modern vertebrates.

Lampreys

- Lampreys attach to fish using a suckerlike mouth. The lamprey's rasping sucker and tongue scrape the surface of the fish to draw blood and break down tissues on which the lamprey feeds.
- Sea lampreys return to freshwater to breed. Their larvae undergo prolonged development before entering the sea to grow into adults.

Hagfish

- Hagfish locate dead or dying prey using their tentacles, which are sensitive to touch and smell.
- Once a prey fish is found, the hagfish uses its toothed tongue to bore into the side of the victim, or enters via the mouth. It then consumes the prey from the inside.
- Lacking biting jaws, the hagfish loops its body into a knot to provide leverage to pull away chunks of flesh.

Jawless fish

Anaspid
(*Jamoytius*)

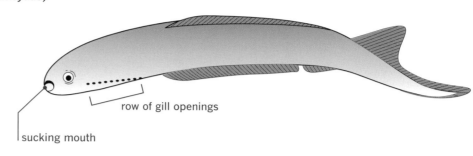

row of gill openings

sucking mouth

Lamprey

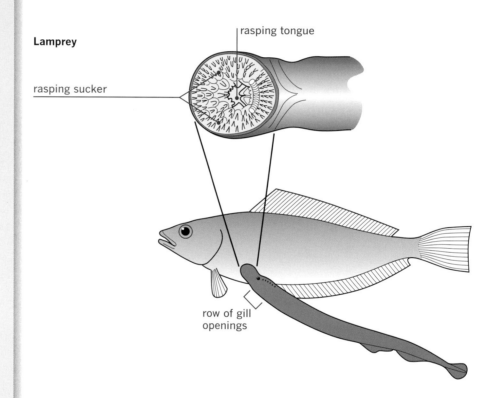

rasping tongue

rasping sucker

row of gill openings

Hagfish

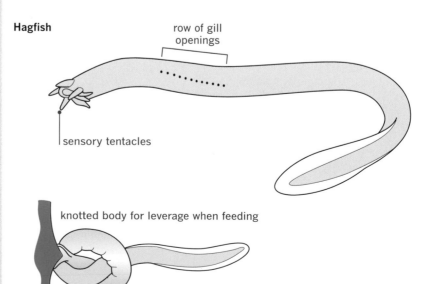

row of gill openings

sensory tentacles

knotted body for leverage when feeding

Jawed fish

A possible evolutionary scheme for modern fish

Key words

agnathan
Chondrichthyes
jawed fish
Osteichthyes

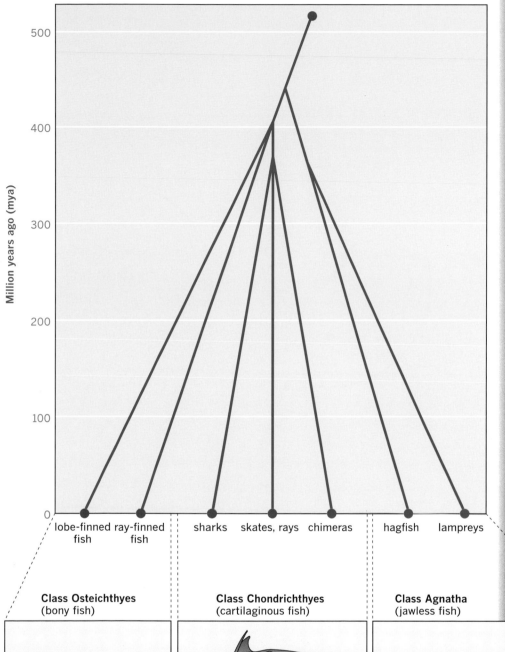

Million years ago (mya)

500
400
300
200
100
0

lobe-finned fish | ray-finned fish | sharks | skates, rays | chimeras | hagfish | lampreys

Class Osteichthyes
(bony fish)

Class Chondrichthyes
(cartilaginous fish)

Class Agnatha
(jawless fish)

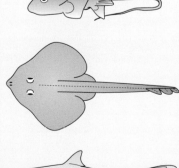

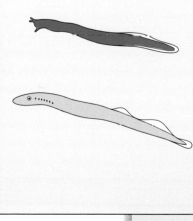

Evolution of jaws

- The evolution of jaws and paired fins is associated with at least four groups of ancient fish that had evolved by the Silurian (443–417 mya) and Devonian (417–354 mya) periods.
- Jaws evolved from skeletal frameworks that supported the gills.
- Jaws were a major advance, enabling fish to bite and chew rather than simply filter or suck.
- The evolution of paired fins—pectoral fins at the shoulder and pelvic fins near the vent—was another major advance. These conferred much greater stability and maneuverability.
- Placoderms were among the first fish with jaws and paired fins. They emerged in the Silurian period and dominated the seas of the Devonian.
- Placoderms had primitive jaws with jagged bony edges that served as teeth. Their jaws opened by means of a joint between the head and the body that allowed the head to rock backwards and opened the mouth.
- Competition from sharks and bony fish is thought to have caused the extinction of the placoderms.
- Sharks and sharklike fishes are the oldest jawed fishes still in the oceans today. They are also cartilaginous.
- Modern cartilaginous fish and bony fish have paired fins, though in some forms these fins have been secondarily lost.

© Diagram Visual Information Ltd.

Key words

cartilaginous fish
Chondrichthyes

Cartilaginous fish

- *Cartilaginous fish* have a skeleton composed entirely of cartilage, rather than bone.
- Cartilaginous fish belong to the vertebrate class Chondrichthyes.
- There are two modern subclasses:
    Elasmobranchii (elasmobranchs), e.g., sharks, dogfish, skates, and rays; and
    Holocephali (holocephalans), e.g., chimeras or ratfish.

Features of sharks, skates, and rays

- Ampullae of Lorenzini (bioelectric sensors)
- Toothlike placoid scales
- Gill slits
- Large, fat-rich liver to assist buoyancy
- Spiral valve in intestine increases surface area for food absorption
- Claspers (in male)
- Caudal fin with upper lobe usually larger than lower

Cartilaginous fish

Features of sharks, skates, and rays

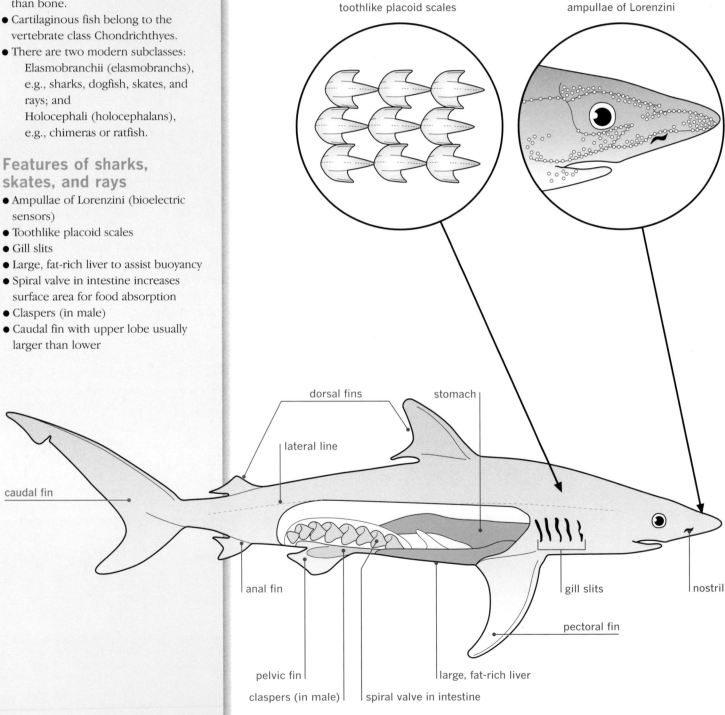

toothlike placoid scales

ampullae of Lorenzini

dorsal fins

stomach

lateral line

caudal fin

anal fin

pelvic fin

claspers (in male)

spiral valve in intestine

large, fat-rich liver

gill slits

pectoral fin

nostril

© Diagram Visual Information Ltd.

Diversity of cartilaginous fish

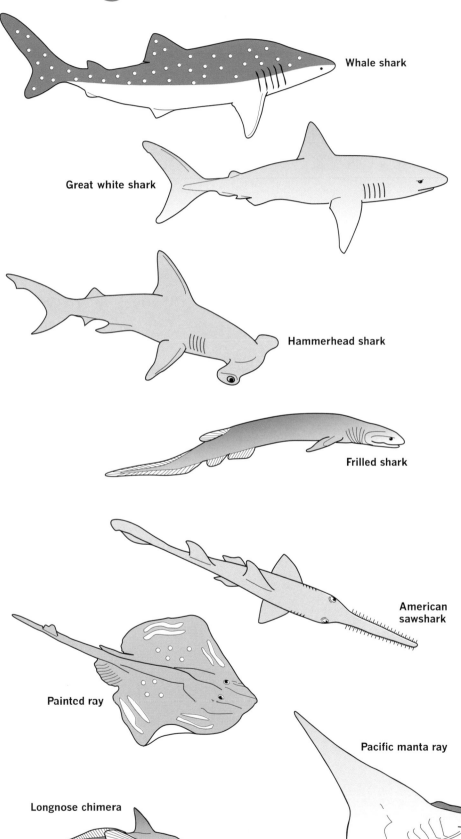

Whale shark

Great white shark

Hammerhead shark

Frilled shark

American sawshark

Painted ray

Pacific manta ray

Longnose chimera

Key words

cartilaginous fish
Chondrichthyes
shark

Cartilaginous fish diversity

- There are about 950 species of cartilaginous fish of which about 920 are elasmobranchs (subclass Elasmobranchii) and 34 are holocephalans (subclass Holocephali).
- The diversity of cartilaginous fish has declined since the Permian period (250–300 mya). Nevertheless, it is still a diverse group. Examples of cartilaginous fishes can be found from the shallowest to the deepest parts of the Ocean.

Examples of cartilaginous fish

Whale shark, *Rhincodon typus*. A plankton feeder and the world's largest fish.

Great white shark, *Carcharodon carcharias*. Its preferred diet includes oil-rich fish and fat-rich mammals, such as seals.

Hammerhead shark, *Sphyrna zygaena*. Its hammerhead probably serves to separate sensory organs and so enhance "stereo" sensory acuity.

Frilled shark, *Chlamydoselachus anguineus*. A slow-moving deep-water shark.

American sawshark, *Pristiophorus schroederi*. The saw is probably swept back and forth to stun and kill fish or uncover bottom-dwelling invertebrates.

Pacific manta ray, *Manta hamiltoni*. A plankton feeder.

Painted ray, *Raja microcellata*. Feeds predominantly on bottom-dwelling fish and shellfish.

Longnose chimera, *Harriotta raleighana*. This small, slow-moving fish lives in deep water and feeds on bottom-dwelling animals, which it detects with its long snout.

© Diagram Visual Information Ltd.

Shark attacks

© Diagram Visual Information Ltd.

Key words

shark

Facts and figures

- In 2004, the International Shark Attack File (ISAF) recorded 61 unprovoked shark attacks on humans, with seven fatalities. In that same year, tens of millions of sharks were killed by humans.
- Of about 400 species of shark, fewer than 40 are implicated in attacks on humans. In some cases, these attacks follow provocation.
- The number of shark attacks per year is directly related to the number of person-hours spent in the sea.
- More attacks are recorded in warm waters. This is partly because potentially dangerous sharks are more prevalent there, but also because of the much greater number of person-hours spent in the water.
- The three species most often implicated in shark attacks (where the species is identified) are the great white shark (*Carcharodon carcharias*), the tiger shark (*Galeocerdo cuvier*), and the bull shark (*Carcharhinus leucas*).

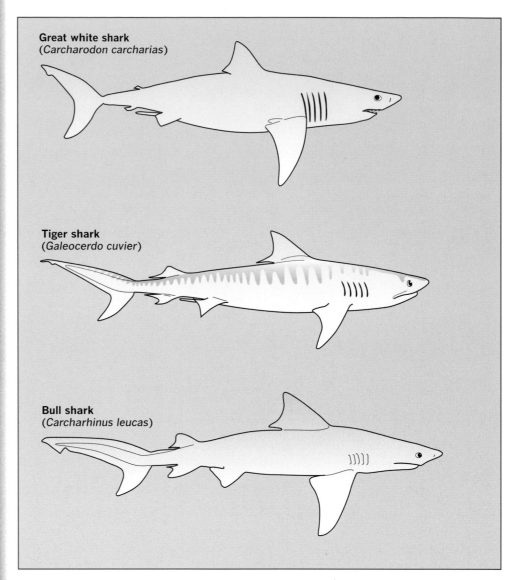

Great white shark
(*Carcharodon carcharias*)

Tiger shark
(*Galeocerdo cuvier*)

Bull shark
(*Carcharhinus leucas*)

Confirmed unprovoked shark attacks around the world, 1994–2004

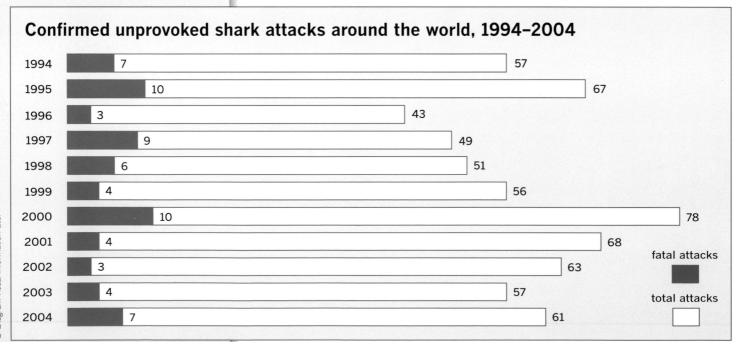

Year	fatal attacks	total attacks
1994	7	57
1995	10	67
1996	3	43
1997	9	49
1998	6	51
1999	4	56
2000	10	78
2001	4	68
2002	3	63
2003	4	57
2004	7	61

Bony fish

Features of bony fish

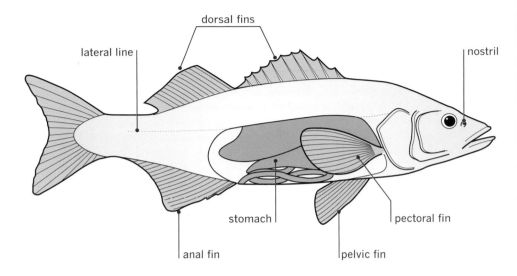

- dorsal fins
- lateral line
- nostril
- stomach
- pectoral fin
- anal fin
- pelvic fin

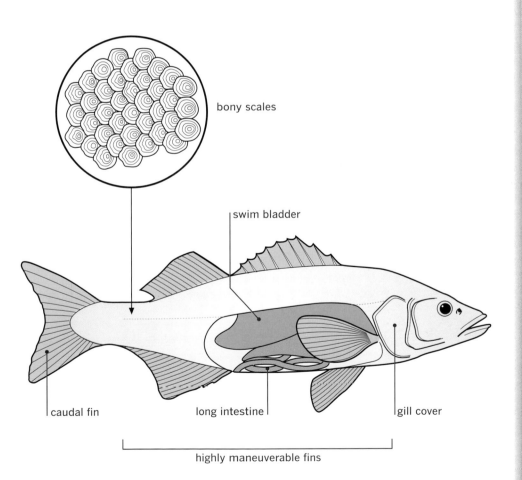

- bony scales
- swim bladder
- caudal fin
- long intestine
- gill cover
- highly maneuverable fins

Key words

bony fish
lobe-finned fish
Osteichthyes
ray-finned fish

Bony fish

- *Bony fish* have a skeleton composed entirely of bone. This distinguishes them from the class of fish with skeletons made of cartilage.
- Bony fish belong to the vertebrate class Osteichthyes.
- There are two modern classes:
  class Sarcopterygii (lobe-finned fish), e.g., freshwater lungfish and the coelacanth; and
  class Actinopterygii (ray-finned fish), which includes almost all modern bony fish.

Ray-finned fish

- Ray-finned fish have straight, bony rays projecting from the body to support their fins.
- Modern ray-finned fish have bony skeletons, widely gaping jaws, thin scales, highly mobile fins, a symmetrical tail, and swim bladders.

Lobe-finned fish

- There are only seven known species of sarcopterygians (lobe-finned fish).
- Their fins are supported by scaly lobes containing bones and muscles. These fleshy lobes are thought to have given rise to the limbs of backboned animals that live on land today.
- Lobe-finned fish first appeared about 400 million years ago.

© Diagram Visual Information Ltd.

© Diagram Visual Information Ltd.

Key words

bony fish
lobe-finned fish
Osteichthyes
ray-finned fish

Bony fish diversity

● There are about 23,000 species of living bony fish of which nearly all are actinopterygians (class Actinopterygii) and only seven are sarcopterygians (class Sarcopterygii).
● Their versatile anatomy and physiology has enabled actinopterygians (ray-finned fish) to exploit most marine environments.

Examples of bony fish

Coelacanth (*Latimeria chalumnae*) A lobe-finned fish believed to have been extinct for about 65 million years until a freshly-caught specimen was identified in 1938.

Giant Maori wrasse (*Cheilinus undulatus*). An inhabitant of tropical and subtropical waters, including coral reefs. It grows to about 7 feet (2.2 m) long and weighs up to about 420 pounds (190 kg).

Northern bluefin tuna (*Thunnus thynnus*). A fast-swimming pelagic predator. During long migrations it covers straight-line distances of more than 40 miles (65 km) a day.

Northern anchovy (*Engraulis mordax*). A small, pelagic fish, it filters the water for zooplankton and larger phytoplankton.

Sharksucker (*Echeneis naucrates*). It attaches itself to sharks and other large fish and hitches a ride. It is a generalist feeder, sometimes feeding on the scraps of food left by the larger fish.

Seahorse (*Hippocampus*). An inhabitant of floating or attached seaweed. Unusually, the male incubates fertilized eggs in a pouch and gives birth to live young.

European eel (*Anguilla anguilla*). It spawns in the Sargasso Sea and migrates to fresh water during its larval development, returning to ocean water when adult.

Atlantic halibut (*Hippoglossus hippoglossus*). The largest of the flatfish, it reaches 8 feet (2.5 m) and 690 pounds (315 kg).

Diversity of bony fish

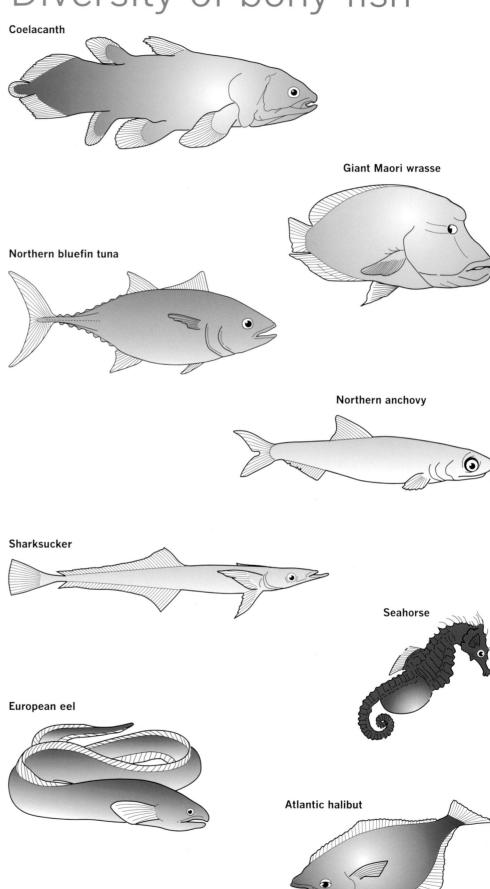

Coelacanth

Giant Maori wrasse

Northern bluefin tuna

Northern anchovy

Sharksucker

Seahorse

European eel

Atlantic halibut

Marine reptiles

Indo-Pacific crocodile

Marine iguana

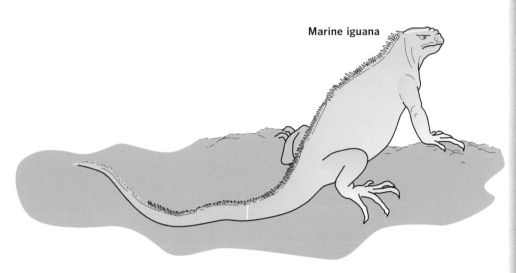

Leatherback turtle

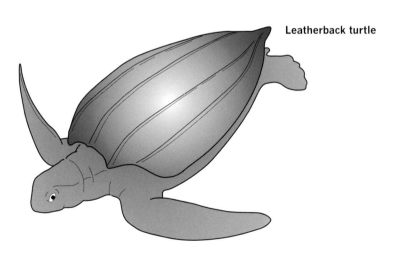

Yellow-bellied sea snake

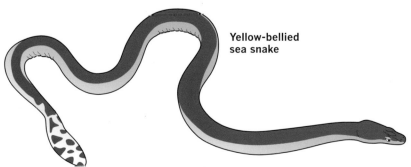

Key words

reptile

Marine reptiles

- From 180 to 90 million years ago various reptiles, such as ichthyosaurs and plesiosaurs, were dominant marine predators.
- Reptiles, however, originated on land. They are less well suited to life in the sea than many other animal groups.
- Reptiles are unable to expel large quantities of salt through their kidneys. They have evolved salt-secreting glands in the head region to expel excess salts.
- Today, of about 6,000 remaining species of reptile, only about 80 are truly marine. Of these, more than 70 are snakes.

Crocodiles

- Two species of crocodile have wide distributions in brackish water: the American crocodile, *Crocodylus acutus*, and the Indo-Pacific crocodile, *Crocodylus porosus*.

A marine lizard

- Only one species of lizard, the marine iguana, *Amblyrhynchus cristatus*, is truly marine.

Marine turtles

- Seven species are recognized. All lay eggs onshore and some species, such as the green turtle, *Chelonia mydas*, carry out long migrations.

Sea snakes

- About 60 species are well adapted to marine life, while a further dozen or so feed in shallow coastal waters but spend part of their time on land.
- Many of the true marine snakes, such as the yellow-bellied sea snake, *Pelamis platurus*, have a small mouth and inject potent venom to immobilize their fish prey rapidly. *Pelamis* gives birth to young at sea and may be the world's most abundant reptile.

© Diagram Visual Information Ltd.

Key words

seabird

Seabirds

- Birds, like reptiles and mammals, originated on land.
- Those birds best adapted to marine life are regarded as "true" seabirds. True seabirds have adaptations such as salt-secreting glands and webbed feet.
- Seabirds require a land base on which to nest, lay eggs, and rear their young.
- Of the 9,000 living species of bird, fewer than 350 are true seabirds.
- There are four major orders of true seabirds: Sphenisciformes (penguins); Procellariiformes (tubenoses, such as petrels and albatrosses); Charadriiformes (includes auks, gulls, puffins, and terns); and Pelecaniformes (includes cormorants, frigate birds, gannets, and pelicans).
- Shorebirds, or waders, are important predators on sandy and muddy shores. They are not however true seabirds, so are not discussed here.

Penguins

- The 17 species of penguin all live in the Southern Hemisphere.
- Among seabirds, they are the best adapted for swimming underwater because their wings have evolved to become flippers.
- The emperor penguin, *Aptenodytes forsteri*, is the deepest-diving of all birds and can capture prey at depths down to 820 feet (250 m).

Tubenoses (petrels, shearwaters, and albatrosses)

- *Tubenose* refers to the nostrils that are fused into a single tube along the top of the bill.
- This group contains the largest true seabird, the wandering albatross, *Diomedea exulans*, and some of the smallest, such as the little shearwater, *Puffinus assimilis*.
- All tubenoses are ocean-going, only returning to land to breed.

© Diagram Visual Information Ltd.

Seabirds

Emperor penguin

Wandering albatross

Little shearwater

Great black-backed gull

Arctic tern

Brown pelican

Great cormorant

Charadriiformes

Auks, gulls, puffins, and terns
- This diverse order contains more species of seabird than any other.
- The great black-backed gull, *Larus marinus*, is a generalist predator and scavenger.
- The Arctic tern, *Sterna paradisea*, by contrast, uses its slender beak to catch small fish from the sea surface.

Pelecaniformes

Cormorants, frigate birds, gannets, and pelicans
- Diverse in appearance, these birds all have webbed feet.
- The brown pelican, *Pelecanus occidentalis*, aerial dives to catch fish.
- The great cormorant, *Phalacrocorax carbo*, surface dives and pursues its prey underwater.

Seabird feeding strategies

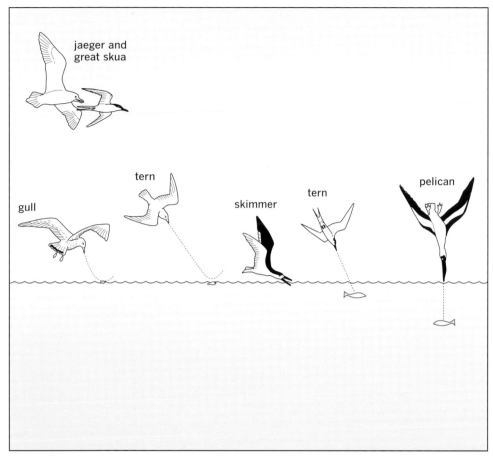

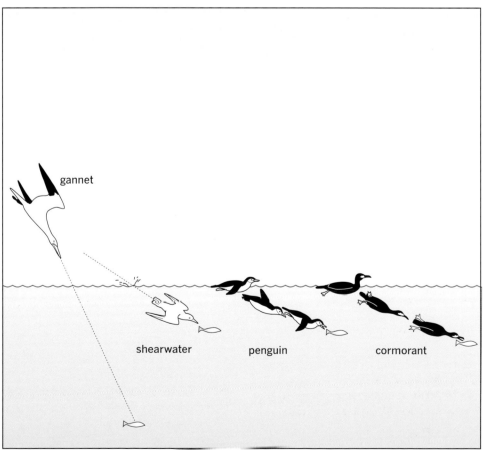

Key words

seabird

Feeding strategies

- Seabirds exhibit a wide range of specialized hunting techniques.
- Each is an adaptation to exploit a particular type of prey item, thereby reducing competition with birds of other species.

Aerial piracy

- Some seabirds acquire a proportion of their food by stealing catches made by other seabirds. This is referred to as "kleptoparasitism." Some also prey on young seabirds or take eggs.
- Jaegers, great skuas, and frigate birds are examples of seabirds that use these feeding strategies.

Surface feeding

- Surface feeding involves taking food or prey from the ocean's surface.
- Some birds surface feed while in flight by either skimming the surface with an open beak or dipping down to grab floating food. In-flight surface feeders are the most acrobatic seabirds and include gulls, terns, and skimmers.
- Other birds surface feed by landing and then taking any food around them.

Plunge diving

- Plunge divers catch food by diving into the water from the air. They rely on speed to attain depth and have little control under water.
- Terns, pelicans, and gannets are examples of plunge divers.

Pursuit diving

- Pursuit divers catch food by diving from the surface and then using specially adapted wings or feet to propel themselves underwater.
- Many of these birds are either weak fliers or cannot fly at all. Examples are penguins and cormorants.

© Diagram Visual Information Ltd.

© Diagram Visual Information Ltd.

Key words

mammal

Whales, dolphins, and porpoises (cetaceans)

- Cetaceans are the most highly-adapted marine mammals and give birth underwater.
- There are two suborders: Odontoceti (toothed whales, including the sperm whale, dolphins, and porpoises), and Mysticeti (baleen whales, such as the humpback whale).

Manatees and the dugong (sirenians or sea cows)

- Sirenians are related to modern-day proboscideans (the order that includes elephants), are well-adapted to an aquatic life and give birth in water.
- There are two families: Trichechidae (three species of manatee) and Dugongidae (one species of dugong).

Seals, sea lions, and walruses (pinnipeds)

- Pinnipeds are most closely related to terrestrial carnivores.
- There are three families: Otariidae (sea lions and fur seals), Phocidae (true seals, such as the Weddell seal) and Odobenidae (walrus).

Marine-adapted otters

- Two species of otter are marine-adapted.
- The sea otter, *Enhydra lutris*, may remain at sea throughout its life, while the little-known marine otter, *Lutra felina*, regularly comes ashore.

Polar bear

- Of the bear family only the polar bear is marine-adapted.
- It has partially-webbed front paws and is a strong swimmer, but spends most of its time on ice floes or on land.

Marine mammals

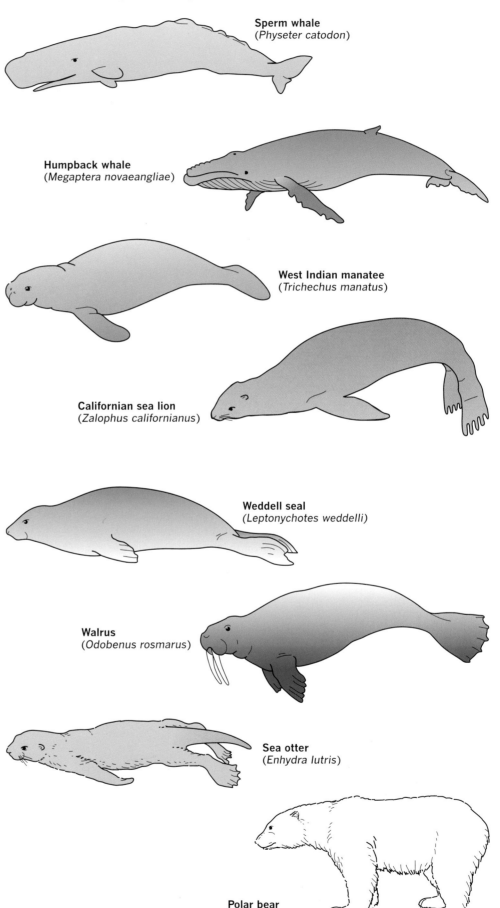

Sperm whale
(*Physeter catodon*)

Humpback whale
(*Megaptera novaeangliae*)

West Indian manatee
(*Trichechus manatus*)

Californian sea lion
(*Zalophus californianus*)

Weddell seal
(*Leptonychotes weddelli*)

Walrus
(*Odobenus rosmarus*)

Sea otter
(*Enhydra lutris*)

Polar bear
(*Ursus maritimus*)

Sea otters

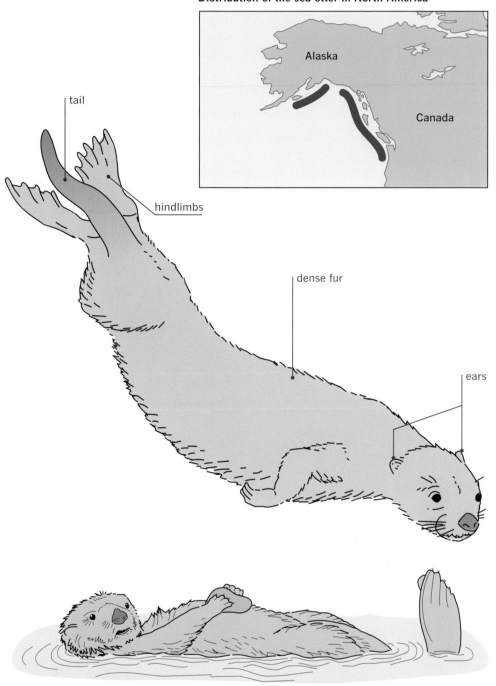

Distribution of the sea otter in North America

Alaska

Canada

tail

hindlimbs

dense fur

ears

Key words

adaptation
mammal

Distribution and ecology

- The sea otter, *Enhydra lutris*, is distributed in coastal waters across the North Pacific, from Siberia to central California. It has been reintroduced into some areas where historically it was in decline due to hunting.
- It primarily feeds on invertebrates, unlike its freshwater relatives, which primarily feed on fish.
- It is commonly associated with kelp beds where it may play an important role in controlling populations of sea urchins. In the absence of sea otters, sea urchins have been known to decimate kelp beds, encouraging a boom and bust cycle of algal growth.

Adaptations

- Although the sea otter has adapted behaviorally to a marine existence, it shows relatively few structural and physiological marine adaptations.
- The sea otter remains at sea for most of its life, but can stay submerged for only a few minutes.
- Its fur is the densest of any mammal, but sea otters lack a layer of blubber beneath the skin and must groom themselves regularly to grease the hairs and trap air in their coats.
- In comparison to river otters (which spend a proportion of their time on land), sea otters do show some adaptation for an aquatic existence.
- The ears are folded and valvelike rather than cupped and projecting.
- The hindlimbs are flipperlike and fully webbed as opposed to the partially-webbed feet of river otters.
- The tail is short and horizontally flattened, rather than long and pointed.

Tool users

- The sea otter is one of the few animals to use a "tool."
- The otter floats on its back balancing a stone on its chest. It uses the stone as an anvil on which to crack open hard-shelled invertebrates such as sea urchins, abalone, clams, mussels, and crabs.

Threats

- Between 1741 and 1911, sea otters were heavily exploited for their fur. In 1911, the Fur Seal Treaty was signed, legally protecting sea otters as well as seals. The sea otter has recovered well, with overall population numbers in the 10,000s.
- The sea otter is susceptible to coastal pollution. In 1989, at least 1,000 sea otters were killed by the Exxon Valdez oil spill in Prince William Sound, Alaska.

© Diagram Visual Information Ltd.

© Diagram Visual Information Ltd.

Key words

adaptation
mammal
sirenian

Distribution and ecology

- The dugong is found in the Indian and western Pacific oceans.
- The three manatee species are found in parts of the Atlantic Ocean and associated rivers and estuaries; the Amazonian manatee is a freshwater-only species.
- Dugongs graze predominantly on seagrasses, while manatees consume a wide variety of aquatic plants—both floating and attached.

Adaptations

- Manatees and dugongs (also called sirenians or sea cows) are well adapted to an aquatic existence.
- Their hair is sparse; they have no external ear flaps; their forelimbs are akin to strong paddles; and the tail is flattened horizontally: the dugong like the flukes of a whale, and the manatee like the paddle of a beaver.
- Like whales, sea cows give birth in the water.
- Sea cows can stay submerged for up to 10–20 minutes.
- Sea cows have a thin blubber layer and lack heat exchange structures to conserve body heat; this may explain why surviving species are only tropical or subtropical.

Threats

- Historically, sea cows—slow and bulky—have been hunted for their meat, skin, and oil-rich blubber. Dugongs grow to 10 feet (3 m) and 925 pounds (420 kg), and manatees to 15 feet (4.5 m) and 1,320 pounds (600 kg).
- The largest sirenian, Steller's sea cow, was hunted to extinction by the 1760s—within 30 years of its discovery by Europeans.
- All species are susceptible to near-shore pollution and habitat loss from coastal development. Every year, some Florida manatees are killed by collisions with powerboats.

Manatees and dugongs

Manatee
(*Trichechidae*)

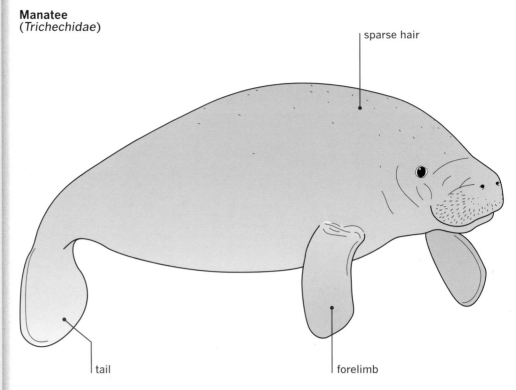

sparse hair

tail

forelimb

Dugong
(*Dugongidae*)

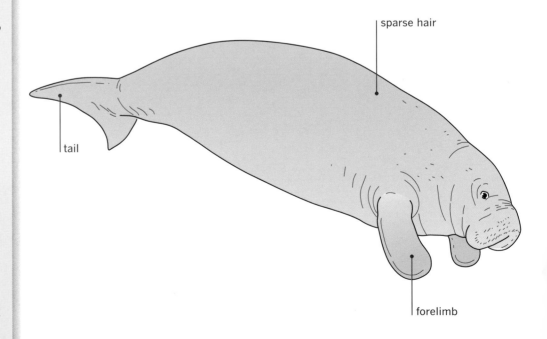

sparse hair

tail

forelimb

Seals, sea lions, and walruses

Walrus
(*Odobenus rosmarus*)

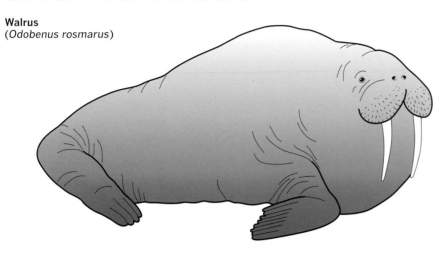

Key words

adaptation
mammal
pinnipedia

Classification

- Seals, sea lions, and walruses are pinnipeds (order Pinnipedia: from the Latin meaning "wing-footed").
- There are three families:
  Phocidae (true or earless seals, 19 species);
  Otariidae (eared seals, 14 species; sea lions and fur seals);
  Odobenidae (walrus, one species).

Adaptations

- Pinnipeds (seals, sea lions, and walruses) are comparatively well adapted to an aquatic existence:
- Their fur is short and dense, especially in fur seals.
- There is a thick layer of insulating blubber (thinner in fur seals).
- Some species of true (earless) seal are very deep divers: the Weddell seal, *Leptonychotes weddellii*, has been recorded at 2,300 feet (700 m) with dive times in excess of 80 minutes; the Southern elephant seal, *Mirounga leonina*, at 5,580 feet (1,700 m) with dive times up to 120 minutes.
- True (earless) seals show greater adaptation to a marine existence than eared seals, suggesting they made the land-to-sea transition earlier. Both types of seal give birth on land.

True (earless) seals and eared seals

Harp seal
(*Phoca groenlandica*)

Californian sea lion
(*Zalophus californianus*)

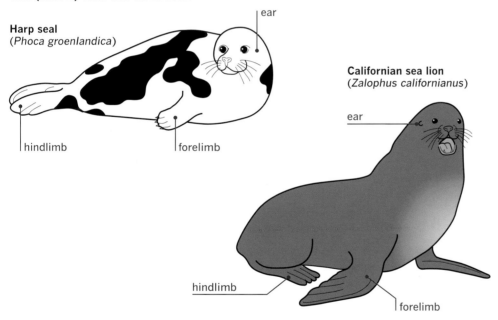

Comparison of true (earless) seals and eared seals

True (earless) seals	Eared seals
External ear absent	External ear present
In water, they use hindlimbs in a similar manner to a fish's tail, with powerful side-to-side strokes.	In water, they swim using forelimbs and steer using hindlimbs.
On land, they cannot rotate their hindlimbs forward, but propel themselves with their front flippers.	On land, the hindlimbs are rotated forward and are used for walking.
In most species, the young are born at an advanced stage of development. In some species, the young can swim within a matter of hours.	In general, the young are born at an earlier stage of development and spend a longer time on land before taking to the water.

© Diagram Visual Information Ltd.

© Diagram Visual Information Ltd.

Whales, dolphins, and porpoises

Key words

adaptation
baleen whale
cetacean
mammal
toothed whale

Classification

- Whales, dolphins, and porpoises are cetaceans (order Cetacea: derived from Latin *cetus* and Greek *ketos* meaning "large sea creature" or "sea monster").
- Technically, all cetaceans are whales. Strictly, "dolphin" refers to certain smaller whales with conical-shaped teeth (members of the family Delphinidae). "Porpoise" refers to smaller whales with spade-shaped teeth, blunt snouts, and other structural differences, although the name is sometimes used to refer to any small cetacean.
- There are two suborders:
  Odontoceti (toothed whales, about 70 species);
  Mysticeti (baleen whales, 11 species).

Features of cetaceans

1. Except for sirenians (sea cows), cetaceans are the only mammals that spend their entire lives in water and give birth in water. Cetaceans are the mammals best adapted to an aquatic existence.
2. The body is streamlined and lacks hair. Below the skin is a thick layer of insulating blubber (subcutaneous fat);
3. The tail with its two horizontal flukes moves up and down to propel the animal forward.
4. The hindlimbs are absent or vestigial. The forelimbs serve as flippers for steering.
5. Nostrils are located on top of the head and exit through one or two blowholes;
6. No external ear.

Sperm whale

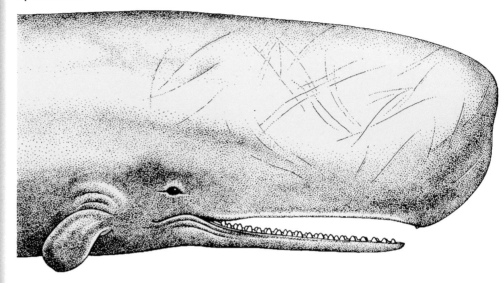

Blue whale

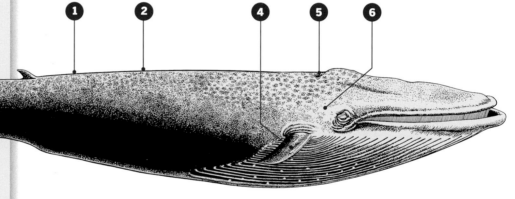

Right whale

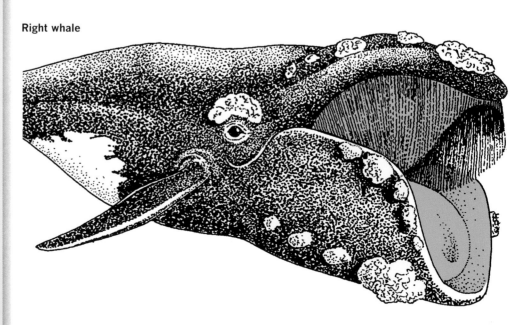

Toothed whales

Diversity

The six families of suborder Odontoceti:

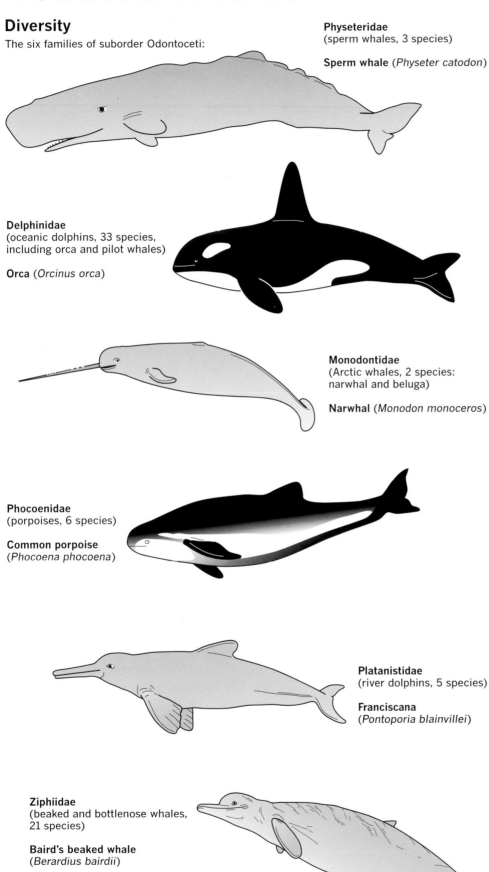

Physeteridae
(sperm whales, 3 species)

Sperm whale (*Physeter catodon*)

Delphinidae
(oceanic dolphins, 33 species,
including orca and pilot whales)

Orca (*Orcinus orca*)

Monodontidae
(Arctic whales, 2 species:
narwhal and beluga)

Narwhal (*Monodon monoceros*)

Phocoenidae
(porpoises, 6 species)

Common porpoise
(*Phocoena phocoena*)

Platanistidae
(river dolphins, 5 species)

Franciscana
(*Pontoporia blainvillei*)

Ziphiidae
(beaked and bottlenose whales,
21 species)

Baird's beaked whale
(*Berardius bairdii*)

Key words

mammal
toothed whale

General features

- The toothed whales, or odontocetes, belong to the suborder Odontoceti (derived from the Greek *odontos* for "tooth").
- Odontocetes have a single blowhole.
- Dentition varies considerably by species. Most narwhals have only two teeth, whereas many dolphin species have more than a hundred.
- Most toothed whales consume fish, squid, and larger crustaceans. Orcas, however, hunt other marine mammals, especially seals.
- Toothed whales produce a wide repertoire of sounds, both for communication and echolocation.
- Most odontocetes are highly social, and some hunt in coordinated pairs or larger groups. Orcas, and some dolphins and other species, are known to maintain close family and friendship bonds throughout their lifetimes.
- Of the dolphins, the bottle-nosed species is the most familiar to humans, with its renowned friendliness and ability to perform tricks.
- Dolphins are believed to be among the most intelligent animals on Earth.

Features of narwhals

- The narwhal (*Monodon monoceros*) lives in the very cold waters of the Arctic, sometimes traveling in large groups.
- They only have two teeth, one of which in males protrudes and grows into a long spiral tusk that can reach almost nine feet (2.7 m) long.
- It is not known exactly what this tooth is used for, but early sightings of the narwhal may have given rise to unicorn legends.

© Diagram Visual Information Ltd.

© Diagram Visual Information Ltd.

Key words

baleen whale
mammal
plankton

General features

- The baleen whales, or mysticetes, belong to the suborder Mysticeti ("moustached" whales).
- The "baleen" is a keratinous substance that replaces teeth: it is composed of hundreds of vertical plates attached to the upper jaw. The plates are flexible structures with hairlike projections, and are used to filter small prey items from the water.
- The 11 species of baleen whale covers most of the larger whales, including the blue whale, *Balaenoptera musculus*, which reaches 200 tons (180 tonnes) in weight and 110 feet (33 m) in length, and is probably the largest animal that has ever lived.
- Mysticetes have two blowholes lying side by side.
- Most baleen whales consume krill and other zooplankton, plus schooling fish or small squid. Gray whales feed on bottom-living amphipods, crabs, mollusks, and polychaete worms, which they suction from the seafloor.
- Baleen whales produce a wide repertoire of sound for communication. Humpback whales produce loud noises to scare and gather schools of fish.
- Baleen whales are social animals. Humpbacks sometimes work together in a coordinated group to form a "bubble net" to gather together fish or zooplankton for consumption.

Baleen whales

Diversity
The four families of suborder Mysticeti:

Balaenidae
(right whales, 2 species)

Eubalaenidae
(Pygmy right whale, 1 species)

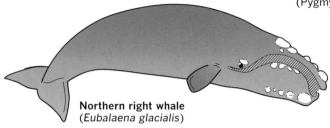

Northern right whale
(*Eubalaena glacialis*)

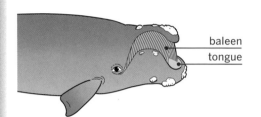

baleen
tongue

**Mouth:
cross section**

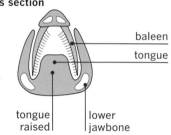

baleen
tongue

tongue raised   lower jawbone

Eschrichtiidae
(Gray whale, 1 species)

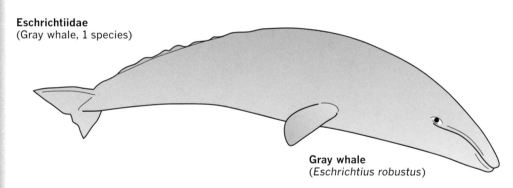

Gray whale
(*Eschrichtius robustus*)

Balaenopteridae
(rorqual whales, 6 species;
including blue whale and humpback whale)

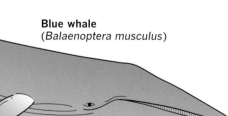

Blue whale
(*Balaenoptera musculus*)

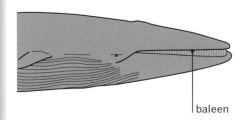

baleen

**Mouth:
cross section**

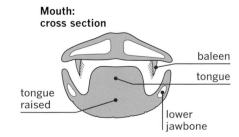

baleen
tongue

tongue raised

lower jawbone

Echolocation

The mechanism of echolocation in dolphins

Key words

adaptation
echolocation
mammal
toothed whale

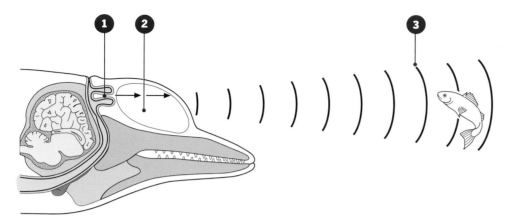

1 Clicks are produced by passing air across soft tissues in the nasal passages.

2 The melon—a fatty structure—focuses the clicks as a narrow beam of sound.

3 Echolocation clicks reach a target prey item.

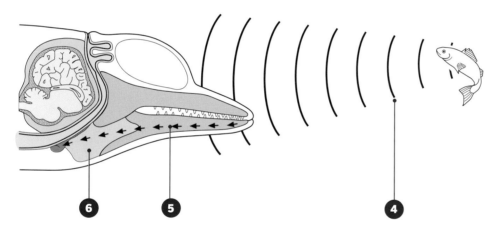

4 The returning echo provides information on distance, size, and reflective properties of the prey item.

5 Returning echoes are channeled to the inner ear via a fat body in the lower jaw.

6 An acoustic window of thin bone amplifies vibrations in the fat body.

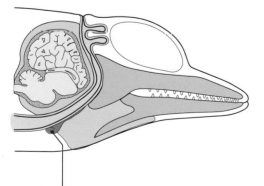

7 The inner ear interprets sound transmitted through the lower jaw.

Echolocation

- *Echolocation* is the detection of objects by the use of reflected sound.
- Dolphins and other marine mammals use echolocation because sound provides a better method of sensing the environment than light under water.
- Dolphins and other toothed whales (odontocetes) generate loud sounds and then listen for the echo of these sounds.
- Bottlenose dolphins produce broadband echolocation clicks in the range 20–220 kilohertz (kHz), and can detect target items as small as 0.06 inches (1.5 mm) in diameter.

Stun gun theory

- According to one hypothesis—yet to be verified—loud clicks produced by toothed whales could be used to stun prey.
- This might help explain how comparatively slow-swimming sperm whales are able to catch fast-swimming squid.

© Diagram Visual Information Ltd.

Fish migration

Fish migration routes

© Diagram Visual Information Ltd.

Key words

anadromous	spawning ground
catadromous	
current	
larva	
migration	

Migration

- Migration is a means of ensuring reproductive success and optimizing feeding.
- For animals that migrate, feeding grounds are commonly distinct from breeding grounds.
- Adults and young may feed on different food resources, in different locations, which reduces competition between them.

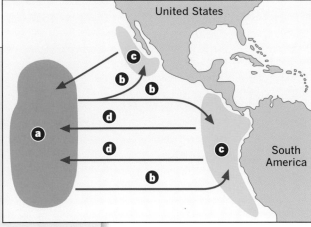

→ prevailing ocean currents

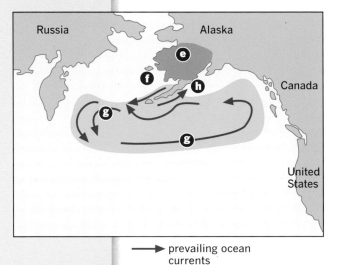

→ prevailing ocean currents

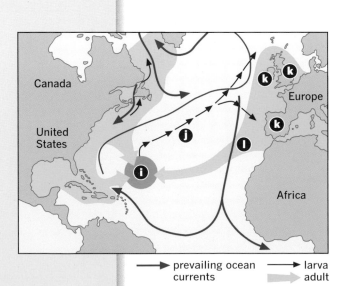

→ prevailing ocean currents

→ larva
adult

Skipjack tuna

Several distinct populations of Skipjack tuna (*Katsuwonus pelamis*) live in the warm Pacific. The eastern Pacific population migrates between central Pacific spawning grounds and near-coastal feeding areas.

ⓐ Young hatch in spawning grounds where they stay and grow for several months.

ⓑ The juvenile fish, about 12 inches (30 cm) long, migrate east, carried part or most of the way on the North and South Equatorial Countercurrents.

ⓒ The fish spend a year in rich feeding grounds where they mature.

ⓓ As young adults, the tuna migrate westward to the spawning grounds, carried on the equatorial currents. Adults repeat the migration pattern, but do not travel at the same time or to exactly the same eastern feeding areas as juveniles.

Pacific salmon

Seven species of salmon (*Oncorhynchus*) live in the North Pacific. They are anadromous (spend most of their lives in the sea but migrate to freshwater to breed). Pacific salmon spawn once and then die. The Sockeye salmon (*Oncorhynchus nerka*) migrates between Alaskan waters and the central extreme North Pacific.

ⓔ Young hatch in freshwater spawning grounds near where they live and grow for about two years.

ⓕ As juvenile salmon (smolts) they migrate to the ocean and enter a period of intense feeding and rapid growth.

ⓖ The salmon ride prevailing currents as they grow to maturity.

ⓗ When mature, they return to their original freshwater spawning grounds to breed and die.
At sea, salmon probably navigate using geomagnetic clues and subtle changes in water quality. Approaching freshwater, they recognize the "flavor" of their home stream.

European freshwater eel

The European eel (*Anguilla anguilla*) like its North American counterpart (*Anguilla rostrata*) is catadromous (spends most of its life in freshwater but migrates to the sea to breed).

ⓘ Young hatch in the waters of the Sargasso Sea.

ⓙ The leptocephalus (leaf-shaped) eel larvae travel north and then east on the Gulf Stream to reach the coasts of Western Europe.

ⓚ The larvae metamorphose into young elvers and enter rivers and move upstream to feeding areas where they will live for up to ten years.

ⓛ They return to the deep waters of the Sargasso Sea to spawn and then die.

Turtle migration

Green turtle migration

The best-documented feat of long-distance navigation by the Green turtle (*Chelonia mydas*) takes place between the east coast of Brazil and Ascension Island—a 5-mile (8-km) wide island in the middle of the South Atlantic.

Precise migration routes are not known. More information is available on female turtles because they can be readily tagged on their nesting beaches. Males remain at sea.

Key words

current
migration
seagrass

(a) Adult males and females arrive at Ascension Island and may mate offshore. Pregnant females come ashore to dig a hole in the sandy beach and lay their eggs in batches of about one hundred. Young turtles hatch 6–8 weeks later and head straight for the sea.

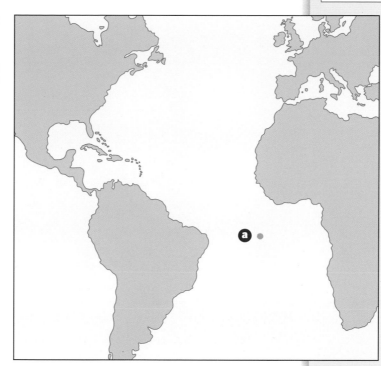

(b) The young turtles probably migrate on the South Atlantic Equatorial Current to reach feeding grounds near the Brazilian coast.

(c) After a year, green turtles begin to congregate on feeding grounds along the Brazilian coast, where they graze on seagrasses.

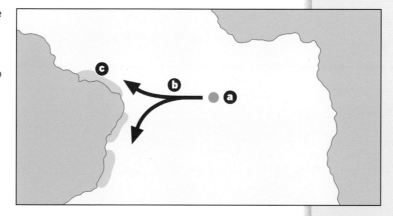

(d) Adult turtles migrate to Ascension Island to complete the life cycle. Adult females make the journey every 2–3 years.

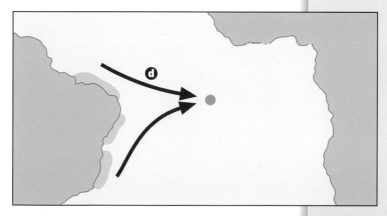

Marine turtles

- Marine turtles hatch from eggs laid on remote sandy beaches.
- In some turtle species, adults complete their migratory cycle by traveling hundreds of miles from feeding grounds to reach the nesting beaches where they originally hatched.

Magnetic compass

- Turtles navigate with the help of an internal geomagnetic compass.
- Researchers studying the loggerhead turtle have established that this compass is probably set when hatchlings leave their nest.
- In laboratory studies, changing the orientation of a magnetic field causes young turtles to change their swimming direction.
- New hatchlings run toward the surf attracted by the reflection of light from the Moon and stars. The geomagnetic compass is probably set at this stage and will aid the turtles in navigation.
- In the surf zone, the hatchlings travel out to sea guided by incoming waves using their newly-established geomagnetic compass.

© Diagram Visual Information Ltd.

© Diagram Visual Information Ltd.

Key words

Arctic
hemisphere
migration
plankton
seabird

subarctic

Arctic tern migration

- The Arctic tern (*Sterna paradisaea*) is arguably the world's greatest migrator.
- When adult, it makes annual migrations of 20,000 miles (32,000 km) north–south across both hemispheres and back again.

Navigation methods

- The more experienced navigators in a flock of migrating birds may pool their resources— both innate and those based on experience— for the benefit of the entire flock.
- Birds navigate using visual cues such as wave patterns and land topography.
- During the day, some species of bird can orientate themselves by the position of the Sun as it passes overhead from east to west.
- At night, they can navigate by taking into account the position of major constellations.
- In many seabirds, smell is important in both navigation and finding food.
- At least some bird species can detect and orientate themselves to Earth's magnetic field.

Seabird migration

Arctic tern migration

Southward migration routes

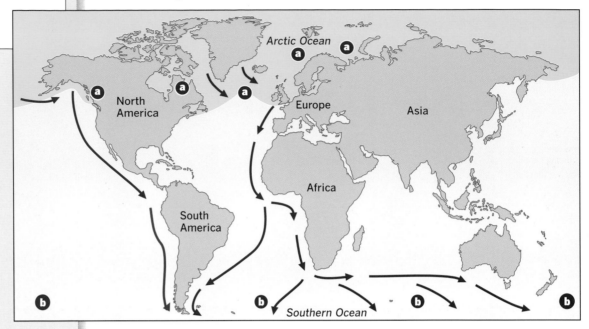

ⓐ Arctic terns nest in summer along the northern coasts of Europe and North America.

ⓑ In the autumn, they migrate to the extreme south of the South Atlantic, and the Southern Ocean.

ⓒ They arrive in the austral (Southern Hemisphere) summer. Here, they take advantage of rich plankton productivity to feed voraciously.

ⓓ In the austral late summer, the terns migrate northward, returning to their Arctic and subarctic breeding and feeding grounds in the northern spring.

Northward migration routes

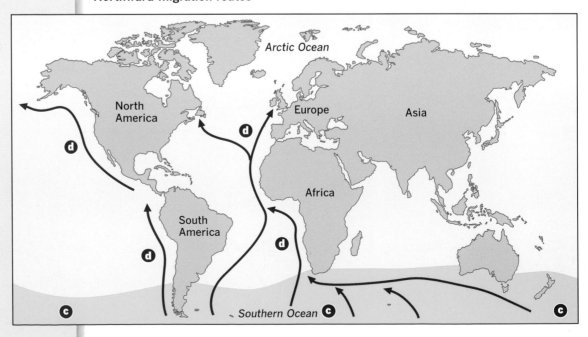

Whale migration

Humpback whale migration

Most Southern Hemisphere Humpback populations form genetically distinct populations that only rarely exchange members. There is greater intermixing between the various populations in the Northern Hemisphere. Northern and Southern Hemisphere humpbacks rarely, if ever, meet.

a Humpback whales in the Northern Hemisphere feed in subarctic waters in the northern summer.

b They winter, mate, and calve in subtropical waters.

c Southern Hemisphere humpbacks feed in Southern Ocean waters in the austral summer.

d They winter, mate, and calve in tropical and subtropical waters.

Gray whale migration

Eastern Pacific gray whales migrate between the waters off Baja, California, and the Bering Sea. For adults unaccompanied by calves, the migration cycle is an eight-month, 10,000-mile (16,000-km) round trip.

e Eastern Pacific gray whales feed on bottom-living amphipod crustaceans in the Bering Sea during the northern summer.

f They migrate to their winter breeding and calving grounds in autumn.

g Whales are conceived in the waters off Baja, California, and are born there about 13 months later.

h On the return journey to the Bering Sea, mothers with newborn calves tend to take a slower, safer route farther from land. Males, and females without calves, follow the coast more closely.

Key words

baleen whale	subtropical
hemisphere	tropical
mammal	
migration	
subarctic	

Whales

- All baleen whales, except the bowhead whale, *Balaena mysticetus*, migrate between cold-water feeding areas and warm-water breeding areas.

- The bowhead whale calves in polar seas. Two species—the gray whale, *Eschrichtius robustus*, and the humpback whale, *Megaptera novaeangliae*—make long migrations along predictable routes.

- Migrating to warm waters in winter may be a means of conserving heat loss when food is less abundant in cooler waters. Calf survival may also be better in warm waters.

Humpback whale migration

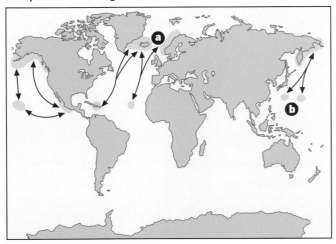
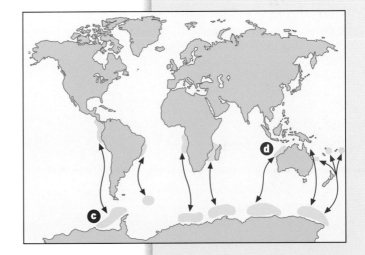

Gray whale migration

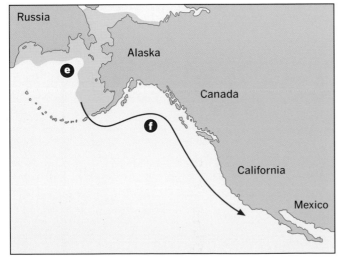
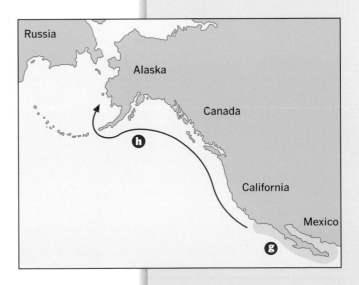

© Diagram Visual Information Ltd.

© Diagram Visual Information Ltd.

Key words

fauna
mangrove
subtropical
tropical

Mangroves

- Mangrove forests develop on tropical and subtropical shores where muddy sediments accumulate. Like the salt marshes of cooler climatic zones, they are also associated with estuaries.
- Mangrove bushes and trees create a network of roots and shoots that form a three-dimensional lattice at the interface of land and sea.

Mangrove swamp environments:

Arboreal fauna

a A community of terrestrial and semi-terrestrial animals lives in the branches of mangroves. They feed on each other and/or the animal life in the water below.

Marine hard-bottom fauna

b Sessile animals attach to the large surface area offered by the mangrove root system above the surface of the mud.

Marine soft-bottom fauna

c In the mud below the mangrove trees, a variety of animals burrows through the surface, bringing oxygen to the otherwise oxygen-poor mud.

Marine fauna visitors

d Pelagic and planktonic animals enter and leave on the rising and falling tides. Water channels between mangrove stands provide nurseries for commercially important fish, shellfish, and crustaceans.

Mangrove swamps

Mangrove swamp environments

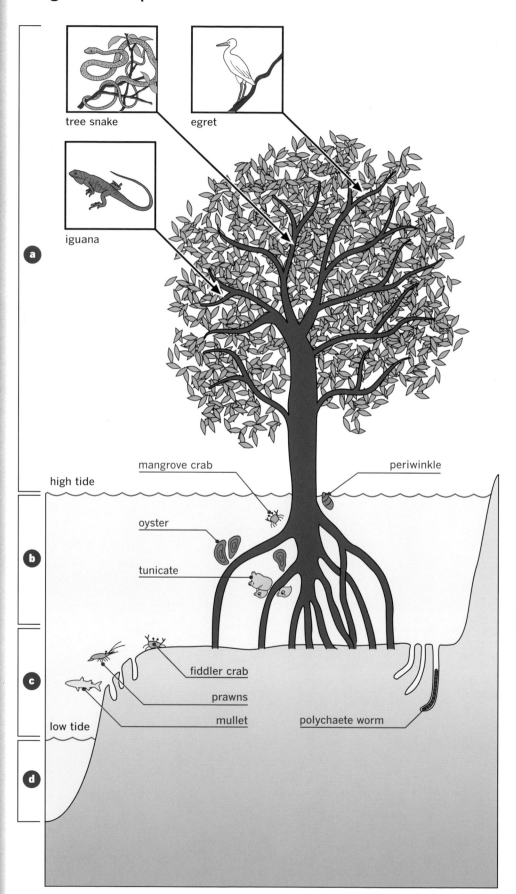

tree snake

egret

iguana

mangrove crab

periwinkle

oyster

tunicate

high tide

fiddler crab

prawns

mullet

polychaete worm

low tide

Mangrove forests and salt marshes

Key words

erosion	salt marsh
estuary	subtropical
latitude	temperate
mangrove	tropical
polar	

Distribution of mangrove forests

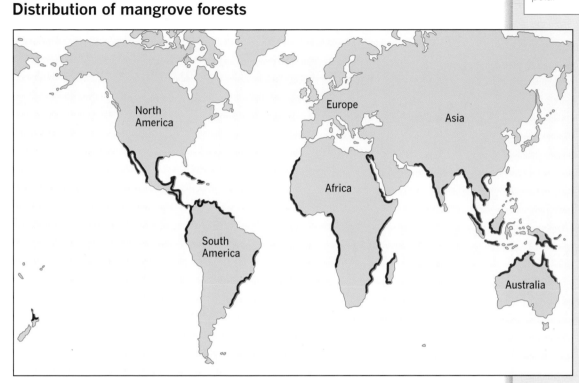

Mangrove forests

- Mangrove forests are found between latitudes 30°N and 30°S.
- They are found on tropical and subtropical shorelines in the upper tidal range.
- Shallow and aerial roots enable them to survive in oxygen-poor mud.
- Mangrove forests filter nitrates and metals from runoff and help stabilize coastlines against erosion.
- They offer vital nursery grounds for commercially important fish, crustaceans, and shellfish.
- They provide a habitat for birds, reptiles, mammals, insects, and amphibians.

Distribution of salt marshes

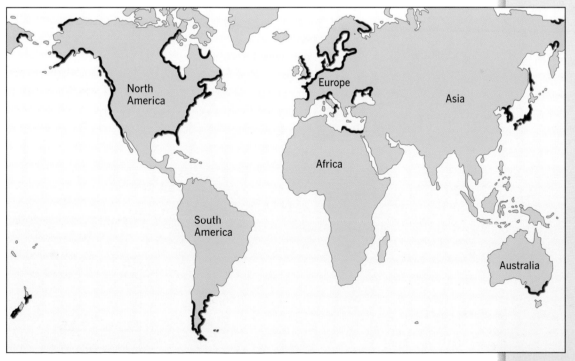

Salt marshes

- Salt marshes are found between latitudes 30°–65°N and 30°–65°S.
- They are dominated by salt-tolerant grasses such as the cordgrasses.
- They are found along sheltered, low-lying coastal strips, often near estuaries.
- They are inhospitable for terrestrial predators and grazers so they are a safe haven for birds.
- They are nursery grounds for many commercially important fish species.

© Diagram Visual Information Ltd.

Key words

algae   plankton
coral   polyp
exoskeleton   reef
hard coral   soft coral
photosynthesis

Hard corals

- Hard coral polyps lay down an exoskeleton of calcium carbonate (chalk). Individuals in a colony are connected by a septum of living material. When the polyp dies, the skeleton remains and forms the hard stony foundation of the coral reef.

- Hard corals are animal, vegetable, and mineral. Symbiotic algae (zooxanthellae) live within the tissues of the hard coral. They provide the hard coral with organic foods and enhance the coral's chalk-secreting ability. The coral provides the algae with a safe home and nutrients to aid photosynthesis.

- Coral polpys feed using tentacles to trap small planktonic organisms. Hard corals cannot, however, survive without their algal partners. Their dependency on algal photosynthesis means that corals are restricted to sunlit waters. Under thermal stress or pollution, corals may eject their algal partners and die (coral bleaching).

Soft corals

- Soft corals produce chalky skeletal elements (spicules) within their tissues rather than secrete an exoskeleton. They do not have the symbiotic association with algae (zooxanthellae) and so they do not lay down a hard exoskeleton.

- Consequently, soft corals are not reef-building but they can live and grow in the absence of strong sunlight.

© Diagram Visual Information Ltd.

Coral polyps

Coral polyp colony

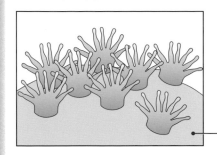

calcium carbonate exoskeleton

Coral polyp

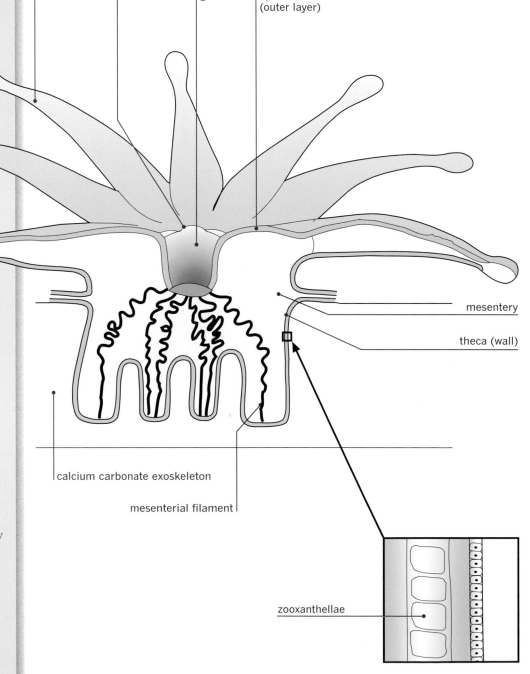

tentacle   mouth   gullet   epidermis (outer layer)

mesentery

theca (wall)

calcium carbonate exoskeleton

mesenterial filament

zooxanthellae

Coral reef formations

1 Fringing reef

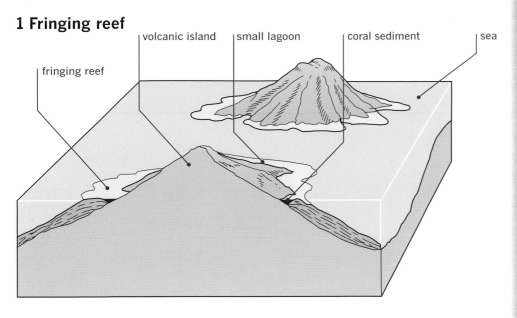

fringing reef | volcanic island | small lagoon | coral sediment | sea

2 Barrier reef

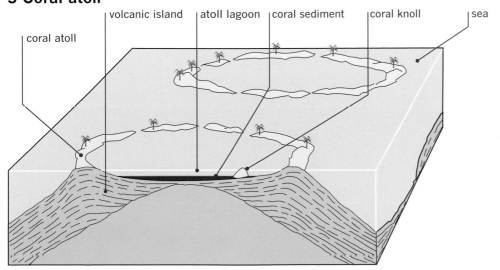

barrier reef | lagoon | volcanic island | coral sediment | sea

3 Coral atoll

coral atoll | volcanic island | atoll lagoon | coral sediment | coral knoll | sea

Key words

atoll	reef
barrier reef	seamount
coral	subtropical
fringing reef	tropical
lagoon	volcanic island
larvae	

Coral reef formation

- The three major types of coral reef follow a developmental sequence:

1 Fringing reef

- A *fringing reef* is a reef that develops directly alongside the line of a coast.
- They are common in tropical and subtropical waters where there is a hard surface on which coral larvae can settle.
- The largest fringing reef is found along the coasts of the Red Sea. It is 2,500 miles (4,000 km) in extent.

2 Barrier reef

- A *barrier reef* is separated from the shore by a lagoon of open water.
- They develop where the coastline is gradually subsiding alongside a fringing reef.
- The largest barrier reef system is Australia's Great Barrier Reef. It is about 1,250 miles (2,000 km) long and for most of its length is separated from the mainland by a lagoon that is at least 25 miles (40 km) wide.

3 Coral atoll

- A *coral atoll* is a final stage in coral-reef development on volcanic islands.
- As the volcanic island subsides, its fringing reef becomes a barrier reef and then, as the island subsides below the sea surface, a ring of coral called an atoll is formed.
- Coral atolls are associated with the volcanic islands of the Indian and Pacific oceans.
- If the rate of subsidence outstrips the rate at which coral grows, the coral will die at sunlight-deprived depths. The coral atoll then becomes a seamount.

© Diagram Visual Information Ltd.

Distribution of coral reefs

Key words

algae	reef
coral	salinity
estuary	sediment
hard coral	subtropical
isotherm	tropical
photosynthesis	

Hard coral distribution

- Hard corals are restricted to warm, clear, sunlit seawaters with near-normal salinity.
- Almost all coral reefs are found in subtropical and tropical waters within the boundaries of the 68°F (20°C) summer isotherm.
- The requirement of light for algal photosynthesis means that hard coral is typically restricted to a maximum depth of about 165 feet (50 m).
- Dilution of seawater by freshwater inhibits the establishment of coral. Sediment also readily smothers a coral reef. Typically, large gaps occur in coral reefs in the vicinity of estuaries.

Coral forms

Types of coral

a Example of a "branching" coral form   **c** Example of a "table" coral form

b Example of "brain" coral form

Hard coral distribution

▢ area within 68°F (20°C) summer isotherms

••••• area over which coral reefs are found

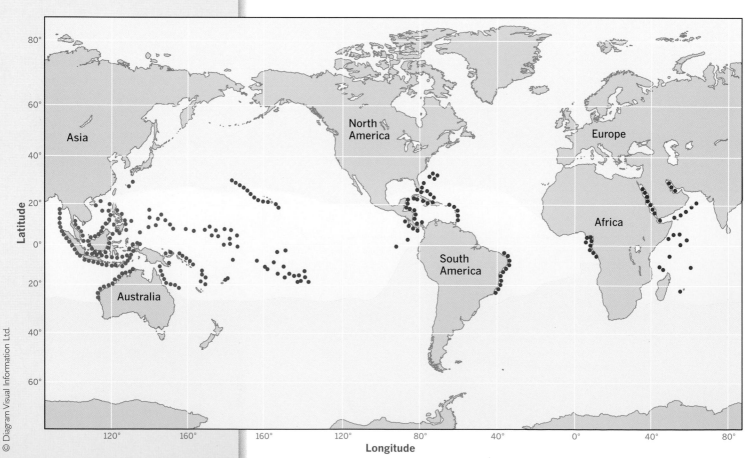

© Diagram Visual Information Ltd.

Coral reef zones

(a) Reef face

The outer edge of a coral reef. This typically exhibits vertical zonation.

(1) Reef crest or algal ridge. Encrusting coralline algae rather than coral often inhabits this region of great turbulence.

(2) Massive or compact hard corals that can withstand surge conditions are prevalent toward the upper part of the reef face.

(3) More delicate hard corals are found to a depth of approximate 165 feet (50 m). At moderate levels, coral forms are branches, columns, or whorls growing upwards toward the light. At deeper levels, corals may grow in flattened sheets (laminar formation) to catch available light.

(4) Beyond about 165 feet (50 m) sunlight penetration is insufficient for hard coral growth. Soft corals and sponges predominate here.

Key words

coral	reef flat
lagoon	reef zone
reef	shore
reef crest	vertical zonation
reef face	

Reef habitats

- Coral reefs are complex structures. The kinds of coral that grow within them depend on depth, turbulence, and other factors.
- The various zones of a coral reef provide different habitats for a wide range of marine life.

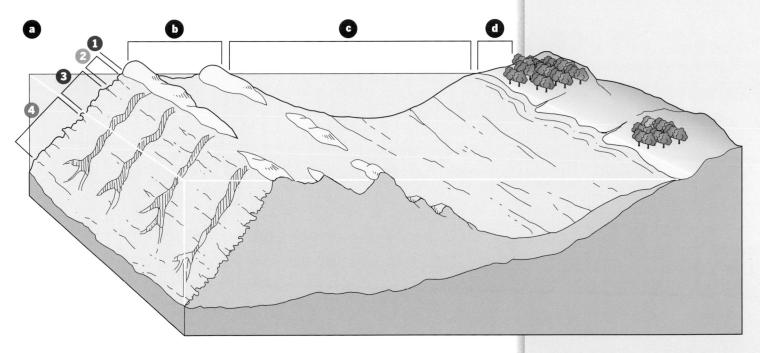

(b) Reef flat

The landward edge of a fringe or barrier reef. Relatively protected from wave action, and being close to the sea surface, this region usually contains an extensive selection of corals.

(c) Lagoon

The open water between reef and land may cover a fine floor of coral sand that harbors seagrasses and seaweeds. Where the seafloor is hard, clumps of coral may grow to the surface to form coral knolls (pinnacles).

(d) Beach

On the nearby shore, palm trees may grow in the coral sand or mangroves may grow in the mud.

The threat of pollution

- Coral reefs and the diverse ecosystems they support are highly vulnerable to degradation by human pollution.
- Oil, pesticides, fertilizers, and other chemicals discharged by human industry poison corals, or indirectly destroy them by increasing algal blooms that blot out the sunlight they require.
- Reefs close to large coastal cities such as Hong Kong and Singapore have already disappeared. Conservation initiatives are underway in some areas however, e.g., the Florida Keys National Marine Sanctuary, which is working to limit the impact of human activities on the Florida reefs.

© Diagram Visual Information Ltd.

© Diagram Visual Information Ltd.

Key words

bacteria
chlorophyte
epiphyte
seagrass
sediment

temperate
tropical

Seagrasses

- *Seagrasses* are flowering marine plants related to lilies. They are descended from true land plants.
- Seagrass flowers are pollinated underwater and the resulting seeds are dispersed on water currents.
- Seagrasses are more successful than seaweeds at exploiting soft-bottom sediments because they have roots.
- Their branching stems can extend horizontally to form rhizomes that give rise to new shoots.

Distribution

- Seagrass meadows are commonly found in sandy subtidal areas of quiet water.
- Of the 50 or so species of seagrass, most are found in tropical waters.
- Dominant temperate species, such as eelgrass (*Zostera*), give way in warmer waters to tropical species such as manatee grass (*Syringodium*) and turtle grass (*Thalassia*).

Seagrass community

- Microscopic diatoms known as *epiphytes*, cyanobacteria, and chlorophytes (green algae) grow on the surface of seagrass blades.
- Green turtles and sea cows consume seagrasses. Many more animals eat seagrass epiphytes.
- Most creatures in the seagrass community feed on seagrass and dead or decaying plant material. Fungi and bacteria are decomposers consumed by larger microbes that, in turn, are consumed by larger deposit feeders such as sea cucumbers, clams, and polychaete worms.
- Suspension feeders, such as sea squirts, bryozoans, and hydroids, live attached to seagrass blades.
- Crabs, lobsters, and fish such as mullet are omnivores grazing within seagrass communities.

Seagrass meadows

Seagrass features

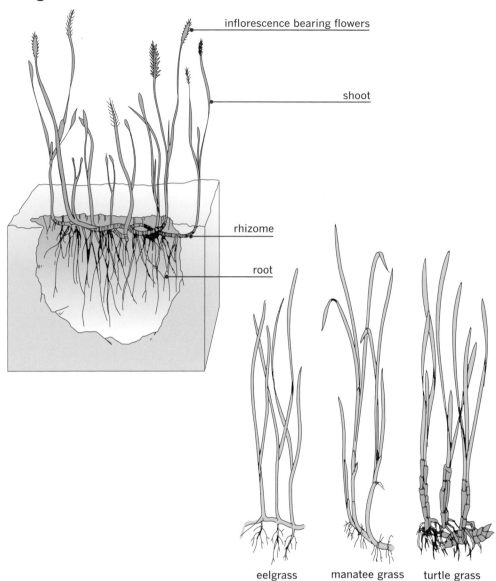

inflorescence bearing flowers

shoot

rhizome

root

eelgrass   manatee grass   turtle grass

Seagrass productivity

- Seagrasses live in clear, shallow water where light intensity is high.
- Seagrasses have true roots, which means they can extract nutrients from the sediment. Seaweed and phytoplankton rely on the supply of nutrients in seawater.
- Cyanobacteria living on the surface of seagrass blades can "fix" nitrogen. This means that they are able to absorb nitrogen from the environment and convert it into a form that can be used by plants as food.
- These combined effects mean that seagrass productivity can reach as high as 4 kg C/m²/year in tropical waters.

Economic importance

- Seagrass meadows provide nursery grounds for fish, crustaceans, and bivalve mollusks. On North American coasts, for example, commercial stocks of menhaden and salmon live in seagrasses during their subadult years.
- By encouraging sedimentation and acting as wave and current breaks, seagrass meadows protect many coastlines from erosion.

Kelp forests

Kelp features

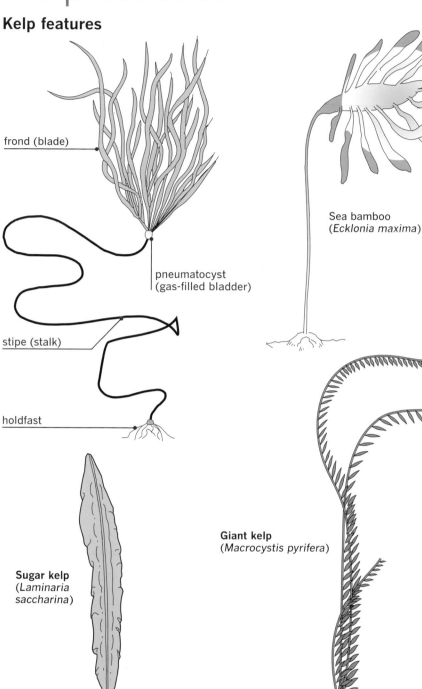

frond (blade)

pneumatocyst
(gas-filled bladder)

stipe (stalk)

holdfast

Sea bamboo
(*Ecklonia maxima*)

Sugar kelp
(*Laminaria
saccharina*)

Giant kelp
(*Macrocystis pyrifera*)

Key words

algae
epiphytes
kelp
polar
temperate

Kelp

- *Kelp* refers to certain genera of brown algae.
- Large kelps—such as *Macrocystis* and *Nereocystis*—create a floating surface canopy. Smaller kelps—such as *Ecklonia* and *Laminaria*—grow from dense "beds" below the surface.
- Typically, a kelp plant has a flexible stipe (stalk) to which are attached fronds (blades: the equivalent of leaves). The plant is attached to the hard substrate by a holdfast. Some kelps have one or more gas-filled floats (pneumatocysts) that buoy up the fronds to reach the light.

Distribution

- Kelp grow subtidally on a hard substrate in temperate and polar regions, particularly where there is reasonable water circulation.
- They are found in similar habitats to those occupied by coral reefs in warmer waters. Kelp are grown where water temperatures are lower than 68°F (20°C).

Kelp forest community

- Where kelp growth is dense and tall the canopy traps much of the available light, creating a dimly lit understory.
- Kelp fronds provide food for sea urchins and some snails and sea slugs.
- Diatoms known as *epiphytes* grow on fronds, as well as bryozoans, hydroids, and filter-feeding polychaetes. Small snails and crustaceans graze or hunt on the fronds.
- Seafloor inhabitants include crabs, sea stars, sea squirts, sponges, various bivalve mollusks, and octopuses.
- Fish are abundant at all levels, and crabs and otters also find concealment here from larger predators.
- Various suspension-feeders, including polychaete worms, crustaceans, and brittlestars, are found on holdfasts and the nearby seafloor.

Kelp forest productivity

- The giant kelp *Macrocystis pyrifera*, can grow to 165 feet (50 m), with a daily growth rate of 12 inches (30 cm).
- In clear, moderately nutrient-rich water, productivity can reach 2 kg C/m²/per year.

Economic importance

- Some kelps are used as cattle feed, land fertilizers, and even as human food.
- Alginates are extracted from kelps and are used as emulsifiers, thickeners, and stabilizers in products ranging from cosmetics and foodstuffs to medicines.
- In the United States and Canada, more than 22,000 tons (20,000 tonnes) dry weight of giant kelp is harvested annually.

© Diagram Visual Information Ltd.

© Diagram Visual Information Ltd.

Key words

bacteria   white smoker
black smoker
chemosynthesis
hydrothermal
  vent

White smokers

- A *white smoker* is a deep seafloor hydrothermal vent.
- They are known as white smokers because minerals dissolved in the water they expel make them look like miniature volcanoes belching white smoke.
- Communities of marine creatures were found around these vents living far beyond the reach of sunlight.
- White smokers discharge water rich in hydrogen sulfide, often with dissolved oxygen and nitrate, at temperatures of 36–73°F (2–23°C).
- The biological communities associated with such vents include 3-foot (1 m) long vestimentiferan worms and 12-inch (30 cm) clams.
- Biomass in these vent communities is at least a thousand times higher than in the seafloor communities normally found at this depth.
- Chemosynthetic bacteria— both free-living and those living symbiotically inside worms, clams, and other animals—are the energy source for the vent community.
- Chemosynthesis—the production of organic compounds using energy derived from the oxidation of inorganic compounds—is the energy source for such communities, rather than photosynthesis (the production of organic compounds utilizing sunlight energy).

Hydrothermal vents

Hydrothermal vent environment

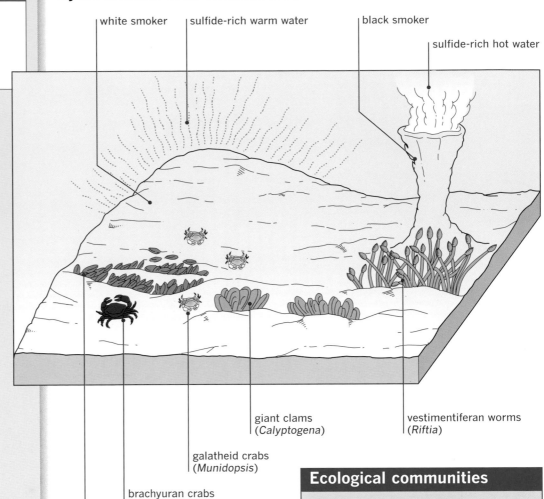

white smoker   sulfide-rich warm water   black smoker

sulfide-rich hot water

giant clams
(*Calyptogena*)

vestimentiferan worms
(*Riftia*)

galatheid crabs
(*Munidopsis*)

brachyuran crabs
(*Bythograea*)

giant mussels
(*Bathymodiolus*)

Ecological communities

- The biological communities associated with both white and black smokers appear to contain members with similar ecological roles, although the species involved do vary. Large clams, mussels, and/or vestimentiferan worms are typically a dominant feature of eastern Pacific vents.

Types of hydrothermal vents

Black smoker
- Black smokers are another form of deep seafloor hydrothermal vent.
- They discharge dark-colored water and often produce chimneys of deposited material around the vent mouth.
- The water discharged from a black smoker is hot: 518–716°F (270–380°C); and typically rich in hydrogen sulfide and certain metals

such as iron and manganese, but without oxygen or nitrate.
- Their flow rates are much higher than those of white smokers.

Shallow water vents
- Hydrothermal vents releasing water rich in sulfides are found in intertidal areas off Southern California.
- These vents support mats of sulfide-oxidizing bacteria that are grazed by limpets.

Hydrothermal vent communities

Giant tube worm
(*Riftia pachyptila*)

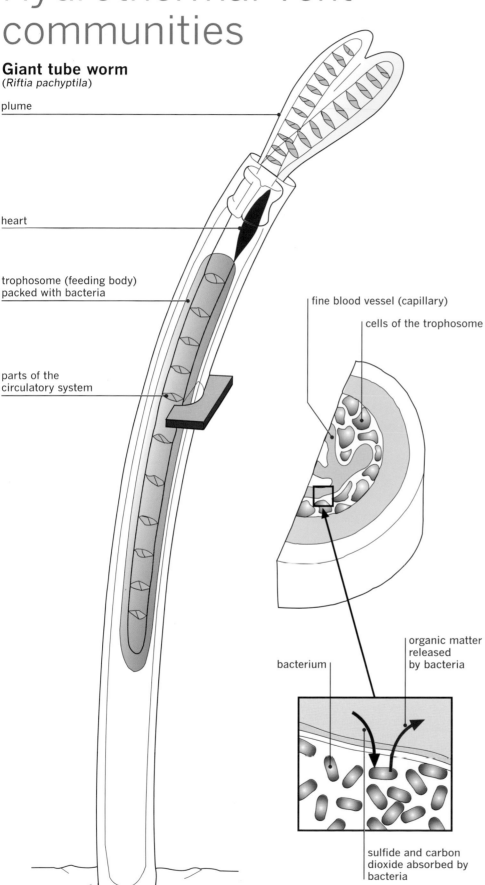

plume

heart

trophosome (feeding body)
packed with bacteria

parts of the
circulatory system

fine blood vessel (capillary)

cells of the trophosome

bacterium

organic matter
released
by bacteria

sulfide and carbon
dioxide absorbed by
bacteria

Key words

bacteria
chemosynthesis
hydrothermal
vent

Tube worms

- The tube worm (*Riftia pachyptila*) comprises the bulk of the biomass in many eastern Pacific hydrothermal vent communities.
- The species can grow to 3 feet (1 m) in length and 2 inches (5 cm) or more in diameter.
- The worm lacks a functional mouth and gut. Instead, a feeding body, the "trophosome," packed with symbiotic bacteria, apparently provides the worm's nutritional requirements.
- The dry weight of bacteria inside the trophosome is greater than that of the worm's body itself.
- The bacteria oxidize hydrogen sulfide and, by chemosynthesis, manufacture organic matter.
- The worm absorbs hydrogen sulfide (highly toxic to most organisms) and carries it in the blood bound to hemoglobin.
- The worm exchanges gases with its surroundings (absorbing oxygen and hydrogen sulfide and excreting carbon dioxide) using its gill-like plume, which is richly supplied with hemoglobin-rich blood.

Other members of the hydrothermal vent fauna

- Some other vent animals, notably large clams (*Calyptogena*) and mussels (*Bathymodiolus*), also contain symbiotic bacteria that supply them with food by chemosynthesis. These mollusks also filter feed.
- Many members of the hydrothermal vent community are filter feeders. They consume small clumps of bacteria that break off the bacterial mats that grow in and around the hydrothermal vents.
- Other community members, such as gastropod mollusks, graze directly on bacterial mats.
- Predators include vent fish and crabs.

© Diagram Visual Information Ltd.

© Diagram Visual Information Ltd.

Key words

bacteria	hydrocarbon
chemosynthesis	seep
cold seep	
continental slope	
gas hydrate	

Cold seeps

- A *cold seep* is a location on the ocean floor where hydrocarbon-rich fluids seep into seawater.
- Unlike black and white smokers, cold seep emissions are at the same temperature as the surrounding seawater.
- Cold seeps support communities similar to those found at black and white smokers. Chemosynthetic bacteria support animals that include sea stars, crabs, clams, mussels, shrimps, and anemones.
- Cold seeps are thought to emit at a slow and dependable rate, unlike black and white smokers, which are volatile and short-lived. Tube worms living near cold seeps are thought to have lifespans of 170 to 250 years.

Hydrocarbon seeps

- Oil and gas seeps at depths of 2,000–2,300 feet (600–700 m) on the continental slope of the Gulf of Mexico were found to support an abundance of chemosynthetic bacteria that used hydrogen sulfide and/or methane as their energy source.
- A new species of polychaete worm, called the "iceworm," was discovered in burrows inside mounds of gas hydrate (an icelike substance formed when methane or other hydrocarbon molecules are trapped in a chemical lattice at low temperature and high pressure).

Cold-water seep communities

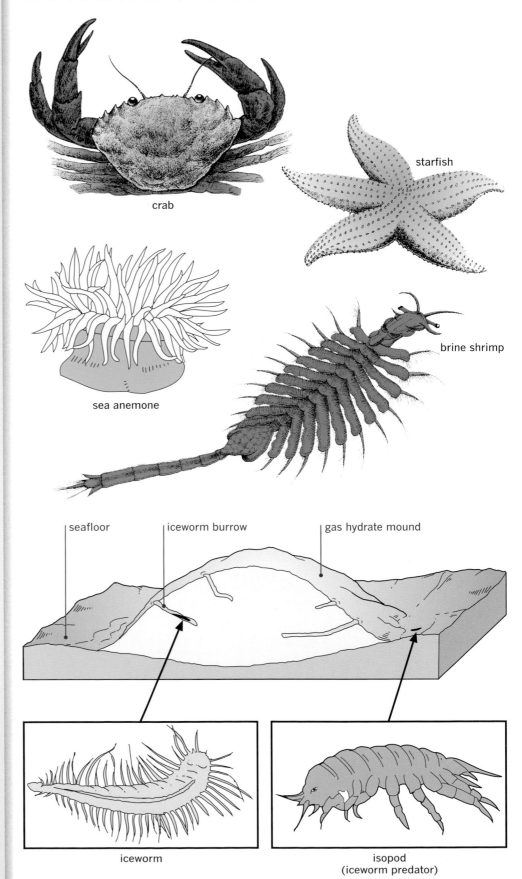

crab

starfish

sea anemone

brine shrimp

seafloor   iceworm burrow   gas hydrate mound

iceworm

isopod
(iceworm predator)

Latitude

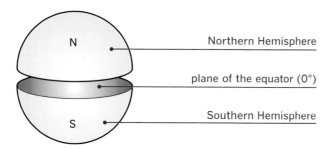

Northern Hemisphere

plane of the equator (0°)

Southern Hemisphere

Key words

Antarctic Circle
Arctic Circle
equator
hemisphere
latitude
line of latitude

midnight Sun
nautical mile
parallel
Tropic of Cancer
Tropic of
  Capricorn

Lines of latitude

- *Latitude* is an angular measurement describing distance north or south of the equator on Earth's surface.

- Latitude is a measure of the angle that the perpendicular (line at right angles) from a location on Earth's surface makes with the plane of the equator.

- Perpendiculars from Earth's surface do not always intersect the center of the globe because Earth is not perfectly spherical—it is flattened at the poles.

- A latitude measurement always falls within the range 0 degrees (on the equator) to 90 degrees north or south (at the North or South poles).

- Each degree of latitude may be subdivided into 60 "minutes." Minutes are usually expressed to one or two decimal places. For example 25°37.5' N(orth) or S(outh). Minutes were formerly subdivided into 60 "seconds."

- One minute of latitude is approximately equivalent to one nautical mile on Earth's surface.

- All points at a given latitude are said to constitute a "line of latitude." Lines of latitude are also known as "parallels."

- The "Tropic of Cancer" and the "Tropic of Capricorn" are lines of latitude at 23°27'N and 23°27'S respectively. It is only possible for the Sun to be directly overhead at latitudes between the Tropic of Cancer and the Tropic of Capricorn.

- The "Arctic Circle" and the "Antarctic Circle" are lines of latitude at 66°33'N and 66°33'S respectively. It is only possible for the Sun to be above the horizon for 24 hours ("midnight Sun") above and below these latitudes.

- A latitude measurement must be combined with a longitude measurement to give location on the surface of Earth.

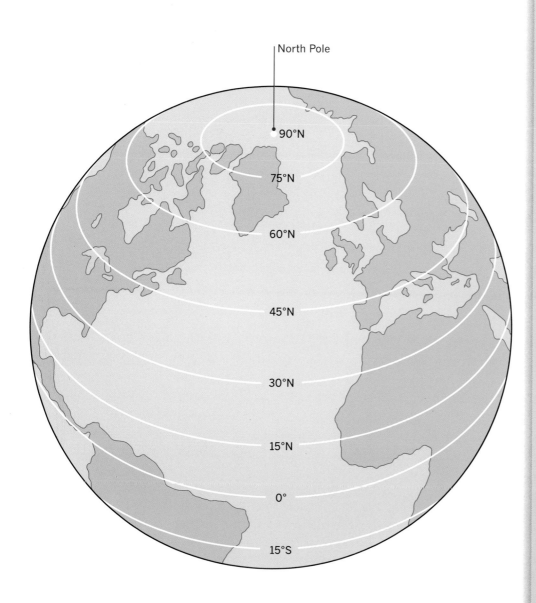

North Pole

90°N
75°N
60°N
45°N
30°N
15°N
0°
15°S

© Diagram Visual Information Ltd.

© Diagram Visual Information Ltd.

Longitude

Key words

equator	line of longitude
Greenwich	longitude
meridian	meridian
hemisphere	prime meridian
international date	time zone
line	

Lines of longitude

● *Longitude* is an angular measurement describing distance east or west of a north–south line known as the "prime meridian."

● The prime meridian is an arbitrary line running between the North and South poles that was designated the line of zero degrees longitude at an international conference in 1884. It is also known as the "Greenwich meridian" because it runs through Greenwich, England.

● The longitude of a location is a measure of the angle that its meridian makes with the prime meridian at the center of Earth and in the plane of the equator.

● A longitude measurement always falls into the range zero degrees (on the prime meridian) to 180 degrees east or west.

● Each degree of longitude may be subdivided into 60 "minutes." Minutes are usually expressed to one or two decimal places. For example 46°50.5' E(ast) or W(est). Minutes were formerly subdivided into 60 "seconds."

● All points at a given longitude are said to constitute a "line of longitude." Lines of longitude are also known as "meridians."

● Lines of longitude are perpendicular (at right angles) to lines of latitude.

● One degree of longitude varies from 0 miles (0 km) at the poles to 69 miles (111 km) at the equator.

● Earth spins on its axis once every 24 hours, so all 360 degrees (180 degrees east plus 180 degrees west) of longitude pass beneath the Sun each day. One hour of time is therefore considered equivalent to 15 degrees of longitude, and the world's time zones are based on this equation.

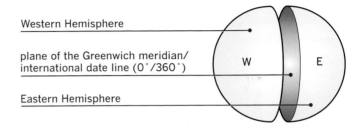

Western Hemisphere

plane of the Greenwich meridian/ international date line (0°/360°)

Eastern Hemisphere

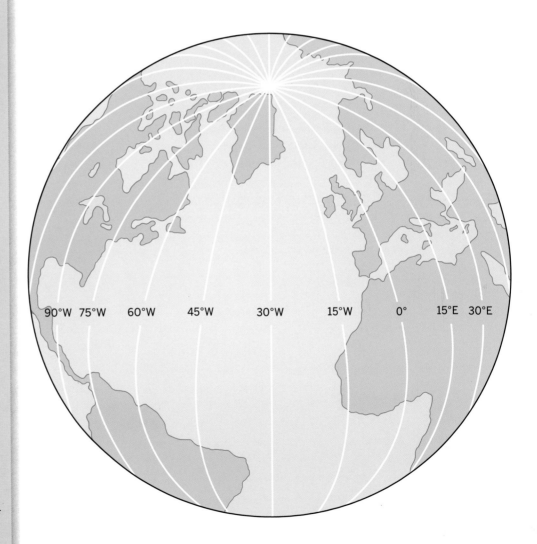

90°W 75°W 60°W 45°W 30°W 15°W 0° 15°E 30°E

Modern navigation

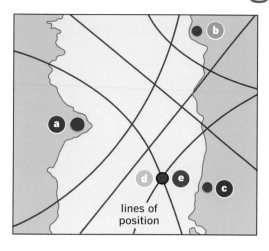

LORAN system

a Master station

b Secondary station 1

c Secondary station 2

d Intersecting radio signals

e Vessel's position

lines of position

Key words

Global
Positioning   radio direction
  System (GPS)   finding
radar

LORAN

- *LORAN* (from "LOng RAnge Navigation") is used by ships approaching land from the sea. A receiver onboard ship compares radio signals sent from one or two "master" stations and two "secondary" stations on land. The ship's position is the point where the relative signals intersect, and is marked on a chart.
- The system has a maximum range of about 2,000 miles (3,200 km) and is accurate to within 50 yards (45 m).

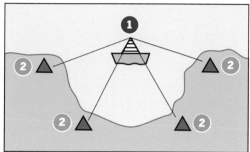

Radio direction finding (RDF)

1 Loop aerial

2 Beacons

Radio direction finding (RDF)

- Radio waves can be considered to travel on a straight-line axis and can be used like a line-of-sight bearing.
- As a ship's radio receiver's aerial is rotated, the intensity of radio signals from beacons increases and decreases relative to the bearings of the beacons.
- By recording the bearings of two or more land-based radio beacons, a ship's position fix may be obtained.
- The range of RDF is less than that of LORAN.

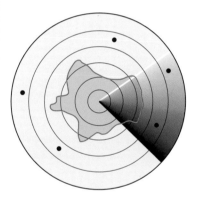

Radar

Radar

- This system is based on transmitting radio signals toward an object and detecting the signals that bounce back.
- The time interval between transmission and reception of signals gives a measure of distance.
- Reflected signals can also be displayed on a screen, giving the direction and distance of the object from the ship, and acting as an aid that helps to avoid collisions.

Satellite systems

- In the TRANSIT system, electronic equipment onboard a ship measures the change in frequency of radio signals from orbiting satellites as they move toward or away from the ship. It is based on the "Doppler Effect," just as the sound of an emergency vehicle's siren changes pitch with motion toward or away from the hearer. Navigation computers fix the ship's position by analyzing signals from several satellites. This system is accurate to within 100 yards (90 m).

- Global Positioning System (GPS) satellites constantly broadcast their position and time. Computerized receivers on vessels analyze the data from at least three different satellites to pinpoint the ship's position with an accuracy of about 66 feet (20 m).

Satellite systems: GPS

1 Satellite 1

2 Satellite 2

3 Satellite 3

4 Broadcast signals

5 Vessel's position

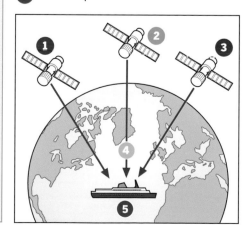

© Diagram Visual Information Ltd.

Early diving apparatus

© Diagram Visual Information Ltd.

Key words

diving bell
diving suit

Diving equipment

- The earliest diving equipment consisted of nothing more than a rock and a rope. Divers would tie a rope around their waist and reach the bottom by holding on to a heavy boulder. No air was supplied to these divers—they simply held their breath. Sponge divers in the Mediterranean and pearl divers in the Indian Ocean still use this technique.

- Historians are not sure when specialized diving equipment was first used. According to legend, Alexander the Great used a diving bell to visit the seabed in the fourth century BCE.

- The origin of diving suits is also obscure. According to manuscripts, suits with air hoses running to the surface were in use in the 15th century. It is not known if these suits were practical or even if they were ever actually used.

- The first documented use of a diving bell came in 1690 when Edmund Halley designed an open-bottomed chamber, supplied with air from the surface, that was tested at 60 feet (18 m) for 90 minutes.

- The first true diving suit was made by German engineer Augustus Siebe in about 1837. Early diving suits were made of waterproofed canvas or leather, often strengthened with wooden hoops inside, and the helmet was metal (usually copper) to withstand water pressure.

- Later, suits were "armored" to enable them to withstand water pressure at greater depths. These suits were made entirely of steel or other high tensile materials.

1430

This illustration of a diving suit from an anonymous manuscript is one of the earliest to show the use of a flexible air hoses that would enable the diver to stay submerged for extended periods. The staring eyes may represent glass goggles that would allow clearer vision underwater. This diver appears to be involved in salvaging valuable cargo.

1680

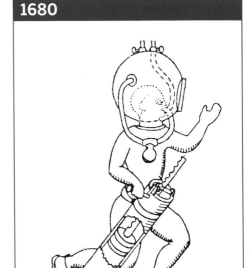

This design shows important developments in the evolution of the modern diving suit. Air from the surface is piped into a rigid, metal helmet. There are also two pipes running to the surface—one for inhaling, and one for exhaling. Lastly, the diver has webbed footwear to make locomotion through the water easier.

c. 1837

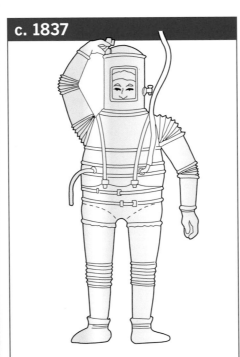

Although not the first armored diving suit, this design was the first to include articulated joints. It also incorporated weighted boots to prevent the diver from floating off the bottom. Articulation proved to be a difficult problem to solve since it introduces weak points to the suit at the joints.

1914

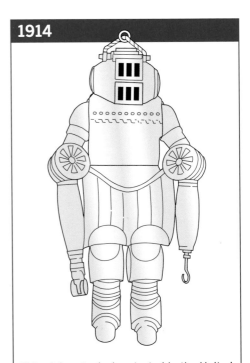

This elaborate design, tested in the United States, is one of many developed at the beginning of the 20th century to solve the problems of resistance to high pressure and articulation. The joints are massively armored and the body is designed to provide maximum pressure resistance.

Scuba diving apparatus

Scuba diver

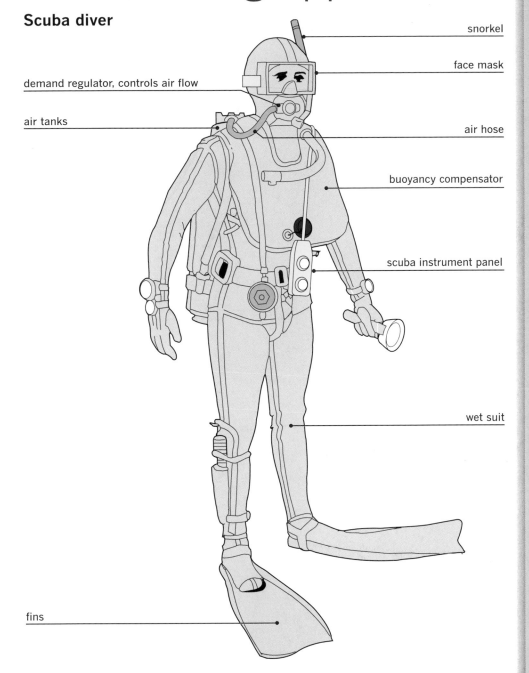

- snorkel
- face mask
- demand regulator, controls air flow
- air tanks
- air hose
- buoyancy compensator
- scuba instrument panel
- wet suit
- fins

Key words

aqualung
*decompression
 sickness*
diving suit

Scuba diving

- *Scuba* is an acronym of "Self-Contained Underwater Breathing Apparatus."
- A scuba diver wears metal tanks that hold compressed air. They supply air to the diver at the same pressure as the surrounding water pressure. The diver uses air more quickly at deeper depths.
- The diver exhales used air into the water.
- British inventor William James made the first scuba unit in 1825, but Frenchmen Jacques-Yves Cousteau and Emile Gagnan did not develop the aqualung used today until 1942.

Risks and limits

- There are risks associated with scuba diving including: injury to the lungs caused by over-expansion during rapid ascent, nitrogen narcosis, and decompression sickness.
- These can easily be avoided if divers dive safely within agreed dive plans.
- Recreational or sport divers dive to a maximum depth of 130 feet (42 m) and use nondecompression diving.

How a scuba unit works

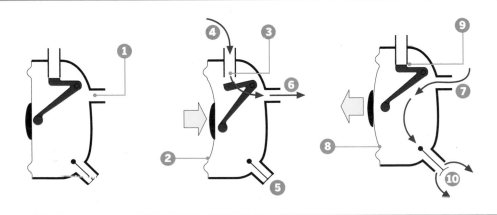

1. Diver breathes in via mouthpiece.
2. Flexible diaphragm pulled inward, pushing inlet valve 3 open.
3.
4. Air from tanks enters.
5. Exhaust valve closed.
6. Air reaches diver.
7. Diver breathes out.
8. Diaphragm pushed back, allowing inlet valve 9 to close.
9.
10. Exhaust valve pushed open, releasing used air.

© Diagram Visual Information Ltd.

Rebreathing apparatus

© Diagram Visual Information Ltd.

Key words

aqualung
diving suit
rebreather

Rebreathers

● A *rebreather* is a form of scuba equipment that recycles the air breathed out by the diver instead of expelling it into the water.

Scuba breathing (open circuit)

a Tank contains air.

b Diver inhales air.

c Diver exhales air with increased carbon dioxide content into water.

Rebreather (closed circuit)

d Tank **1** contains air.

e Tank **2** contains pure oxygen.

f Diver inhales air.

g Diver exhales air with increased carbon dioxide content.

h Carbon dioxide is removed from exhaled air by "scrubber" compound (e.g., soda lime).

i Oxygen from tank **2** is added to exhaled air and the diver rebreathes exhaled air.

Rebreather advantages

● Lighter and less cumbersome.
● Allows longer safe-dive time.
● No bubbles means better visibility for underwater filming and is less liable to scare underwater sea creatures.

Rebreather disadvantages

● Expensive.
● Complex mechanism that needs more maintenance.
● Defective devices can cause the diver to breathe the scrubber compound.

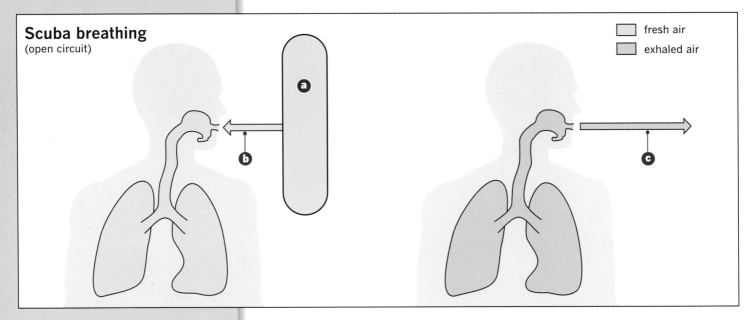

Scuba breathing
(open circuit)

fresh air
exhaled air

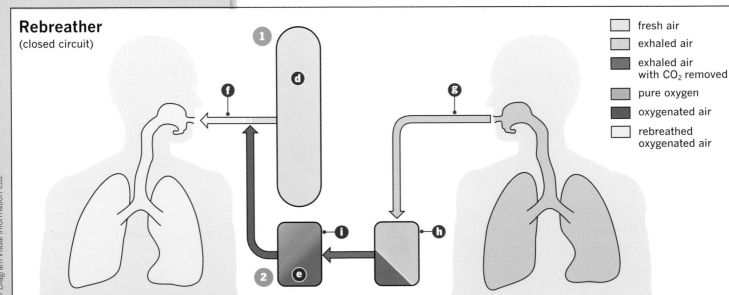

Rebreather
(closed circuit)

fresh air

exhaled air

exhaled air with CO_2 removed

pure oxygen

oxygenated air

rebreathed oxygenated air

Modern deep-sea diving

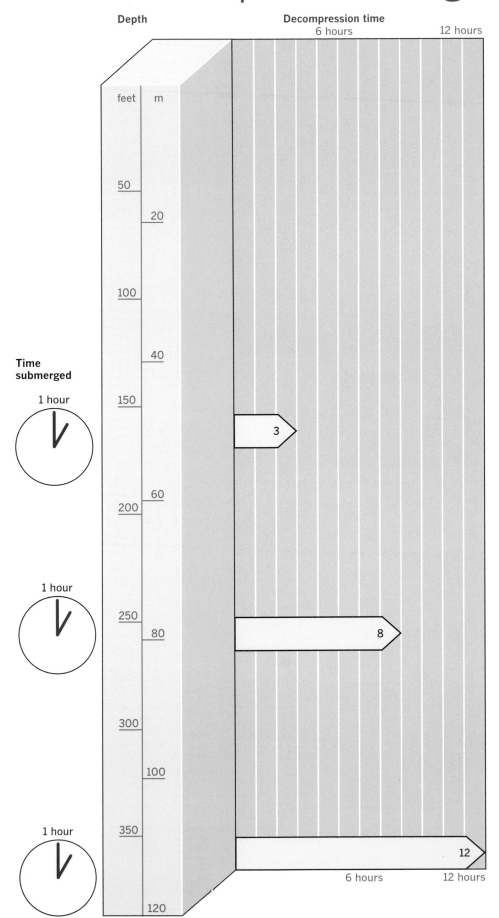

Depth

Decompression time

6 hours   12 hours

feet   m

50
20

100

Time submerged

40

1 hour

150

3

60

200

1 hour

250

80

8

300

100

1 hour

350

12

120

6 hours   12 hours

Key words

heliox   (ROV)
hyperbaric diving
remotely
  operated
vehicle

The petroleum industry

- Modern deep-sea diving is particularly important in the petroleum industry, where divers are needed to inspect and repair underwater pipelines, or perform other tasks that cannot yet be carried out by remotely operated vehicles (ROVs).
- Deep-sea diving is a high risk, but therefore well-paid occupation, using cutting-edge science and technology.

Onshore research

- Before deep dives are made, extensive research is carried out into the effects of the extreme pressures and necessary decompression times for such dives. This research is carried out onshore in compression/decompression chambers at "hyperbaric" diving research centers.
- There are major hyperbaric centers at Duke University Medical Center, Durham, NC; Marseilles, France; Hamburg, Germany; Bergen, Norway; Toronto, Canada; and elsewhere.

Equipment

- Diving suits are usually made of canvas, and helmets of copper or fiberglass, which is more lightweight. For very deep dives, suits are armored.
- Special mixtures of gas, such as hydrox (hydrogen and oxygen), and heliox (helium and oxygen), are used for deep dives. The hydrogen or helium replaces atmospheric nitrogen, which is toxic at high pressures.
- Hoses from the surface supply breathing gas, hot water to warm the diving suit, electricity or high-pressure air (pneumatics) to operate tools, gases for welding tools, and cables for voice links and video equipment.

© Diagram Visual Information Ltd.

© Diagram Visual Information Ltd.

Key words

diving bell
nuclear
  submarine
submarine
submersible

Submersibles

- A *submersible* is any type of vehicle that travels underwater.
- A *submarine* is a shiplike submersible that mainly has military uses. Other submersibles are vessels for exploring the ocean depths.

Diving bells

- In the 1620s, Dutchman Cornelius van Drebbel built a wooden rowboat covered with waterproof hides that was used as the first true submersible.
- The diving bell was also developed at this time.

Early submersibles

- The first propeller-driven submarine was invented in 1776 by American David Bushnell.
- Called *The Turtle*, it was a wooden, egg-shaped vessel, weighted at the bottom, in which the single passenger turned crankshafts by hand to rotate the propellers.

Fulton's *Nautilus*

- In 1800, American Robert Fulton built the *Nautilus*, a 21-foot (6.4 m) long copper-covered vessel that was a sailboat on the surface, but which, with the sails removed and the hatch covered over, became a submarine.

Powered submersibles

- In 1875, American John Philip Holland developed *Holland I*, a metal-hulled one-man manually propelled craft that was 16 feet (5.3 m) long, 2 feet (0.6 m) deep, and 20 inches (50 cm) wide. Holland later developed a 53-foot (16 m) long submarine powered by gasoline and electric batteries.
- Britain launched the first diesel-powered submarine in 1908.
- The world's first nuclear submarine, *Nautilus*, was built in the United States in 1955.

Historical submersibles

Diving bells

Early submersibles

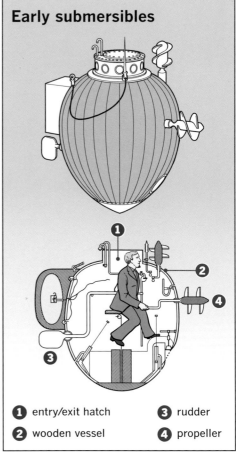

1. entry/exit hatch
2. wooden vessel
3. rudder
4. propeller

Fulton's *Nautilus*

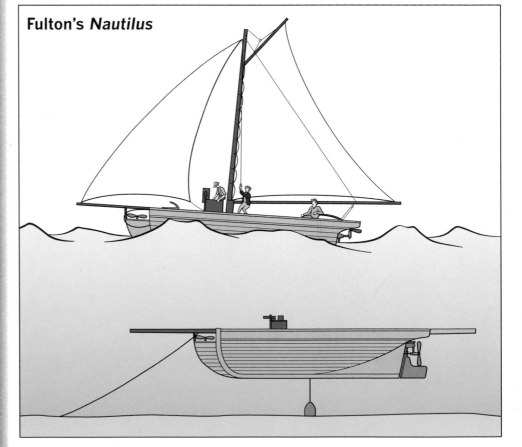

Modern submarines

Nuclear submarine

Key words

autonomous underwater vehicle (AUV)

nuclear submarine

remotely operated vehicle (ROV)

submarine

submersible

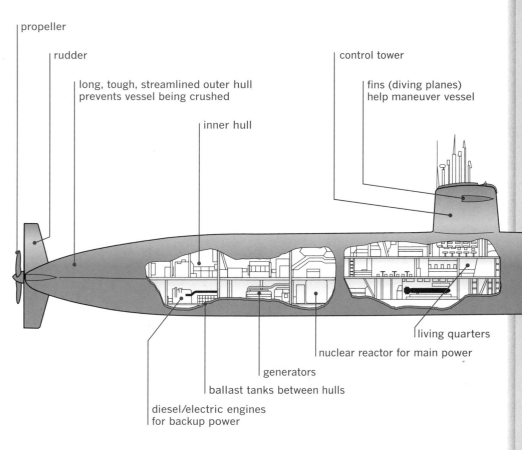

propeller

rudder

long, tough, streamlined outer hull prevents vessel being crushed

inner hull

control tower

fins (diving planes) help maneuver vessel

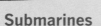

living quarters

nuclear reactor for main power

generators

ballast tanks between hulls

diesel/electric engines for backup power

Modern submersibles

● Today's nuclear submarines are used by the military, and deep-sea submersibles are used for scientific research and exploration.

● Deep-sea submersibles include both remotely operated vehicles (ROVs) and autonomous underwater vehicles (AUVs).

Submarines

● Modern submarines range in length from 200–600 feet (61–183 m) and are about 30 feet (9 m) in width. They have a crew of up to 200 and can stay submerged for months at a time.

● The fastest submarines can reach speeds of 45 knots (51 miles per hour; 83 kmph) and can dive to depths in excess of 2,600 feet (800 m).

Descending and ascending

● Ballast tanks are usually filled with air.
● To descend, the tanks are flooded with seawater.
● To ascend, compressed air is used to push out the water.

Descent

valves open— air pushed out

valves open— tanks fill with water

Ascent

compressed air pumped in

valves closed

valves open— water forced out

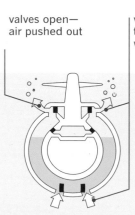

© Diagram Visual Information Ltd.

© Diagram Visual Information Ltd.

Key words

hydrothermal vent	remotely operated vehicle (ROV)
nuclear submarine	

Deep-sea submersibles

- Vehicles capable of submerging beneath the surface of the sea, moving under their own power, and then re-emerging at will, were first conceived as weapons of war.
- In 1963 the *Thresher*, a U.S. Navy nuclear submarine, sank in 8,000 feet (2,400 m) of water in the Atlantic, killing all onboard. When it was realized that there was no vehicle capable of making a rescue attempt at that depth and that the majority of the seafloor was unknown to science there was a great impetus to design and build deep-water research vehicles.
- The U.S. Navy built two submersibles capable of rescuing submarine crews at depths as great as 5,000 feet (1,500 m). The *Deep Submergence Rescue Vehicle-1* (*DSRV-1*) *Mystic* was launched in 1970, and the *DSRV-2 Avalon* in 1972.

Alvin

- *Alvin* is a crewed submersible built by the U.S. Navy and usually operated by the Woods Hole Oceanographic Institution. It is also known as *Deep Submergence Vehicle 2* (*DSV 2*).
- Launched in 1964, it has made more than 3,500 dives reaching depths of 13,120 feet (4,000 m).
- *Alvin* carries a crew of three and can be fitted with a wide array of sensory and recording equipment.
- The submersible is often used in association with the remotely operated vehicle (ROV) *Jason*.
- In 1966 *Alvin* was used to locate and recover a nuclear weapon lost in the Mediterranean Sea.
- In 1977 scientists on board *Alvin* made the first studies of hydrothermal vents and hydrothermal vent communities in the deep Pacific.
- In 1985–86 *Alvin* was used extensively in the exploration of the wreck of the *Titanic*.

Crewed submersibles

Crewed submersible *Alvin*

External view

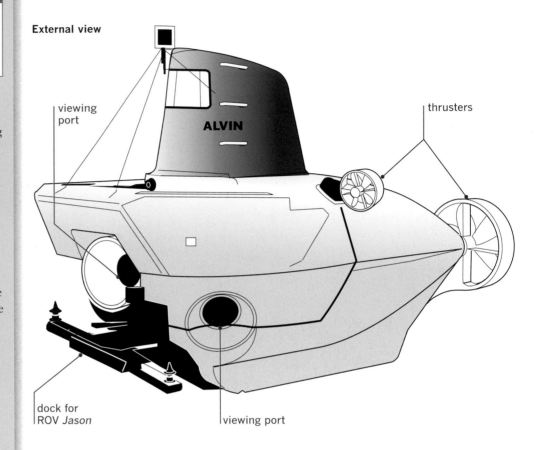

viewing port

thrusters

ALVIN

dock for ROV *Jason*

viewing port

Cross section

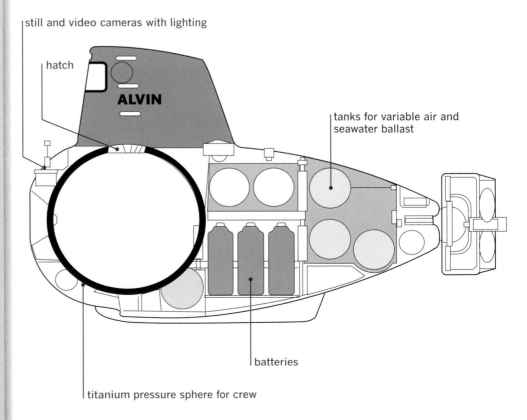

still and video cameras with lighting

hatch

ALVIN

tanks for variable air and seawater ballast

batteries

titanium pressure sphere for crew

Uncrewed submersibles

Remotely Operated Vehicle *Jason*

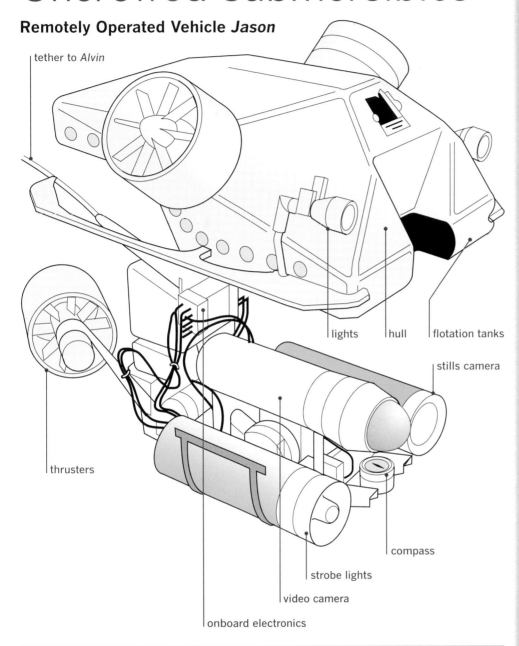

tether to *Alvin*

lights

hull

flotation tanks

stills camera

thrusters

compass

strobe lights

video camera

onboard electronics

Key words

autonomous
underwater
vehicle (AUV)

remotely
operated
vehicle
(ROV)
submersible

Remotely Operated and Autonomous Vehicles

- There are two varieties of uncrewed submersible used in underwater exploration—remotely operated vehicles (ROVs) and autonomous underwater vehicles (AUVs).

ROVs

- ROVs are robotlike submersibles smaller than crewed underwater vehicles.
- They have greater maneuverability than crewed vehicles and are able to stay submerged for longer.
- Instruments able to record temperature, chemical, and light intensity data can be mounted on ROVs as well as lights, video cameras, sonar instruments, and manipulators.
- They are tethered to a surface vessel or a crewed submersible via a cable that enables a remote pilot to control the vehicle and enables data to be transmitted live to observers.

Jason

- The ROV *Jason* is a highly successful vehicle operated by the Woods Hole Oceanographic Institution.
- It was developed in the early 1980s and in 1985–86 it was used in conjunction with the crewed submersible *Alvin* to explore the wreck of the *Titanic* in deep waters of the North Atlantic.

AUVs

- AUVs are the latest development in deep-sea exploration technology.
- They are self-contained and fully autonomous.
- Once programed they can submerge and carry out repetitive measurement over a large area for long periods.
- Because they are untethered, AUVs are able to penetrate confined spaces, such as caves or the interior of wrecked hulls.

Autonomous Benthic Explorer (*ABE*)

- *ABE* is an autonomous underwater vehicle (AUV) operated by the Woods Hole Oceanographic Institution.

- *ABE* has conducted surveys of the seafloor at depths of 7,200 feet (2,200 m). It is capable of making pre-programed repeated measurements over a long period of time.

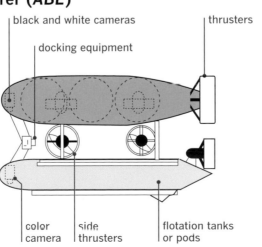

black and white cameras

docking equipment

thrusters

color camera

side thrusters

flotation tanks or pods

© Diagram Visual Information Ltd.

© Diagram Visual Information Ltd.

Key words

autonomous underwater vehicle (AUV)	remotely operated vehicle (ROV)
diving suit	submersible

Scuba diver
- Maximum depth: 656 feet (200 m)
- Has no protection against high pressure.

Deep-diving suit
- Maximum depth: 1,476 feet (450 m)
- Pressurized, self-contained suit with articulated limbs and manipulators.

Nuclear submarine
- Maximum depth: 3,280 feet (1,000 m)
- Actual operating depths and survivable depths are military secrets.

Alvin
- Maximum depth: 14,763 feet (4,500 m)
- U.S. crewed submarine with titanium pressure hull.

Seacliff II
- Maximum depth: 19,684 feet (6,000 m)
- Crewed U.S. submersible.

Jason
- Maximum depth: 19,684 feet (6,000 m)
- Uncrewed U.S. remotely operated vehicle.

Shinkai 6500
- Maximum depth: 21,325 feet (6,500 m)
- Crewed Japanese submersible; deepest diving crewed vehicle currently in operation.

Kaiko
- Maximum depth: 35,797 feet (10,911 m)
- Uncrewed Japanese remotely operated vehicle reached this depth in 1995.

Trieste
- Maximum depth: 35,802 feet (10,912 m)
- Crewed vehicle; made the deepest ever dive, to Challenger Deep—the deepest known point of the Mariana Trench in the Pacific—in 1960.

Submarine vehicles

Maximum operating depths

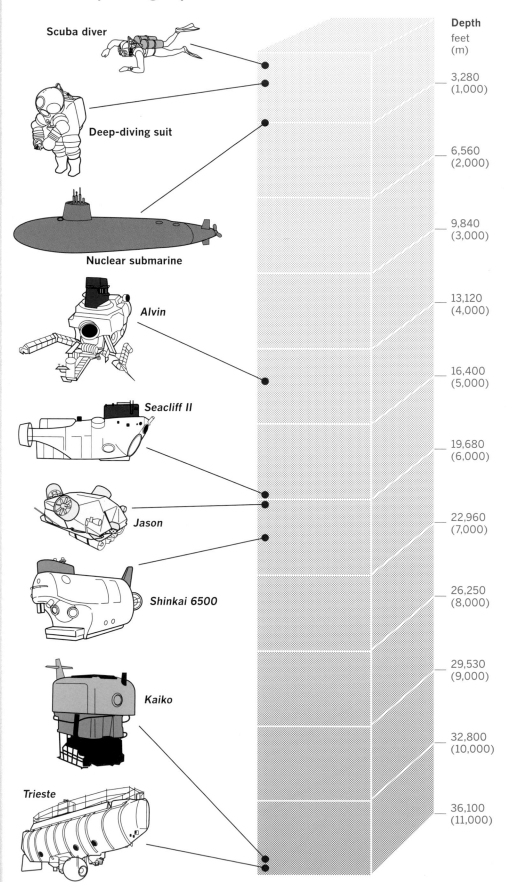

Scuba diver

Deep-diving suit

Nuclear submarine

Alvin

Seacliff II

Jason

Shinkai 6500

Kaiko

Trieste

Depth feet (m)
3,280 (1,000)
6,560 (2,000)
9,840 (3,000)
13,120 (4,000)
16,400 (5,000)
19,680 (6,000)
22,960 (7,000)
26,250 (8,000)
29,530 (9,000)
32,800 (10,000)
36,100 (11,000)

Satellite technology

Measuring ocean roughness

1 Satellite

2 Microwave radiation

3 Sea surface

4 Scatterometer picks up reflected microwaves

Measuring sea surface slope

1 Satellite (in position for first measurement)

2 Microwave radiation

3 Sea surface

4 Altimeter picks up reflected microwaves

5 Satellite (in position for second measurement)

Key words

active sensing
passive sensing
remote sensing
satellite

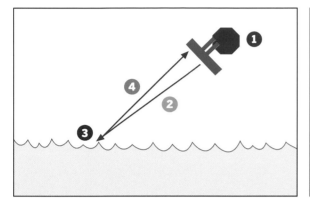

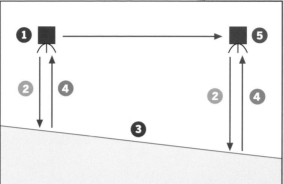

Remote sensing

- Satellites can carry equipment that pick up signals or radiation from the surface of Earth to create global pictures so that large-scale phenomena may be observed.

- Satellite sensing allows areas that are otherwise inaccessible to be observed, for example mid-oceans, deserts, mountain tops, and areas around Antarctica and the Arctic during winter.

- Remote sensing satellites rely on electromagnetic radiation to convey information. There are three distinct wavebands of electromagnetic radiation that are not fully absorbed or scattered by the atmosphere, and these are the foundation of remote sensing. The "spectral windows" involved are the visible waveband, parts of the infrared waveband, and microwaves, which include radar.

- Remote sensing satellites orbit Earth at altitudes ranging from 300 miles (480 km) to 22,400 miles (36,000 km).

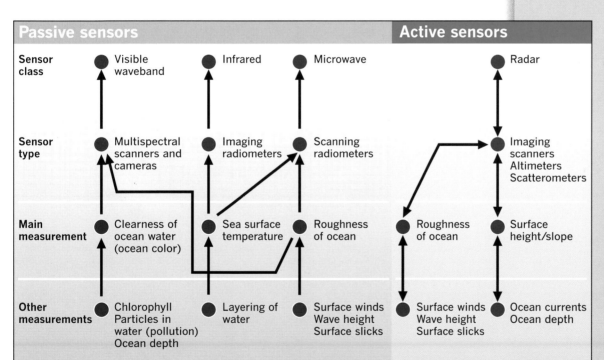

Passive sensing

- Passive remote sensing detects natural radiation from the surface of the land and sea. This includes visible, infrared, and microwave radiation.

- Sensors include cameras, scanners, spectrometers, and radiometers.

Active sensing

- Active sensing satellites transmit electromagnetic radiation to Earth's surface then detect its reflection. They use only microwave radiation, which includes radar.

- Sensors include imaging scanners, altimeters, and scatterometers.

© Diagram Visual Information Ltd.

© Diagram Visual Information Ltd.

Key words

active sonar
passive sonar
sonar

Sonar techniques

- *Sonar* is an acronym of "SOund NAvigation and Ranging."
- It refers to the use of sound to discover the location and distribution of underwater objects or features.
- It can also be used to generate underwater images and measure the speed of objects.
- Sound can be used in this way because it travels more efficiently through water than it does through air. Radar does not work well in water.
- There are two main types of sonar—*passive sonar* and *active sonar*.

Passive sonar

- Passive sonar detects sound waves given off by objects. It involves listening to underwater sounds from marine mammals, such as whales, or from submarines or other underwater vessels.
- Ancient mariners used to listen to whale song through the hulls of their ships, but it was not until WWI that a simple underwater microphone was made to listen out for enemy subs.
- Passive sonar can primarily determine the direction of objects. Submersibles and submarines mainly use passive sonar as it does not reveal their position underwater.

Active sonar

- With active sonar, sound is emitted into the ocean in short bursts or "pings" and the reflections detected.
- The distance to an object is calculated from the echo transmission and return interval and the speed of sound in water (about 1 mile per second; 1.6 km/s).
- Active sonar is more often used by surface ships than submersibles.

Sonar techniques

Passive sonar

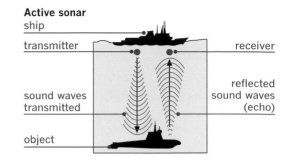

Active sonar

Types of active sonar

Echo sounders

- Weak, high-frequency pings are used to discover distances from objects.
- Echo sounders are suspended from ships, lowered onto the sea from helicopters, or attached to buoys, which transmit the recordings by radio to ships or shore stations.

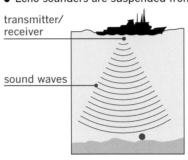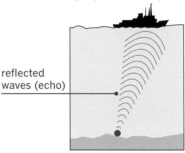

Seismic reflection profilers

- These mostly use high-energy, low-frequency explosives to create sound waves, which are reflected from rock layers in the seabed. They can find the thickness of rock beds and indicate the type of rock.

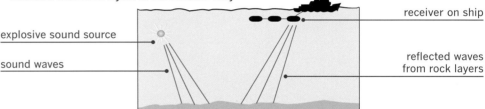

Side-scan sonars

- These cameras build up a picture or image of surfaces or objects. They are used to map the topography of the seabed.
- Strips of seabed up to 37 miles (60 km) wide and 16,400 feet (5,000 m) long can be mapped at a time.
- Side-scan sonar can also be used to study fish populations, including their size, number, and species.

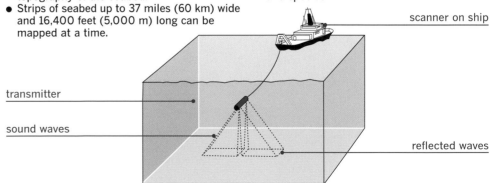

Acoustic Doppler Current Profilers (ADCPs)

- These systems became a widely used oceanographic tool in the 1980s. They use sound to measure current direction and speed by making use of the doppler shift. Sound waves change in pitch if the water through which they are traveling is in motion. The size and direction (up or down) of the shift can be used to calculate current speed and direction. ADCPs are either mounted on the bottom of a ship, or anchored to the seabed.

World fish catch

Ranking of fishing zone catches, 2003
Million tons (million tonnes)

1 Pacific, Northwest 24.14 (21.90)

2 Pacific, Western Central 11.84 (10.74)

3 Pacific, Southeast 11.61 (10.53)

4 Atlantic, Northeast 11.32 (10.27)

5 Indian Ocean, Eastern 5.89 (5.34)

6 Indian Ocean, Western 4.71 (4.27)

7 Atlantic, Eastern Central 3.63 (3.29)

8 Pacific, Northeast 3.22 (2.92)

9 Atlantic, Northwest 2.56 (2.32)

10 Atlantic, Southwest 2.27 (2.06)

11 Pacific, Eastern Central 2.06 (1.87)

12 Atlantic, Western Central 1.94 (1.76)

13 Atlantic, Southeast 1.92 (1.74)

14 Mediterranean and Black Sea 1.62 (1.47)

15 Pacific, Southwest 0.77 (0.70)

16 Atlantic, Antarctic 0.14 (0.13)

17 Indian Ocean, Antarctic 0.01 (0.01)

18 Pacific, Antarctic 0.002 (0.002)

Key words

fishing zone

Fishing zones

● For the purposes of economic analysis, the world's total fishing production is divided into oceanic fishing catch zones by the United Nations Food and Agriculture Organization (FAO).

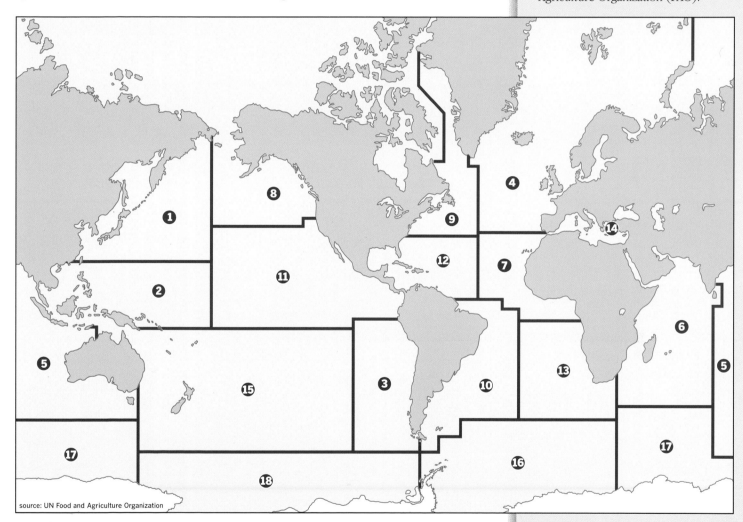

source: UN Food and Agriculture Organization

Worldwide catches from marine fisheries
Million tons (million tonnes)

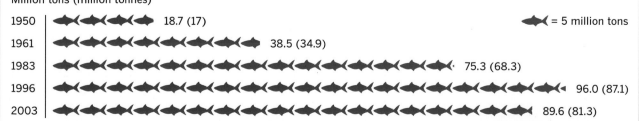

Year	Catch
1950	18.7 (17)
1961	38.5 (34.9)
1983	75.3 (68.3)
1996	96.0 (87.1)
2003	89.6 (81.3)

= 5 million tons

© Diagram Visual Information Ltd.

© Diagram Visual Information Ltd.

Key words

fishing zone
fish stocks
overfishing

Fish in the world food supply

- The United Nations Food and Agriculture Organization (FAO) estimates that fish provides 20 percent of total protein intake for half the world's population.
- Demand is constantly increasing with an ever-growing world population.
- Much of the production that meets this demand is now made by aquaculture (both inland and marine), since the world's natural fish stocks have been drastically reduced by overfishing in the latter part of the twentieth century.

Overfishing

- Overfishing can be defined as occurring when so many fish are being caught in an area that there are not enough fish left to breed and produce replacements.
- In terms of economics, overfishing can occur before this level of negative growth is reached, if the increased cost of fishing is not matched by a continual increase in the quantities of fish available to be caught.

1 31% Under or approaching full exploitation

2 44% Fully exploited; likely to become over-exploited

3 16% Over-exploited; catches likely to fall

4 6% Depleted; rapid fall in catches evident

5 3% Recovering slowly from depletion

World fish stocks

Northwest Atlantic
million tons
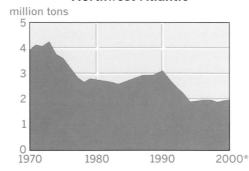

Northeast Atlantic
million tons
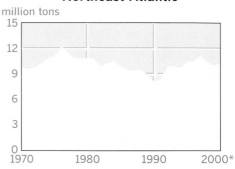

Eastern Central Atlantic
million tons
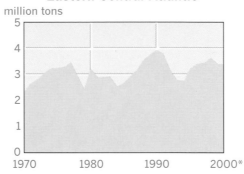

Southeast Atlantic
million tons
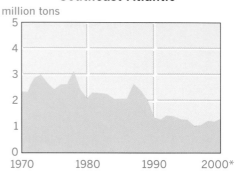

Northwest Pacific
million tons
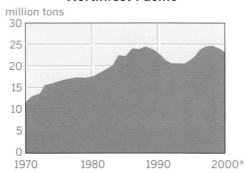

Northeast Pacific
million tons
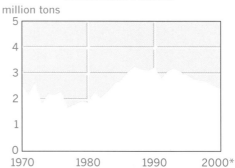

Western Central Pacific
million tons
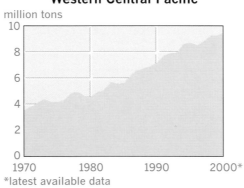

*latest available data

Southwest Pacific
million tons
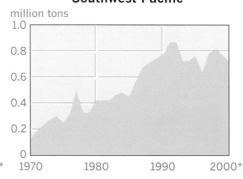

Status of world fish stocks

Aquaculture

Key words

aquaculture
mariculture

Aquaculture

- *Aquaculture* is defined by the United Nations as the farming of aquatic organisms, including fish, mollusks, crustaceans, and aquatic plants.
- Farmed stocks are included in aquaculture statistics only if they are owned, cultivated, and harvested exclusively by an individual or corporation.
- *Mariculture* is aquaculture that takes place exclusively in a marine environment.
- Aquaculture is an increasingly important source of the world's food supply, particularly for developing nations. According to the Food and Agriculture Organization of the United Nations (FAO) aquaculture provided 3.9 percent of global fish supplies in 1970 and 29.9 percent in 2002.
- Aquaculture production has grown at an average rate of 8.9 percent per year since 1970. This compares to an annual growth rate of 1.2 percent for capture fisheries and 2.8 percent for farmed meat production on land.
- China dominates world aquaculture, producing many times more fish than the rest of the world put together.

a

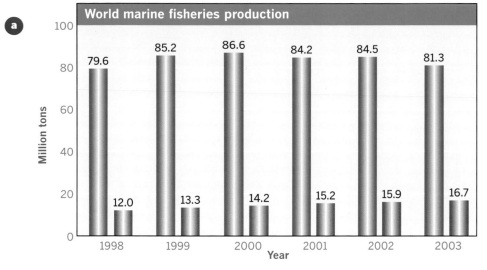

World marine fisheries production

b

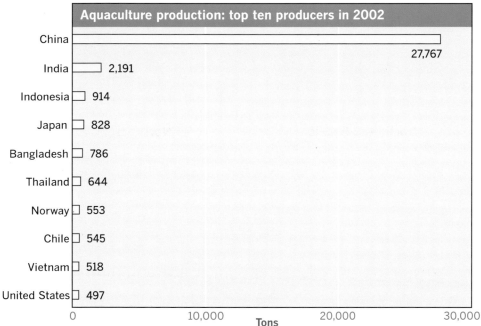

Aquaculture production: top ten producers in 2002

Country	Tons
China	27,767
India	2,191
Indonesia	914
Japan	828
Bangladesh	786
Thailand	644
Norway	553
Chile	545
Vietnam	518
United States	497

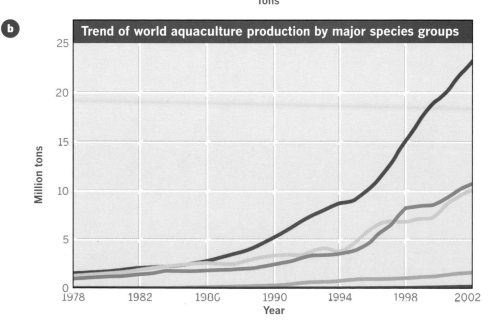

Trend of world aquaculture production by major species groups

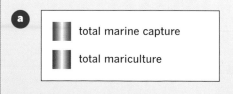

a
- total marine capture
- total mariculture

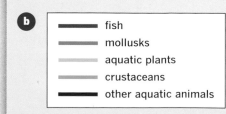

b
- fish
- mollusks
- aquatic plants
- crustaceans
- other aquatic animals

© Diagram Visual Information Ltd.

© Diagram Visual Information Ltd.

Key words

whaling

Commercial whaling

- Commercial whaling was begun in the first or second century CE by the Japanese.
- In Europe, the Basques and Norwegians began whaling between 800 and 1000 CE.
- By the 18th century, whaling had spread to most of the world's oceans.
- Modern whaling began in the middle of the 19th century with the introduction of rocket-powered harpoon guns and faster, steam-powered vessels.
- In the 20th century factory-ship whaling reduced many populations of whales to near extinction and eventually resulted in a total worldwide ban on commercial hunting.
- Catches of the five most commonly hunted whales rose steadily during the 20th century.
- Depletion of whale numbers and international agreement caused a sharp downturn in hunting in the mid-1970s.
- An international moratorium on commercial whaling was agreed in 1982 and came into effect in 1986.
- Today the moratorium is still in place. Small numbers of whales are allowed to be hunted for scientific research only, and some traditional subsistence cultures are granted a small catch allocation. No commercial whaling has taken place since 1986.
- At the beginning of the 21st century large areas of the world's oceans are whale sanctuaries.
- Japan and Norway have repeatedly requested that the ban on commercial whaling be lifted. To date, neither have managed to secure the two-thirds majority of the International Whaling Commission needed for such a decision.

Decline of whaling

Whale catches (1900–86*)
*No commercial whaling has taken place since 1986

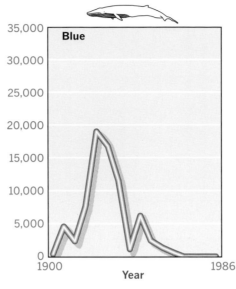

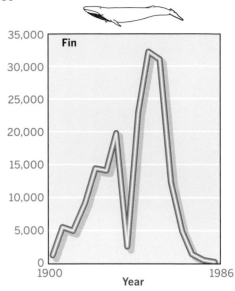

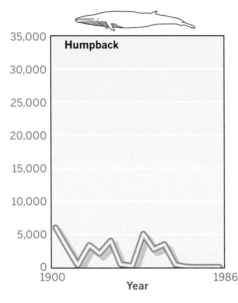

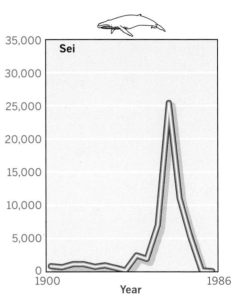

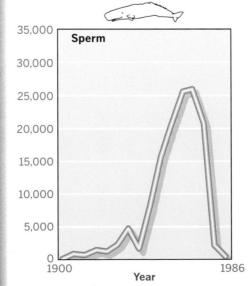

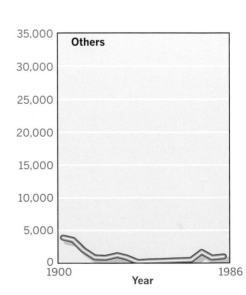

Mineral wealth

Minerals dissolved and suspended in seawater

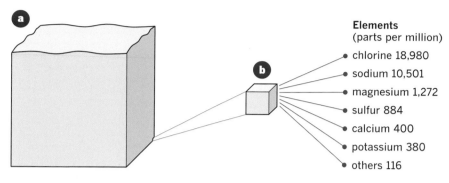

Elements
(parts per million)

- chlorine 18,980
- sodium 10,501
- magnesium 1,272
- sulfur 884
- calcium 400
- potassium 380
- others 116

Elements in seawater

a 1,000,000 gallons of seawater

b Proportion of dissolved and suspended elements

Sediments and deposits on the ocean floor

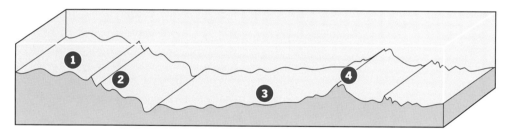

Minerals on the ocean floor

1 Continental shelf—heavy metals, sands, and gravels

2 Continental slope—sands and gravels, gas hydrates in polar regions

3 Abyssal plain—manganese nodules, gas hydrates

4 Mid-ocean ridge—metal sulfide deposits

Sediments and deposits in rocks beneath the ocean floor

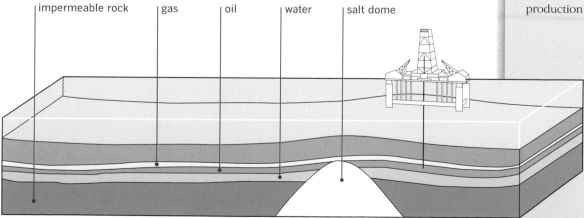

impermeable rock | gas | oil | water | salt dome

Key words

abyssal plain	mid-ocean ridge
continental shelf	mineral
continental slope	sediment
manganese nodule	

Minerals in seawater

- Seventy-three of the 93 naturally occurring elements are found in seawater in measurable amounts.
- Sodium chloride (salt), magnesium, and bromine are the most commonly extracted substances.
- Iodine in seawater is naturally concentrated in seaweed, which can then be harvested by people.

Sediments and deposits

- Manganese nodules represent a huge untapped source of manganese, cobalt, and other elements.
- Gold, diamonds, and other heavy elements are concentrated in shallow waters by the sorting action of waves.
- Large quantities of potentially exploitable metal sulfides are present around hydrothermal vents on mid-ocean ridges.
- Gas hydrates are a potentially huge source of energy.
- Ore-bearing sands and gravels are abundant in shallow seas.

Beneath the ocean floor

- Oil and gas deposits beneath the ocean floor are believed to be at least as plentiful as those so far discovered on land.
- Salt and sulfur are also mined from deposits beneath the ocean floor.
- A growing proportion of oil and gas production comes from offshore sites.

© Diagram Visual Information Ltd.

© Diagram Visual Information Ltd.

Key words

desalination
mineral

Desalination

- *Desalination* is the process of removing salts and minerals from water to obtain freshwater.
- In parts of the world where there is little freshwater but cheap fuel, such as the oil-rich Middle East, desalination processes can be economically viable.
- Multiple flash distillation is the most commonly used process.
- Desalination by freezing is also being researched and icebergs have been identified as a potential source of freshwater.
- Desalination is carried out in more than 100 countries. Saudi Arabia accounts for 24 percent of the world's desalination capacity.
- Desalination is often more ecologically desirable than extracting freshwater from sources deep underground, but it can produce hypersaline waste water that can harm marine environments.

Extracting salt

- Separating salt from seawater by evaporation has been carried out by people for thousands of years.
- Salt can also be extracted from seawater by freezing, but the process is expensive in its use of power.
- The separation of salt from seawater by evaporation in the past has left vast underground deposits of salt, which are exploited today by mining.

Magnesium and bromine

- Magnesium is a light metal used in anti-corrosion alloys and munitions.
- Bromine is used in medicine, photography, dyes, and metallurgy—70 percent of the world's bromine comes from the oceans.
- Magnesium and bromine are extracted from seawater by chemical processes.

Exploiting seawater

Flash distillation process

1 Seawater enters the first condenser, which has low pressure and a temperature up to 140°F (60°C), where it boils instantly.

2 Seawater is pumped into a second chamber with a temperature of 160°F (71°C).

3 Seawater enters a third chamber with a temperature of 180°F (82°C).

4 As the steam loses heat it condenses as pure water, which runs off and is collected.

5 Hypersaline water (seawater with a large part of pure water distilled out) is pumped out to sea.

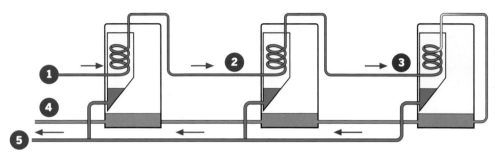

Salt evaporation process

1 Seawater is pumped into shallow pools known as pans.

2 Sunshine and wind evaporate the seawater.

3 Calcium carbonate and calcium sulfate settle out of the seawater.

4 The brine is moved to a second pool where sodium chloride (salt) settles out.

5 More brine is pumped in until a thick deposit of salt can be harvested from the bottom of the pan.

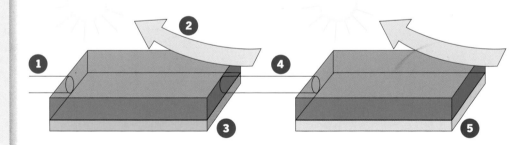

Magnesium extraction process

1 Seawater is mixed in a vast tank with lime so that magnesium hydroxide settles out.

2 Magnesium hydroxide is filtered off and treated with hydrochloric acid to produce magnesium chloride.

3 An electrolytic cell separates dissolved magnesium chloride into pure magnesium and chlorine.

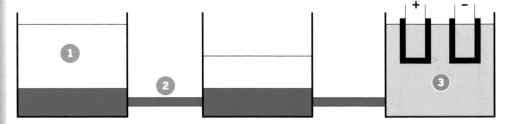

Mining for aggregates

Distribution of exploited aggregates

Key words

aggregate
dredging

- △ gold and diamonds
- ● tin
- ■ other minerals

North America

Europe

Asia

Africa

South America

Australia

Aggregates

- Coarse and fine sediments laid down as sands and gravels are currently the most profitable and widely exploited resources from the ocean floor.
- They are found close to land in shallow waters off the continental shelf.
- Sand and gravel for use in the manufacture of concrete is the most common form of aggregate mining from the seabed.
- Sands rich in aragonite, a compound used in glass and cement production, are dredged in huge quantities from the seas off the Bahamas.
- Tin-rich ores are dredged from the waters around Southeast Asia.
- Barium sulfate is dredged from waters off the coasts of Sri lanka.
- Gold, diamonds, and other heavy minerals are concentrated in shallow waters by the sorting action of waves, but it is rarely economically viable to recover them by dredging.

Dredging

- Dredging is the most common method of recovering valuable resources from the seabed, but it is also carried out for other reasons.
- Dredging is necessary to keep many of the world's most important estuaries open to shipping.
- Very large-scale dredging operations have been used to create new land for development in crowded areas such as Hong Kong and Japan.

Shallow dredging operation

1. dredging vessel
2. mineral-rich sediment
3. boom lowered into the water
4. continuous chain of buckets to collect sediment
5. conveyor belt to deliver sediment onto barges

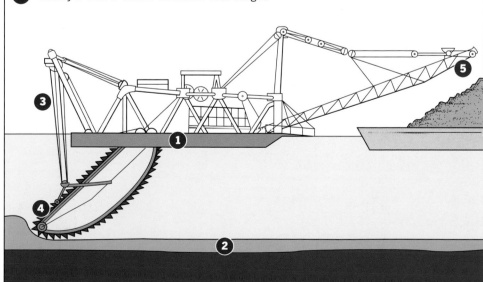

© Diagram Visual Information Ltd.

© Diagram Visual Information Ltd.

Key words

gravimeter
magnetometer
oil rig
sound wave

Methods of offshore oil exploration

General geologic survey

- The known or theoretically inferred geology of the seabed enables geologists to determine the areas worth investigating for oil.
- Aircraft or surface vessels with extremely sensitive equipment are able to detect changes in local gravity (gravimeter) or magnetic fields (magnetometer) that indicate the general nature of the seabed.

Detailed geologic survey

- Sound waves from underwater explosions or releases of high pressure air travel through strata of the seabed and rebound off deep, hard rock.
- Vessels with trailing sonar devices pick up these sound waves and analyze them to determine the presence of features associated with oil and gas deposits.

Test drilling

- A mobile test drilling rig is brought in if the geology is promising.
- The definite presence of oil cannot be determined without test drilling.
- If oil is found in commercial quantities a permanent drilling rig may be erected to exploit the site.

Demand for oil

- World demand for oil is rising steadily. It is unlikely that major new reserves will be found onshore so this demand will have to be met from offshore sources. Oil companies continue to spend billions of dollars in the search for offshore oil reserves.

Oil exploration

Methods of offshore oil exploration

General geologic survey

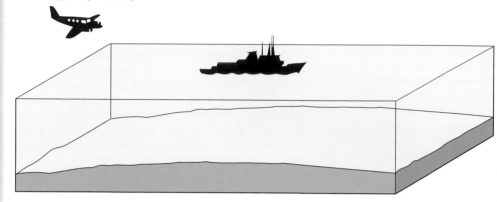

Detailed geologic survey

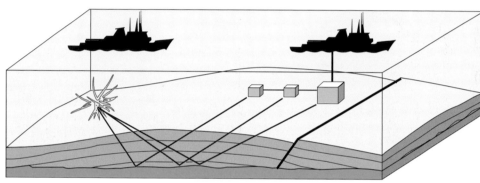

Test drilling

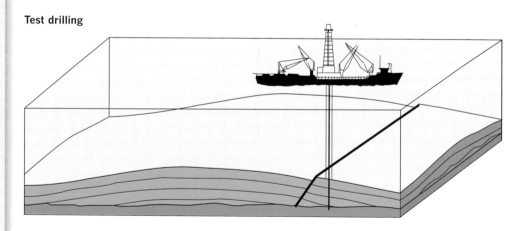

Projected world oil demand
(Million barrels per day)

1995 (69.9)
2000 (77.8)
2005 (83.2)
2010 (90.2)
2025 (121)

Offshore drilling

Jack-up rig **Fully-floating rig** **Gravity platform**

Key words

fully-floating rig
gravity platform
jack-up rig
oil rig

Drilling rigs

- There are two main classes of offshore drilling rigs: exploratory and permanent.
- Exploratory rigs are mobile and their test drills are used to identify the presence of oil deposits.
- If the exploratory rig finds significant deposits, a permanent rig may be brought in to exploit it long-term.

Jack-up rig

- A jack-up rig is free-floating and may have a shiplike hull.
- Once in position to drill, three or four telescopic legs are extended down to the seabed.
- When drilling is finished the legs are retracted and the rig can be towed to a new site.
- The jack-up rig is able to operate in water depths up to 300 feet (100 m).

Fully-floating rig

- A fully-floating rig is mounted on a free-floating, self-powered hull.
- Once in position, several computer-controlled motors all around the vessel keep it on station.
- When drilling is finished the vessel moves to another site under its own power.
- The fully-floating rig is able to operate in waters deeper than 350 feet (120 m).

Gravity platform

- The gravity platform rig is towed to station and then lowered into position. It is not moved once it has started production.
- The sheer weight of its legs and ballast section keeps the rig in position.
- The ballast section may also be used for temporary oil storage.
- Oil may be taken ashore by tankers or a permanent pipeline.
- The gravity platform is able to operate in water depths up to 500 feet (150 m).

© Diagram Visual Information Ltd.

© Diagram Visual Information Ltd.

Key words

estuary	wave power
thermal energy	
tidal power	
tide	
tropical	

Tidal power

- Tidal power stations exploit the predictable daily rise and fall of tides.
- To be economically viable a tidal power station needs to be placed in a bay or estuary with a tidal range greater than 15 feet (3 m).
- As the tide rises, water flows into the estuary through open gates in the power station dam.
- **1** At high tide the gates are closed, creating a large reservoir of water.
- **2** The gates are opened and the pent-up water flows out through electricity-generating turbines in the dam.

Wave power

- It is estimated that energy equivalent to a 50 megaton nuclear explosion is released onto the world's coastlines by waves every day.
- Many designs for machines to harness this power have been built and tested.
- A typical design takes advantage of the rising and falling motion of a wave:
- **1** Water rises in a closed column, forcing air up, which then turns an electricity generating turbine.
- **2** Water falls in the column, sucking air back down and causing it to turn the turbine again.

Thermal energy

- The oceans absorb and store huge quantities of solar energy.
- Thermal energy plants are feasible in tropical regions where the temperature differential between warm surface water and the cold deep water is more than 36°F (20°C).
- Warm water at the surface is used to vaporize liquid ammonia, which then drives electricity-generating turbines.
- The ammonia is condensed using cold water at a depth of 2,000–3,000 feet (600–1,000 m).
- The liquid ammonia is returned to the vaporizing chamber and the cycle is repeated.

Energy from the oceans

Tidal power

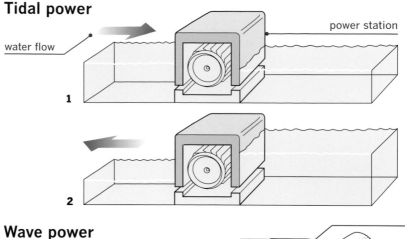

water flow
power station

1

2

Wave power

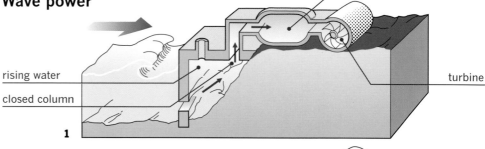

forced air

rising water
closed column
turbine

1

2

Thermal energy

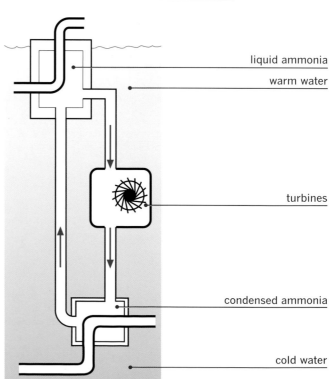

liquid ammonia
warm water
turbines
condensed ammonia
cold water

Shipping industry

Major shipping routes

▬▬▬	over 250 million tons
▬ ▬ ▬	100–250 million tons
•••••	30–100 million tons

Key words

container ship   supertanker
Lighter Aboard
  Ship (LASH)
oil tanker
shipping

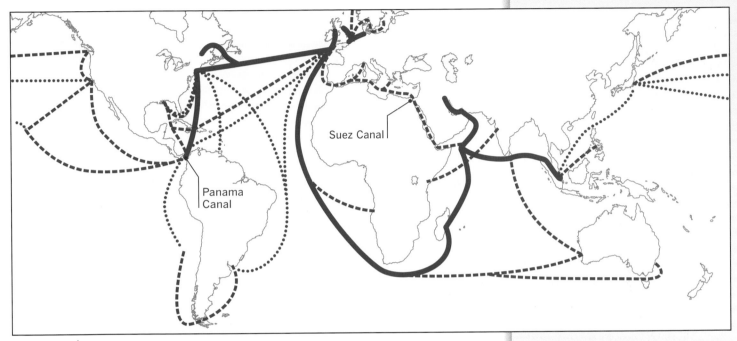

Panama Canal

Suez Canal

Container Ship
● Transports pre-packed metal containers 20 feet by 8 feet by 8 feet (6 m x 2.5 m x 2.5m).
● Typically able to carry over 1,000 containers giving a total capacity of 10,900 tons.
● Loading and unloading to and from trains and trucks is by crane.

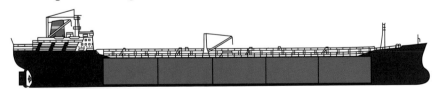

Supertanker
● Transports liquid cargo (usually oil).
● Hull space is divided into separate holds with an overall capacity of more than 450,000 tons.
● Loading and unloading is achieved with pumps.

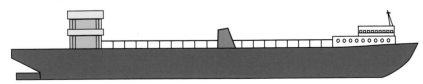

Lighter Aboard Ship (LASH)
● Transports pre-packed barges (lighters) each containing over 300 tons of cargo.
● Typically able to carry 70 to 90 barges giving a total capacity of up to 27,000 tons.
● Barges are loaded and unloaded directly from the water using a traveling crane on the vessel.

Shipping routes
● The most used routes connect the United States with Europe, and both with the oilfields of the Middle East.
● During the closure of the Suez Canal (1967–75) due to the Arab–Israeli conflict, much larger oil tankers were built to make the longer journey to the Middle East oilfields cost-effective. Many oil tankers and cargo vessels are now too large to use the Suez Canal and are forced to take the long route around southern Africa.
● About 13,000 transits of the Panama Canal are made each year, but many modern vessels are also too large to use this waterway.
● There are about 90,000 registered cargo vessels on the world's oceans (2003). About 11,000 of these fly the flag of the United States.
● Rotterdam, Netherlands has the world's busiest port (by volume).
● The busiest port in the United States (by volume) is the port of South Louisiana.

© Diagram Visual Information Ltd.

Key words

abyssal hills Low hills on the seafloor.

abyssal plain The deep and mostly flat region that makes up most of the seafloor.

abyssal zone The seabed of the deep ocean.

abyssopelagic zone The deep, lightless ocean between about 12,000 and 20,000 feet (3,660–6,100 m).

active sensing Sensing that involves transmitting sound, radar, radio, or other waves and the detection of reflections.

active sonar Sonar that detects artificially produced sound waves reflected from objects in the ocean.

adaptation The adjustment of an organism or population to its environment through genetic changes.

aeolian transport Movement by wind.

aggregate A collection of granular material.

agnathan A jawless fish.

algae A large and diverse group of plantlike organisms capable of photosynthesis.

alluvial fan A fan-shaped accumulation of alluvium or sediment usually at the mouth of a river estuary.

anadromous Fish that spend most of their adult lives in a marine environment but breed in freshwater.

anaerobic Not requiring oxygen.

annelid A worm with a cylindrical segmented body.

Antarctic The region south of the Antarctic Circle.

Antarctica The continent within the Antarctic Circle.

Antarctic Circle A line of latitude at 66.5°S.

aphotic zone The ocean below a depth of about 100 feet (30 m) where no sunlight penetrates.

aquaculture The farming of aquatic organisms.

aqualung Breathing equipment used by divers.

Arctic The region north of the Arctic Circle.

Arctic Circle A line of latitude at 66.5°N.

arthropod A member of a large, diverse group of invertebrate animals characterized by segmented bodies and jointed legs.

asthenosphere A partially molten layer of rock immediately below Earth's crust.

atmosphere Earth's envelope of gases.

atmospheric fallout Particles introduced to the atmosphere by volcanic activity or storms that later fall to the surface of Earth or into the ocean.

atmospheric pressure The pressure created by the atmosphere. At sea level atmospheric pressure is about 14.7 pounds per square inch (1.033 kg/cm²).

atoll A ring of coral reef around a subsiding volcanic island. It encloses a lagoon.

authigenesis The spontaneous crystallization of sediment within the water column.

autonomous underwater vehicle (AUV) A robotic vehicle used for deep sea exploration.

bacteria Single-celled organisms that break down the waste materials or bodies of other dead organisms.

bacterioplankton Bacteria that live as plankton.

baleen whale Whales with horny slats instead of teeth that are used to filter plankton from the water.

bar (1) A unit of pressure equal to about one atmosphere. (2) A sandy or muddy ridge across the mouth of a bay or estuary.

bar-built estuary A type of estuary with a sandy or muddy barrier across its mouth.

barrier island An island close to a shoreline formed from sediment.

barrier reef A reef that follows a shoreline and is separated from it by a deep lagoon.

basin A major depression in Earth's surface that contains a sea, an ocean, or part of an ocean.

bathyal zone The seabed of the continental slope.

bathypelagic zone The mid-depth region of the open ocean between about 3,300 and 12,000 feet (1,000 and 3,600 m).

bay A region of the ocean close to and semi-enclosed by land. Usually smaller than a gulf.

bay-head beach A beach in a bay that is largely protected from erosion by headlands.

benthic realm The region near or at the bottom of the ocean regardless of depth.

benthos Organisms that live on or near the bottom of the ocean regardless of depth.

biogenous sediment Sediment that has a biological origin, such as the bodies of dead sea creatures.

biogeochemical cycle The interaction of biological, geological, and chemical processes.

biogeographical zone A region of the ocean that can be defined by the kind of organisms that live there.

biological capture The removal of major ions from seawater by living organism.

bioluminescence The production of light by living organisms.

biosphere The entire volume of Earth's land, air, and ocean that supports or is capable of supporting life.

black smoker A form of hydrothermal vent that emits dark, mineral-saturated water at high temperatures.

blowhole A passageway connecting the roof of a sea cave with the surface of the land above.

bony fish A fish that has a skeleton composed completely of bone.

bottom water Seawater at or near the bottom of the water column.

boulder beach A beach with a belt of shingle and boulders at the base of a cliff.

breaker A wave that breaks into foam on a shore.

brown algae A class of algae that are predominantly brown in color.

calcareous sediment Sediment composed of calcium carbonate usually from the shells of living organisms.

calving The separation of icebergs from a glacier.

carbon cycle The continuous circulation of carbon through the biosphere, hydrosphere, lithosphere, and atmosphere.

© Diagram Visual Information Ltd.

cartilaginous fish A fish that has a skeleton completely composed of cartilage.

catadromous Fish that spend most of their adult lives in a freshwater environment yet breed in the ocean.

cetacean A marine mammal such as a whale, dolphin, or porpoise.

chaetognathan Free-swimming wormlike plankton.

chemosynthesis The process by which chemical energy is used by organisms to make organic compounds from inorganic compounds.

chlorophyte A green alga.

Chondrichthyes The class of cartilaginous fish.

climate The average weather condition for a location over an extended period of time.

cnidarian A marine animal such as a jellyfish, coral, or sea anemone.

coast The region of land influenced by sea.

coastal erosion Erosion of the coast by wave action and currents.

coastline The line that divides an environment in which marine processes are dominant from an environment in which terrestrial processes are dominant.

cold current A current carrying water that is colder than the surrounding water temperature.

cold seep A location where cold water infused with minerals, hydrocarbons, or other compounds flows into the ocean from beneath the seafloor.

cometary theory The theory that the majority of the water in the ocean came from comets.

container ship A freight ship that transports standardized containers.

continental crust The outermost layer of Earth that makes up the landmasses.

continental drift The theory that the continents travel across Earth's surface under the influence of plate tectonics.

continental margin The region of a continent that lies beneath the ocean.

continental rise The gentle slope at the bottom of the continental slope consisting of material that has slid down from the continental slope.

continental shelf The shallow seafloor that extends from the shore to the edge of the continental slope.

continental slope The steep slope that descends from the continental shelf to the abyssal plain.

convergence A region where water masses with different properties (for example temperature) merge.

convergent boundary The boundary between two masses of water with different properties.

coral Marine invertebrate organisms that build reefs.

coral reef A calcium carbonate platform composed of the exoskeletons of generations of coral polyps.

Coriolis effect The tendency for ocean currents and winds to be deflected to the west by the eastward rotation of Earth.

cosmogenous sediment Sediment that originates from meteorites.

crest The highest point of a wave.

crust The outer surface of Earth.

crustacean A group of arthropod marine invertebrates that includes crabs, lobsters, and shrimps.

current A consistent flow of water in the same direction. Currents may be on the surface or deep in the ocean.

decompression sickness A potentially fatal condition that occurs if a diver ascends too rapidly from a deep high-pressure environment.

deep scattering layer (DSL) Horizontal bands at different depths in the ocean that scatter sound. They are caused by concentrations of marine organisms as they migrate through the water column.

depth zone A division of the water column according to depth.

desalination The removal of salts from seawater.

diel vertical migration (DVM) The daily migration of marine organisms through the water column.

diffuse vent A hydrothermal vent that emits heated water across a wide area rather than at a single site.

disphotic zone The depths in the water column to which minimal sunlight is able to penetrate.

dissolved organic material (DOM) Organic material in solution in seawater.

diurnal tide A tide that results in one high tide and one low tide in the same day.

divergent boundary The boundary between two lithospheric plates that are moving away from each other. Usually a mid-ocean or spreading ridge.

diving bell A simple diving chamber filled with pressurized air and open to the water at the bottom.

downwelling Sinking surface water.

dredging The mechanical removal of sediment.

earthquake The energy released by a sudden movement in Earth's crust.

echinoderm One of a group of simple marine animals that includes starfish, sea urchins, and sea cucumbers.

echolocation The use of sound to sense the physical environment.

eddy A rapidly rotating current.

Ekman spiral The tendency for the Coriolis effect to deflect the direction of a current created by winds through a greater and greater angle as depth increases.

Ekman transport The net movement of oceanic surface water resulting from the Coriolis effect.

element One of the 92 naturally occurring substances that are not combinations of other substances.

El Niño An occasional warming of sea surface temperatures across the Pacific Ocean.

epipelagic zone The top layer of the open ocean down to a depth of about 300 to 700 feet (90–210 m).

epiphyte A nonparasitic plant that grows on the surface of another plant.

equator An abstract line around the middle of Earth midway between the North and South poles. The line of latitude at 0°.

© Diagram Visual Information Ltd.

KEY WORDS

erosion The movement of material from one area to another by the action of the ocean, running water, precipitation, ice, or wind.

estuary Where a river meets the sea.

euphotic zone The shallow top layer of the ocean that receives sufficient sunlight for photosynthesis to occur.

eustasy Referring to sea level measured from the center of Earth rather than with reference to any coastline.

evaporation A change in state from a liquid to a gas.

evolution The gradual development of different species.

exoskeleton A hard protective shell of an organism.

fair-weather waterspout A waterspout that forms in association with thunderstorms rather than tornadoes.

fault A fracture in Earth's crust.

fauna The animal life of a region.

fetch The influence of the wind on wave height over a period of time across a stretch of water.

finger rifting A series of small fissures in sea ice that form when one ice floe is forced under another.

fishing zone An administrative area used to measure quantities of fish caught.

fish stocks The quantity of fish available for fishing.

fjord An estuary with a U-shaped cross section formed when seawater floods a valley carved by a glacier.

floe A flat portion of free-floating ice of any size.

flora The plant life of a region.

food chain A sequence of organisms where each member is food for the next member higher in the chain.

food web An interrelated complex of food chains.

frazil Individual ice crystals floating on the sea.

fringing reef A coral reef along a coast that is not separated from the shore by a lagoon.

frond The leaflike part of a seaweed.

fully-floating rig An oil rig that floats.

gas hydrate A crystalline solid composed of gas and water molecules.

geoid The shape that the Ocean's surface would have if there were no perturbing forces such as tides, winds, or currents. Dips and bumps in the surface of this shape are due to local variations in gravity caused by the uneven density of the crust, core, and mantle beneath.

geostrophic current A current produced by Earth's rotation and the Coriolis effect.

geostrophic gyre A circular current produced by Earth's rotation and the Coriolis effect.

glacial sediment Sediment deposited by a glacier.

glacier A large, flowing mass of ice that moves from highlands down toward the sea.

Global Positioning System (GPS) A navigation system that uses signals from orbiting satellites.

global warming A sustained rise in average temperatures across Earth.

Gondwana A supercontinent thought to have existed on Earth between 180 and 100 million years ago, composed of the landmasses that now mainly comprise the continents of the Southern Hemisphere.

gravimeter An instrument for measuring gravity.

gravity platform An oil rig that is held in place by its sheer weight.

grease ice An early stage in the formation of sea ice.

green algae Algae that are predominantly green.

greenhouse gas A gas that traps heat in the atmosphere.

Greenwich meridian Another name for the prime meridian or the line of longitude at 0°.

gulf A region of an ocean enclosed on three sides by land and usually larger than a bay.

guyot A flat-topped mountain under the sea.

gyre A roughly circular current.

hadal zone The very deepest part of the ocean extending to the bottom of the deepest trenches.

hard coral Coral polyps that excrete hard calcium carbonate exoskeletons.

headland A piece of land that protrudes into the sea.

heat capacity The amount of heat required to raise the temperature of a defined quantity of a pure substance by one degree celsius.

heat sink A body that adsorbs and stores heat.

heavy water Water containing a higher than usual concentration of deuterium.

heliox A mixture of helium and oxygen.

hemisphere A half of Earth, bisected at the equator to give the Northern and Southern Hemispheres, or through the poles, to produce the Eastern and Western Hemispheres.

high tide The maximum height reached by a rising tide.

holdfast A rootlike anchor that attaches a marine plant to a firm substrate.

holoplankton Organisms that spend the whole of their life cycle as plankton.

hot spot A weakness in Earth's crust where magma routinely upwells or erupts to the surface.

hydrocarbon An organic compound consisting of only carbon and hydrogen.

hydrocarbon seep An area on the seabed from which hydrocarbons seep into the water column.

hydrogen bonding The cohesive force between hydrogen, oxygen, iron, and nitrogen atoms.

hydrogenous sediment A sediment composed of minerals precipitated from seawater.

hydrosphere All the water on Earth in its liquid form.

hydrothermal vent Vents emitting heated, mineral-rich water on the ocean floor.

hyperbaric diving Diving to depths where pressure is significantly above atmospheric pressure.

hypersaline Having a salt content greater than average seawater (35 parts per thousand).

hyposaline Having a salt content less than average seawater (35 parts per thousand).

ice age A geological period of extensive glacial activity.

iceberg A massive piece of freshwater ice floating in the ocean that has broken away from a glacier.

ice cap A mass of ice that permanently covers an area.

© Diagram Visual Information Ltd.

infiltration The movement of water through a porous medium.

intermediate water Water at mid-depths in the ocean.

internal wave A wave that forms at the boundary of two layers of water with different properties.

international date line A line of longitude approximately antipodean with the Greenwich meridian, conventionally agreed as the starting point of each day.

interstitial space The gaps between grains of sediment.

intertidal zone The area of a shore between the average highest and lowest tides.

island arc A chain of volcanic islands.

island chain A line of islands associated with a geological feature, such as a trench or a hot spot.

isostasy The equilibrium state of lithospheric plates floating on the asthenosphere.

isotherm A line connecting points of the same temperature.

isthmus A narrow strip of land with water on either side connecting two larger areas of land.

jack-up rig An oil rig with legs that can be extended and retracted.

jawed fish A modern group of fish with jaws and paired fins.

jawless fish An ancient group of fish that lack jaws and paired fins.

kelp A family of large brown seaweed.

kelp bed An area in which many kelp plants are established.

keystone predator A predator that feeds on species that compete with each other. Removing a keystone predator results in a reduction in species diversity.

lagoon A shallow body of water separated from the open sea by a reef or a sandbar.

land bridge A stretch of land that allows land-based life to cross from one landmass to another.

larva A stage in an insect's or marine creature's life cycle before maturity.

latent heat of fusion The amount of energy absorbed during melting or lost during freezing.

latent heat of vaporization The amount of energy absorbed during vaporization, or lost during condensation.

latitude An angular measure of distance north or south of the equator.

Laurasia A supercontinent thought to have existed on Earth between 180 and 100 million years ago, composed of the landmasses that now mainly comprise the continents of the Northern Hemisphere.

Lighter Aboard Ship (LASH) A cargo ship that carries smaller, unpowered cargo vessels.

line of latitude A line connecting all locations at the same latitude.

line of longitude A line connecting all locations at the same longitude.

lithosphere All of the rock and nonbiological sediment on Earth.

lithospheric plate One of the solid, but distinct, segments that make up the outer surface of Earth.

lobe-finned fish (or sarcopterygians) An ancient group of fish including coelacanths, which have fleshy-lobed fins capable of supporting weight on land, and which may be the remote ancestors of land tetrapods.

longitude An angular measure of distance east or west of the prime meridian.

longshore current A current running parallel to a shore.

longshore drift A tendency for sediment to be carried along a shore by waves breaking at an angle to that shore.

lowland beach A broad, gently sloping sandy beach.

low tide The lowest height reached by a falling tide.

magma Molten rock beneath Earth's surface.

magnetometer An instrument for measuring magnetic fields.

mammal Any warm-blooded, vertebrate animal whose young are born live and nurtured on milk.

manganese nodule A small, roughly spherical nugget of metal that forms on the deep ocean floor.

mangrove A salt-tolerant tree that grows in the intertidal zone of some tropical and subtropical coasts.

mantle The interior of Earth below the solid crust and above the core.

mariculture The farming of marine organisms.

meiofauna Tiny animals that live in the spaces between grains of a sediment.

meridian Another name for a line of longitude.

meroplankton Organisms that spend only the larval stage of their life cycle as plankton.

mesopelagic zone The open ocean at depths between about 700 and 3,300 feet (210–1,000 m).

microbial loop The activities of marine bacteria and protozoa in breaking down organic detritus and making it available to a food chain.

micrometeorite A meteorite no larger than a particle of sand.

midnight Sun The seasonal polar phenomenon in which the Sun is above the horizon for 24 hours in a day.

mid-ocean ridge A chain of undersea mountains that usually marks the line of a spreading ridge.

migration The periodic or seasonal movement of animals from one location to another.

mineral A naturally occurring, inorganic crystalline solid.

mixed tide A tide with marked differences in the height of daily high and low tides.

molecular size The physical size of a molecule of a substance.

molecule A substance composed of two or more atoms held together by chemical bonds.

mollusk An invertebrate animal with a soft body, muscular foot, and a calcareous shell.

monsoon A wind system in which the prevailing wind direction reverses seasonally.

muddy shore A shore composed of sediment with particles no larger than 0.0025 inches (0.062 mm).

© Diagram Visual Information Ltd.

natural gas A naturally occurring mixture of hydrocarbons used as a fuel.

nautical mile A unit of distance equal to one minute of latitude 1.15 miles (1.85 km).

neap tide The tide with the smallest range between high and low tide. Neap tides occur twice per lunar month at most locations.

nekton All strongly swimming marine organisms capable of moving against currents.

nematode A roundworm.

nemertean A ribbonworm.

nilas A smooth thin layer of flexible sea ice.

nitrogen cycle The continuous circulation of nitrogen through the biosphere, hydrosphere, lithosphere, and atmosphere.

Northern Hemisphere The half of Earth north of the equator.

nuclear submarine A submarine with a nuclear power source.

nutrient Any substance that can be taken in by an organism to promote growth.

Ocean The continuous body of saltwater that covers about 70 percent of Earth's surface.

oceanic crust Earth's crust beneath the ocean.

offshore breeze A wind that blows from the land toward a body of water.

oil rig A platform at sea that supports the equipment needed to drill for and extract oil from the seabed.

oil tanker A vessel designed to carry oil.

onshore breeze A wind that blows from a body of water toward the shore.

orbital The circular path described by a water particle during the passage of a wave.

Osteichthyes A class of fish with skeletons composed partly of bone and partly of cartilage.

outgassing theory The theory that most of the oceans' water originated from gases that escaped from the primeval Earth and condensed in the atmosphere.

overfishing Fishing to the point where the population can no longer be sustained.

pancake ice Unconnected smooth edged discs of ice.

Pangaea The single landmass that is thought to have comprised all the dry land on Earth more than 180 million years ago.

Panthalassa The ocean that is thought to have surrounded Pangaea more than 180 million years ago.

parallel Another name for a line of latitude.

passive sensing Sensing that involves receiving sound or other waves emitted by objects.

passive sonar Sonar that detects sound waves emitted by objects in the ocean.

pelagic realm The open ocean away from coasts, continental shelves, and the ocean floor.

perigee The point in an orbit (e.g. the Moon's) that is closest to Earth.

petroleum A generic term for oil and oil products.

phaeophyte A brown alga.

phosphorus cycle The continuous circulation of phosphorus through the biosphere, hydrosphere, lithosphere, and atmosphere.

photophore An organ that produces bioluminescence.

photosynthesis The process by which plants use sunlight, water, and carbon dioxide to produce carbohydrates as food. Oxygen is a by-product.

phytoplankton Plankton that photosynthesize.

pinnipedia A group of marine mammals with four swimming flippers that includes seals and sea lions.

plankton All drifting or weakly swimming organisms in the water column that rely on currents for transport.

plate boundary The region where lithospheric plates meet and interact.

platyhelminth A flatworm, fluke, or tapeworm.

polar Refers to the regions of Earth north of latitude 66.5°N and south of latitude 66.5°S.

pollution Contamination by harmful substances.

polynya A wide split in an ice floe.

polyp An individual cnidarian.

poriferan A sponge.

precipitation All forms of solid or liquid water that fall from the atmosphere and reach Earth's surface.

prevailing wind A wind that blows more frequently from one direction over a given period.

primary producer An organism that forms part of the lowest link (trophic level) in a food chain.

prime meridian The line of longitude at 0°

protozoa The kingdom of single-celled animal-like organisms.

pycnocline A layer of the water column between the halocline and thermocline through which water density changes with depth.

radar A system that uses radio waves to detect and locate distant objects.

radiation Energy that is radiated or transmitted in the form of waves or particles.

radio direction finding A navigation system that involves fixed radio transmitters on the land.

ray-finned fish (or actinopterygians) The class that includes most modern species of fish, whose fins consist of skin webbed with spines.

realm A volume or area of the ocean within which conditions are similar.

rebreather Diving equipment that recirculates breathing gases instead of expelling them into the water.

red algae Algae with a predominantly red color.

red tide A discoloration of the sea surface caused by high concentrations of microorganisms.

reef A continuous stretch of rock or coral.

reef crest The top of the side of a reef that faces out to sea.

reef face The side of a reef that faces out to sea.

reef flat The edge of the side of a reef that faces the coast.

reef zone A region of a reef with distinct environmental conditions.

© Diagram Visual Information Ltd.

remotely operated vehicle (ROV) A robotic undersea exploration vehicle controlled by a remote operator.

remote sensing The collection of information about an object or event without having physical contact with it.

reptile All cold-blooded vertebrate animals that breathe air at all stages of their life cycles.

respiration The process by which living organisms take up oxygen from the environment and consume organic matter, releasing both carbon dioxide and heat.

rhodophyte A red alga.

rift valley A steep, flat-bottomed depression in Earth's crust. Common at mid-ocean ridges.

river valley A valley created by a river eroding the landscape.

rocky shore A shore dominated by solid rock or large rocky fragments.

runoff Precipitation, snow and ice melt, and all other water that flows from the land into the ocean.

salinity A measure of the quantity of dissolved salts in seawater.

salinometer An instrument for measuring salinity.

salt marsh A coastal wetland dominated by salt-tolerant grasses and other plants.

sand dune A mound or ridge of loose sand heaped up by the wind.

sandy shore A shore composed of sediment with particles in the size range 0.0025 to 0.08 inches (0.063–2.0 mm).

satellite A natural or artificial body in orbit around a planet or other celestial object.

sea A large region of an ocean usually bordered by or partially enclosed by land.

sea arch A natural arch in a headland.

seabird A bird that frequents marine environments.

sea cave A natural cave in a cliff face created by wave action.

seafloor spreading The slow, continual movement of oceanic crust away from a mid-ocean ridge resulting in the widening of an ocean.

seagrass One of a group of flowering marine plants.

sea ice Ice that forms from seawater.

sea level The mean altitude between high and low tides.

seamount A volcanic mountain with a peak that lies below sea level.

season A division of the year according to characteristic changes in climate.

seasonal vertical migration (SVM) The vertical migration of organisms through the water column during a specific season.

sea spray Droplets of seawater blown from the tops of waves.

sea stack A pillar of rock left separate from the mainland by the collapse of a sea arch.

seawater The mixture of water and various dissolved salts found in the ocean.

secondary producer An organism that feeds on primary producers and is in turn food for organisms at higher levels in a food chain.

sediment Fine grains of solid organic or nonorganic material suspended in or settled out of water.

seiche A standing wave in an enclosed body of water.

semidiurnal tide A tidal pattern that produces two high tides and two low tides each day.

shark An ancient group of fish with cartilaginous skeletons.

shelf break The top of a continental slope.

shipping The commercial transportation of goods by sea.

shore General term for the area of land adjacent to a body of water that is submerged at high tide and uncovered at low tide.

shore deposition The movement of sediment onto a shore by wave action or via a river.

shore slope The angle of a shore's slope.

siliceous sediment Sediment composed of silicon dioxide usually from the shells of living organisms.

sirenian General term for dugongs and manatees.

soft coral Coral polyps that do not excrete hard exoskeletons and therefore do not build coral reefs.

solvent A liquid in which other substances may be dissolved.

sonar (SOund NAvigation and Ranging) A system for detecting objects by the use of sound.

sound wave A wave that transmits sound.

spawning ground An area where a particular species of marine organism gathers to reproduce.

spit A low sandbank that extends into the sea.

sponge Any of a group of simple aquatic organisms that have porous structures and skeletons of thorny, interlocking fibers known as spongin.

spreading ridge An mid-ocean ridge where seafloor spreading is taking place.

spring tide The tide with the greatest range between high and low tide. Spring tides occur twice per lunar month at most locations.

standing wave (or **stationary wave**) A wave pattern produced by two waves with the same frequency and wavelength travelling in opposite directions.

strait A narrow strip of water bordered by land that connects two larger bodies of water.

strata Layers of rock.

subarctic Regions bordering the Arctic.

subduction The process of one lithospheric plate descending beneath another.

sublittoral zone The lowest part of the shore only exposed at the lowest tides.

submarine A vehicle capable of carrying a crew beneath or on the surface of the water.

submarine canyon A steep V-shaped trench in the seabed, usually in a continental shelf or slope.

submersible A vehicle capable of operating beneath the surface of the water.

© Diagram Visual Information Ltd.

subpolar The regions adjacent to the Arctic and Antarctic circles from latitudes 50°–70°N, and 50°–70°S respectively.

substrate The hard surface onto which organisms can attach themselves; the seabed.

subsurface current A current that moves water below the surface of the ocean.

subtidal zone The region of the marine environment that is just covered by seawater at low tide.

subtropical The regions adjacent to the Tropic of Cancer and the Tropic of Capricorn, from 35°–40°N, and 35°–40°S respectively.

supertanker The largest kind of oil tanker.

surface current A current that affects water near the top of the water column.

surface tension The tension of a liquid's surface due to the forces of attraction between its molecules.

surface water Water at or near the top of the water column.

swell Waves that have traveled out of the area in which they were generated.

tectonic estuary An estuary that is formed when seawater flows into an area that has subsided due to tectonic processes.

temperate The regions of Earth in which the climate undergoes seasonal changes of temperature and moisture. They lie primarily between 30° and 60° latitude in both hemispheres.

temperature gradient A change in temperature over distance.

terrigenous sediment Sediments formed from material that originated on land (continental crust material).

thermal energy Energy in the form of heat.

thermocline The narrow band in the water column where the temperature gradient is at its maximum.

thermohaline Referring to the combined effects of temperature and salinity.

tidal pool A depression in the intertidal zone that remains filled with seawater at low tide.

tidal power The generation of electricity from tides.

tidal wave The wave motion of the tides. Also another name for a tsunami.

tide The periodic rise and fall of sea level under the gravitational influence of the Moon and Sun.

time zone One of 24 regions of the globe loosely defined by longitude throughout which the same standard time is used.

tombolo An island connected to the mainland by a narrow bar of sand or shingle.

toothed whale Group of whales with conical teeth that feed on fish, squid, or marine mammals.

tornadic waterspout A waterspout formed by a tornado over the ocean.

transform boundary The boundary between two lithospheric plates which are sliding past each other.

transform fault A fault that forms at a transform boundary.

transparency The capacity for a medium, such as water, to allow light to pass through it.

trench A long narrow depression in the seafloor created where one lithospheric plate sinks beneath another.

trochoidal wave A wave with a pointed crest and a rounded trough.

trophic level A group of organisms in a food chain that feed on the next lower group or are fed on by the next higher group.

tropical The regions between 23.5°N and 23.5°S.

Tropic of Cancer A line of latitude at 23.5°N.

Tropic of Capricorn A line of latitude at 23.5°S.

trough The low part of a wave between crests.

tsunami A large sea wave generated by a seismic event.

turbidity A measure of the amount of particulate matter suspended in water.

turbidity current A flowing mass of sediment-laden water.

twilight zone The depths in the water column to which some light penetrates but not enough to allow photosynthesis to take place.

upwelling Bottom water rising toward the surface.

vertical migration The migration of organisms through the water column.

vertical zonation Classifying regions with similar environmental conditions dependent on altitude.

volcanic island An island created by volcanic activity.

volcano A vent in Earth's crust through which magma and gases can escape.

warm current A current that carries water that is warmer than the surrounding water.

water column A hypothetical cylinder of water drawn from the seabed to the water's surface and referred to when describing the conditions at different depths of the ocean.

waterspout A rising and rotating column of water and spray generated by an air vortex.

wave One of a series of periodic oscillations of the surface of a body of water.

wave action The effects of the energy transmitted by waves on the coast.

wave-cut platform A flat terrace extending out to sea from the base of a cliff.

wavelength The distance between successive wave peaks.

wave power The use of waves to generate electrical power.

whaling The commercial capture of whales.

white smoker A form of hydrothermal vent that emits white mineral-saturated water at high temperatures.

Wilson Cycle The processes by which ocean basins form, widen, and then shrink over geologic time periods.

zooplankton Plankton that are animals rather than plants.

© Diagram Visual Information Ltd.

Internet resources

There is a lot of useful information on the internet. Information on a particular topic may be available through a search engine such as Google (http://www.google.com). Some of the sites that are found in this way may be very useful, others not. Below is a selection of Web sites related to the material covered by this book.

The publisher takes no responsibility for the information contained within these Web sites. All the sites were accessible in March 2006.

Alaska Fisheries Science Center
Conducts field and laboratory research to manage local marine resources; includes educational materials.
http://www.afsc.noaa.gov

American Society of Limnology and Oceanography
Advances the science of limnology and oceanography; includes educational resources.
http://aslo.org

Bigelow Laboratory for Ocean Sciences
Oceanography through research and education.
http://www.bigelow.org

British Antarctic Survey
A research center with resources for schools.
http://www.antarctica.ac.uk

Climatic Research Unit of the University of East Anglia
Useful information sheets on climate-related subjects.
http://www.cru.uea.ac.uk

CoastWatch
Provides real-time oceanographic satellite data.
http://coastwatch.noaa.gov

Environmental Technology Laboratory
A NOAA department providing remote sensing instrumentation for oceanographers.
http://www.etl.noaa.gov

FishBase
Everything students need to know about fish species in one database.
http://www.fishbase.org

Fisheries Department of the United Nations Food and Agriculture Organization
A wealth of information about and resources for the world's fisheries.
http://www.fao.org/fi/

Great Barrier Reef Marine Park Authority
Web site of the largest natural feature on Earth.
http://www.gbrmpa.gov.au

Harbor Branch Oceanographic Institution, Inc.
A leading marine science institution with education, research, and conservation programs.
http://www.hboi.edu

Intergovernmental Oceanographic Commission
A UNESCO initiative to improve international co-operation in the study and management of the Ocean.
http://ioc.unesco.org/iocweb/

Intergovernmental Panel on Climate Change
Assesses scientific and socio-economic information relevant for the understanding of climate change.
http://www.ipcc.ch

International Council for the Exploration of the Sea
Coordinates and promotes marine research in the North Atlantic.
http://www.ices.dk

International Hydrographic Organization
Web site of the world's leading organization for the survey and charting of the oceans.
http://www.iho.shom.fr

International Maritime Organization
The UN's specialized agency for shipping.
http://www.imo.org

International Oceanographic Data and Information Exchange
Facilitates the exchange of oceanographic data and information between participating member states.
http://ioc3.unesco.org/iode/

International Tsunami Information Center
An IOC Web site dedicated to the mitigation of the hazards associated with tsunamis.
http://www.prh.noaa.gov/itic/

© Diagram Visual Information Ltd.

INTERNET RESOURCES

International Whaling Commission
The international body that regulates the whaling industry.
> http://www.iwcoffice.org

Marine Technology Society
Dedicated to the development and sharing of information about marine science.
> http://www.mtsociety.org

National Oceanic and Atmospheric Administration
Information and advice on marine and meteorological matters from the government.
> http://www.noaa.gov

National Oceanography Centre, Southampton University
A leading center of research and education in marine science.
> http://www.soc.soton.ac.uk

National Ocean Service
An agency of NOAA concentrating on the nation's oceans, coasts, and marine navigation.
> http://www.nos.noaa.gov

National Sea Grant Library
An archive and lending library of marine science. Some full-text articles are available online.
> http://nsgl.gso.uri.edu

Ocean Planet
An online archival version of the Smithsonian Institution's historic traveling exhibition.
> http://seawifs.gsfc.nasa.gov/ocean_planet.html

Ocean Surface Topography from Space
An exciting NASA Web site with educational resources for the study of oceanic science and the weather.
> http://topex-www.jpl.nasa.gov

Open Directory Project
A comprehensive listing of internet resources.
> http://dmoz.org/Science/Earth_Sciences/
>   Oceanography/

Pelagic Fisheries Research Program
A useful center of fisheries research.
> http://www.soest.hawaii.edu/PFRP/

ReefBase
An excellent information center dedicated to the conservation and management of the world's coral reefs.
> http://www.reefbase.org

Scripps Institution of Oceanography
One of the largest and most important centers in the world for marine science research.
> http://sio.ucsd.edu

Seaspace
A nonprofit corporation with event proceeds funding a marine-related scholarship program, Seaspace is an annual exposition of sports, travel, and scuba diving.
> http://www.seaspace.org

The Global Drifter Center
A NOAA operation managing the deployment of drifting buoys for oceanographic and meteorological research across the globe.
> http://www.aoml.noaa.gov/phod/dac/gdc.html

The Ocean Conservancy
A leading campaign for ocean conservation focusing on overfishing and human pollution as major threats to the marine environment.
> http://www.oceanconservancy.org

United Nations Environment Programme
A UN program with the stated mission "to provide leadership and encourage partnership in caring for the environment by inspiring, informing, and enabling nations and peoples to improve their quality of life without compromising that of future generations."
> http://www.unep.org

University-National Oceanographic Laboratory System
An co-ordinating organization of 61 academic institutions and national laboratories involved in oceanographic research.
> http://www.unols.org

Woods Hole Oceanographic Institution
Dedicated to research and higher education at the frontiers of ocean science, its primary mission is to develop a fundamental understanding of how the oceans function.
> http://www.whoi.edu

© Diagram Visual Information Ltd.

Index

Index of subject headings.

© Diagram Visual Information Ltd.

© Diagram Visual Information Ltd.